Dave Carnell • John Ireland • Ken Mackreth • Helen Moors • Sarah van Wely

evision Guide

www.heinemann.co.uk

✓ Free online support
✓ Useful weblinks
✓ 24 hour online ordering

01865 888080

Heinemann

Heinemann is an imprint of Pearson Education Limited, a company incorporated in England and Wales, having its registered office at Edinburgh Gate, Harlow, Essex, CM20 2JE. Registered company number: 872828

www.heinemann.co.uk

Heinemann is a registered trademark of Pearson Education Limited

First published 2008

This edition published 2010

13
10 9 8 7

British Library Cataloguing in Publication Data
A catalogue record for this book is available from the British Library

ISBN 978 0 435466 81 7

Edited by Nigel Copeland and Stephen Nicholls
Typeset by Tek-Art
Cover design by Wooden Ark Studios
Picture research by Pearson Education
Cover photo/illustration © Pearson Education/Photodisc/Photolink
Printed in China (CTPS/07)

Acknowledgements

The author and publisher would like to thank the following individuals and organisations for permission to reproduce photographs:

Chapter 1 © PA Photos/ David Davies/ PA Wire **p 9**; Chapter 4 © PA Photos **pp 58, 58**; Chapter 5 © Radius Images/ Photolibrary **p 60**; © Corbis/ Kai Pfaffenbach/ Reuters **p 65**; Chapter 6 © Image Source Black/ Alamy **p 68**; Chapter 7 © Getty Images/ AFP/ Carl de Souza **p 80**; Chapter 9 © Photofusion/ Maggie Murray **p 100**; © Rex Features/ Image Source **p 103**; Chapter 10 © PA Photos/ Empics Sport/ Tony Marshall **p 113**; Chapter 11 Part I © Sport England **p 121**; © Sports Council for Northern Ireland **p 122**; © Logo reproduced with permission from the Sports Council for Wales **p 122**; © PA Photos/ Gareth Copley/ PA Archive **p 130**; © Phil Walter/ Getty Images **p 132**; Part III © Corbis/ Hulton-Deutsch Collection **p 142**; © International Olympic Committee **pp 143, 146**; Chapter 12 © Alamy Images/ Digital Vision **p 152**; Chapter 13 © Alamy Images/ Digital Vision **p 160**; © PA Photos/Gero Breloer **p 161**.

Every effort has been made to contact copyright holders of material reproduced in this book. Any omissions will be rectified in subsequent printings if notice is given to the publishers.

Table of Contents

INTRODUCTION

This book has been produced specifically for students revising for OCR's AS Physical Education specification. It contains information on all the topics that are examined in:

Unit G451 An introduction to Physical Education

- Anatomy and Physiology
- Acquiring Movement Skills
- Socio-Cultural Studies relating to participation in physical activity.

This unit is assessed in a two-hour written paper.

AS Unit G451: *An introduction to Physical Education*

60% of the total AS GCE marks 2h written paper 90 marks

Externally set and assessed.

This question paper has **three** sections with **one** question in each section.

Candidates are required to answer **all** parts of the question in each of Sections A, B and C to demonstrate knowledge, analysis and evaluation

Unit G452 Acquiring, developing and evaluating practical skills in Physical Education

- Performing an activity
- Coaching/Leading an activity
- Officiating an activity
- Evaluating and planning for the improvement of performance.

This is an externally set, internally assessed and externally moderated unit. Candidates will be assessed performing one activity and performing, coaching or officiating another different activity. They will also be expected to evaluate and plan how to improve a performance. This practical is worth 80 marks.

This book follows the same structure as *Advanced PE for OCR AS* also published by Heinemann and contains the key information you need to know for your examination and assessment.

This book contains the following features to help you:

KEY TERMS

Key terms – These are emboldened in the text and listed separately. These are the key words and terms that you need to know.

Need to know more? These provide cross references to chapters/pages in *Advanced PE for OCR AS* if you need further information on a topic.

EXAM TIP

These are designed to give you exam help and advice.

CHECK

☐ At the end of each chapter, you will find an overview section with tick boxes, which you can use to help review your revision as well as to check your progress. If you are not satisfied with your level of knowledge and understanding of a particular topic or chapter, then you can revisit those areas.

EXAM PRACTICE

At the end of each chapter, you will find a section of exam-style questions. When you have completed your revision for a chapter, you should answer the questions, which will enable you to test your knowledge and understanding as well as practise your exam technique.

When you have completed the questions, check your answers with those provided at the end of the book. Grading grids similar to those used by examiners are provided for the longer questions.

Remember that in the last part of each of the three questions on your examination paper, you will be assessed on the quality of your written communication. This means that the examiner will be assessing how well you have presented your answer using the following criteria.

- Is it structured into paragraphs and sentences?
- Is the punctuation and grammar correct?
- Is the spelling correct and have you used the correct terminology and technical language?
- Can the examiner understand what you have written?

The last part of each question will be assessed out of ten marks. When you answer a ten-mark question in this book you should make sure that you use paragraphs and sentences, your spelling is correct and you use the correct technical language and terminology. This will help you prepare for your exam.

While this book will help you in your preparation for your examination, there is no substitute for planning and spending time and effort in putting that plan into action. Establish your revision schedule and the learning method most suited to you. Use this revision book to support your plan.

The next section on study skills and exam technique gives you lots of useful information on how to best prepare for the exam.

ACHIEVING PEAK PERFORMANCE

Peak exam performance needs knowledge, application of knowledge and exam technique! Adopting techniques and strategies for exam success is just like learning tactics and strategies for success in sport (e.g. set plays for free throws or kicks).

Here we will look at techniques and tactics that will help you succeed in your written exam. We will also point out how to avoid pitfalls that regularly cause problems and underachievement by candidates.

Let's start by answering some common questions and then look at a number of tips for success.

TEN FREQUENTLY ASKED QUESTIONS:

1. What are 'command words'?

There are several **command words** that you must recognise and respond to correctly. If you **identify** when you should **describe** or fail to efficiently and effectively develop your answer into a **discuss** or **compare** response (when you are asked to) you won't score a max! Table 1 shows some common command words set out in three different levels of demand.

2. Should I just write everything I know about the topic in the question?

Absolutely not, though lots of candidates do this! It is important that you spot and stick to not only the command word (e.g. discuss) and subject being examined (e.g. motivation or Olympic Games) but also, and most importantly, the **exact** aspect of the subject that will get you marks.

3. How exactly should I compare/contrast/identify differences between things?

Let's look at an exam-style question and a couple of 'mock' candidate responses to answer this.

Identify differences between cycling as a physical recreation and cycling as a sport. (4 marks)

Candidate A:
When cycling is done recreationally it is mainly for enjoyment, whereas when it is done for sport it is to win. ***(Examiner's comment: true, and a direct difference identified – so one mark.)*** Cycling as recreation doesn't necessarily need expensive high tech bikes and equipment; however, when done for sport it does. ***(Examiner's comment: again true, and clear difference identified – so a second mark.)*** Finally cycling as recreation does not require high levels of physical fitness, but for sport it does. ***(Examiner's comment: bingo, for the third mark.)*** *A fourth direct identification of differences is needed for the fourth mark.*
Total: three marks out of a possible four.

Candidate B:
When cycling is done as sport it needs high-tech equipment, high levels of physical fitness, might attract sponsorship and even media coverage. ***(Examiner's comment: four accurate points, but no marks yet as no direct differences identified.)*** On the other hand when cycling is done as recreation, no real commitment is needed ***(Examiner's comment: true, but no direct comparison with cycling as sport, so no mark yet.)*** and it doesn't involve sponsorship.

Level 3: Evaluation and synthesis of knowledge	Critically Evaluate	Analyse	Justify	These more demanding commands require you to 'play with' your knowledge: to think about, apply and perhaps link information from different parts of the specification. You should include examples and context and perhaps some independent opinion.	INCREASING COGNITIVE DEMAND (↑)
	Discuss	Assess	To what extent ...		
Level 2: Application of knowledge	Contrast	Explain	Describe	These are discursive commands that require thought and development of key words, phrases or statements.	
	Compare	Identify differences between ...	Give reasons for ...		
Level 1: Knowledge and understanding	Define	List	State	These are straightforward 'recall' commands requiring knowledge. Your AS PE exam paper will have some of these.	
	Identify	What ...	Outline		

Table 1 Command words require different levels of cognitive engagement

(Examiner's comment: again true, and this point now links to the sponsorship point made earlier about sport, so one mark, but more by luck than judgement.)
Total: one mark out of four.

See the importance of effective technique?

4. How important are key words and phrases?

Vitally important! Using key words and phrases in context helps you to get marks efficiently and effectively. Their accurate use in well-written sentences also stops examiners writing 'Vague', 'Repeat' or 'Irrelevant' on your script. The meaning of key words and phrases may even be directly examined for one or two opening marks, e.g. What is meant by a balanced healthy lifestyle?

5. Can I write in bullet points?

Not a good idea! Having said that, if an opening question asked candidates to 'Identify two roles of the media' and they wrote two of the following: inform/educate/entertain/advertise; they would get two marks. But as AS Level is a step up from GCSE most teachers would coach students to always write in full sentences.

To start off you could write in 'bullet sentences' or try thinking/planning in bullet points which you could then develop into full extended sentences (always sticking to the command word).

6. How important are past questions to my revision?

They can be extremely useful, especially to check your efforts against published mark schemes, but watch out that you don't answer a question that you have done in a mock exam or practised as part of your revision rather than the exact question in front of you, which may be similar but not identical.

7. How will my work be marked?

When scripts are marked, examiners carefully read and credit your key points that match those on the mark scheme. It can be useful to think of every point you make as a potential mark; especially in the opening four questions of each section of your AS PE exam.

8. What about the ten-mark 'critically evaluate' or 'discuss' question at the end of each section?

A question that asks you to 'critically evaluate' is asking you to determine the value of something, probably by pointing out its advantages and disadvantages.

Here are a few examples of 'thinking/applying' questions.

1. Critically evaluate the impact of taking part in different types of physical activity on the joints and muscles of the body.
2. Critically evaluate drive theory, inverted U theory and catastrophe theory as explanations for the relationship between arousal and performance of motor skills.
3. Critically evaluate the factors that can influence young people's participation in physical activity.

When critically evaluating something consider the following:

- *What's good about it?*
- *What's bad about it?*
- *What have others said or written about it?*
- *What do you think?*
- *Why do you think that?*
- *What is your evidence?*

You should not only say how good a particular idea is, but try to say exactly why you think that. The very best answers will really 'tussle' with the material, the candidate probably having read about and around the subject as well as having discussed and debated it.

9. What is a 'levels of response' mark scheme?

Your ten-mark question at the end of each section will be marked with a 'levels of response' mark scheme. This gives examiners the chance to credit your critical thinking skills, explanations, development of points, independent opinion and analysis. So the **quality of your answer** will probably be more important than the **quantity you write.** Questions 1–3 in point 8 above would almost certainly be marked with a 'levels of response' mark scheme. On your ten-mark questions, aim for:

- detailed knowledge and understanding of the topic (learn your stuff!)
- detailed discussion of a number of relevant factors
- detailed analysis of one or more relevant factors
- a high standard of written communication.

10. And how should I revise?

Annoying as it may sound – in whatever way works for you! The key is to keep your revision active. Most people find that they need a varied approach. Diagrams and mind maps often help as many people find it easier to remember things when they are visual. Notepads and postcards are also useful for jotting down key points for each topic. You can then use these for revision at 'dead' time/s.

Other tips and strategies

- Keep well hydrated when revising and on the day of the exam; your brain can only function efficiently when your body is well hydrated.
- 'Walk the course' – by skim-reading the whole paper before you start to write.
- Take thinking time – check that you have really read the question properly.
- Read each question really carefully to check exactly what you need to do. What is the subject being examined? What exactly is being questioned about the subject?
- Underline or highlight the three key components of the question (command word, subject, the exact part of the subject that is being examined).
- Make a note of key important points, definitions, acronyms, mnemonics, data/values and/or formulae that you think you might need but might forget.
- Remember to obey the command word/s in the question.
- Develop answers where the command word is **explain** or **discuss**.
- Attempt all parts of each question e.g. identify **and** explain.
- Use examples to support an answer and to demonstrate your knowledge of a topic wherever you can.
- Keep to the point – be specific not vague in your answers. If asked for a definition or explanation of key terms don't repeat the exact words in the question.
- Check the number of marks available and write to suit.
- Plan longer answers when more marks are available, but don't over plan.
- Keep your eye on the clock and pace yourself.
- Attempt every question on the paper; if you run out of time give your answers in bullet points.
- Aim for high-quality written communication, i.e. spelling, punctuation and grammar.
- Make your writing easy to read – please.
- Ignore everyone else in the room.
- Read through, check and edit your work at the end.

Good luck!

Sarah van Wely

CHAPTER 1

The skeletal and muscular systems

LEARNING OBJECTIVES

By the end of this chapter you should be able to demonstrate knowledge and understanding of:

- The different types of joint found in the body
- A variety of anatomical terms to describe a moving body during physical activity
- A range of sporting techniques in terms of joint movements
- The major muscles associated with the main joints of the human body and explain their role as an agonist or an antagonist with reference to specific movements in physical activity
- Full movement analysis of specific movements in physical activity
- The difference between concentric, eccentric and isometric muscular contraction
- The distinction between three types of skeletal muscle fibre in the body and apply the characteristics to suggest reasons why certain individuals choose to take part in special types of physical activity
- The considerable benefits of a warm-up and cool-down on skeletal muscle
- The advantages of lifelong involvement in an active lifestyle in relation to both joint and muscle health and evaluate certain disorders of bones, joint and muscles that can result from participation in different types of physical activity.

Bone is the hardest connective tissue in the body, mainly because it contains deposits of *calcium phosphate* and *calcium carbonate*.

Bone acts as a store for calcium, and as a result of exercise more calcium is deposited, increasing bone density and therefore increasing bone strength.

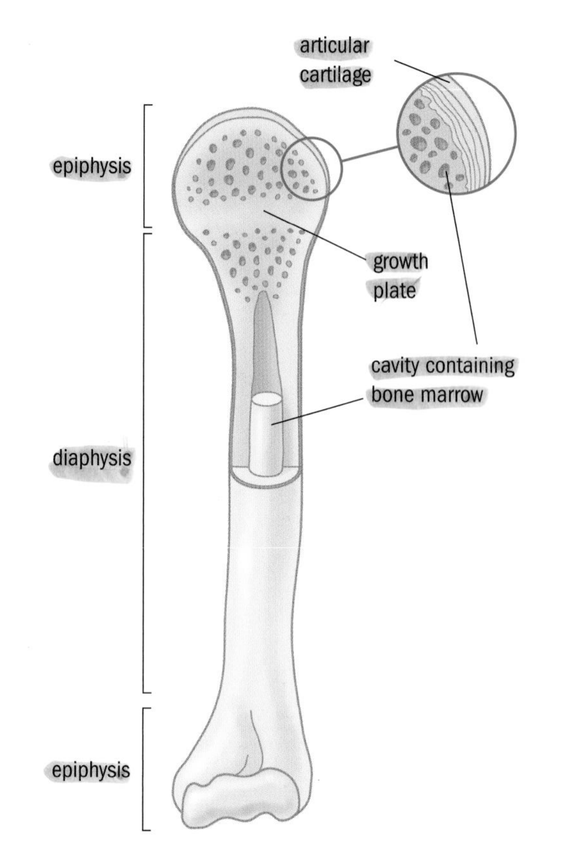

The bone matrix also contains collagen. Collagen gives bone tissue a flexible strength, allowing it to cope with a certain amount of impact.

As you get older the bone contains less collagen and the bone is less dense, resulting in brittle bones that are damaged quite easily.

Fig 1.1 The structure of a long bone during adolescence

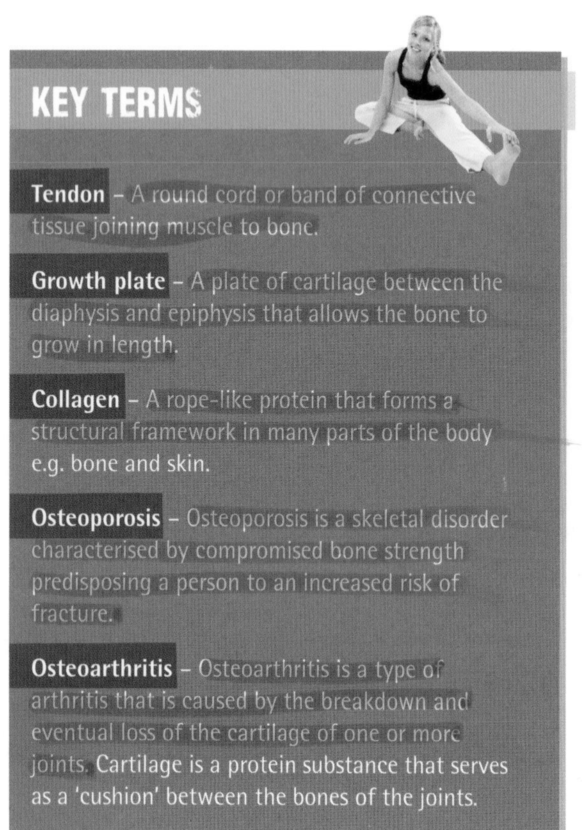

KEY TERMS

Tendon – A round cord or band of connective tissue joining muscle to bone.

Growth plate – A plate of cartilage between the diaphysis and epiphysis that allows the bone to grow in length.

Collagen – A rope-like protein that forms a structural framework in many parts of the body e.g. bone and skin.

Osteoporosis – Osteoporosis is a skeletal disorder characterised by compromised bone strength predisposing a person to an increased risk of fracture.

Osteoarthritis – Osteoarthritis is a type of arthritis that is caused by the breakdown and eventual loss of the cartilage of one or more joints. Cartilage is a protein substance that serves as a 'cushion' between the bones of the joints.

BONE TISSUE

Ossification process

The skeletal frame is initially made out of **cartilage**, which is gradually replaced by **bone**. The ossification process begins in the **diaphysis** (the primary ossification centre in the main shaft of the bone) and then occurs in the **epiphysis** (the secondary site of ossification at the ends of the bone). A plate of **cartilage** is left between the diaphysis and each epiphysis; this is where bones grow in length until **maturation** takes place. The plate is known as the **growth plate** and when growth stops this plate **fuses** and becomes bone.

Growth plate

The growth plate does not fuse until ossification is complete, i.e. the performer has stopped growing. Therefore young performers can run the risk of damaging growth plates with injuries occurring from impact or repetitive overuse. If untreated, growth plate injuries can result in abnormal bone growth (a decrease or accelerated bone growth) or a complete stop to bone growth.

Need to know more? For further information on growth plate injuries, see Chapter 1, page 37 in your Student Book.

Condyloid	Gliding	Pivot	Ball & socket	Hinge
wrist	intervertebral joints	atlas and axis (C1 and C2)	hip joint	elbow joint
		radio ulnar joint	shoulder joint	knee joint
				ankle joint

Table 1 Joints

Synovial joints

The joints identified in the specification have been classified in Table 1.

Although the hip and shoulder are both ball and socket joints and they both perform the same type of movement, the range of movement does differ. This is because more stability is required at the hip joint. In the shoulder movement is gained at the expense of stability and at the hip stability is gained at the expense of movement. It is much harder to displace the hip than the shoulder and this is because of the structure of the joint.

EXAM TIP

Remember to link:

STRUCTURE → FUNCTION → PRACTICAL

Joints: Function vs Stability

You will be expected to be able to analyse the degree of joint stability and joint mobility for each synovial joint. This will be directly attributable to the structure and function of each joint. A comparison of joints is often asked for, typically between the two ball and socket joints of the hip and shoulder.

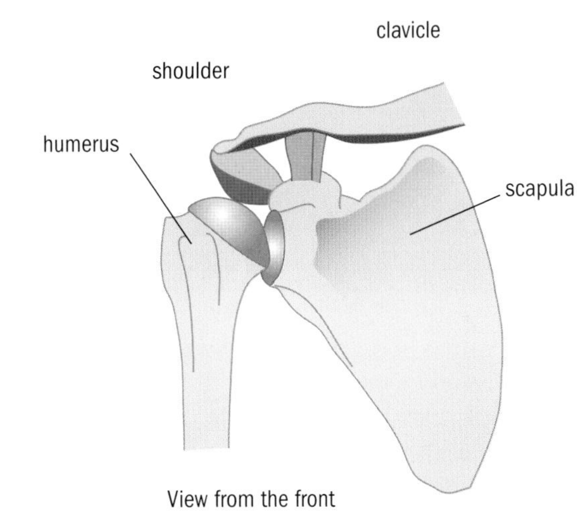

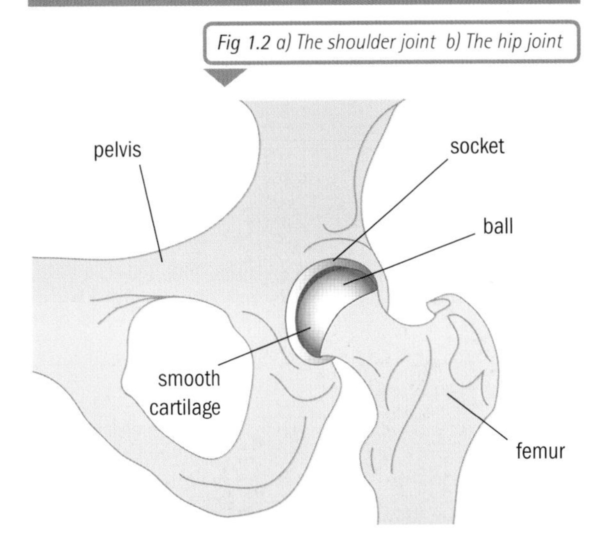

Fig 1.2 a) The shoulder joint b) The hip joint

Shoulder joint	Hip joint
• The socket on the scapula (the glenoid fossa) is small and shallow making the joint less stable. • The joint capsule is very loose (allowing separation between the two bones) allowing more movement. • The head of the humerus is rounded but not as ball-like as the head of the femur; therefore it does not sit as deeply into the glenoid fossa. • The shoulder joint is stabilised by the rotator cuff muscles but these are not as strong as the muscles surrounding the hip. It is relatively easy to dislocate the shoulder joint.	• The socket on the pelvis (the acetabulum) is deep and cuplike in shape making the joint more stable. • A rim of fibrocartilage adds depth to the acetabulum, adding to stability. • The head of the femur is very spherical and fits snugly into the acetabulum. • The joint is supported by five strong ligaments; in particular the iliofemoral ligament (the Y ligament) is extremely strong. • The hip joint is surrounded by large muscle groups that aid stability, e.g. gluteus maximus.

Table 2 Joints: shoulder and hip

Read the extract below from www.shoulderdoc.co.uk written by L. Funk (2006):

'Rugby has the highest risk per player/hour of injury of all sports. The shoulder comprises 20% of all rugby injuries, being the second most commonly injured joint after the knee.'

Think of reasons why the knee and shoulder joints are the most susceptible joints to injury in rugby. Try and give both structural and functional reasons in your answer.

EXAM TIP

Think about how participation in certain sports impacts on joints of the body so that you are able to analyse joints and give relevant practical examples.

Features of a synovial joint

Table 3 below provides a summary of the structural and functional characteristics of the features of a synovial joint.

EXAM TIP

Quite often questions will ask for both functional and structural characteristics/differences to be considered. It is therefore useful to separate out structure from function when you are revising, as it will make it far easier to answer the question under exam conditions.

Joint feature	Structure	Function
joint capsule	fibrous tissue encasing the joint	forming a capsule around the joints adds stability
articular discs of cartilage	c-shaped rims of fibro cartilage	they act as shock absorbers
synovial fluid	a fluid that fills the joint capsule	nourishes and lubricates the articular cartilage
synovial membrane	lines the joint capsule	secretes synovial fluid
articular cartilage	covers the articulating surfaces of the bones	prevents friction between the ends of bones
bursa	a sac filled with synovial fluid located between tendons/ligaments and bone	to reduce friction where tendons, ligaments, muscle or bones might rub together
ligaments	white fibrous connective tissue which attaches bone to bone	by securing the bones of a joint together it adds significantly to joint stability
pads of fat	fatty tissue located between fibrous capsule and bone or muscle	provides a cushion between the joint capsule and the bone/muscle

Table 3 Synovial joint: structural and functional characteristics

KEY TERMS

Flexion – Decreasing the angle of a joint.

Extension – Increasing the angle of a joint.

Abduction – Movement away from the midline of the body.

Adduction – Movement towards the midline of the body.

Rotation – Movement of a bone around its longitudinal axis.

Circumduction – The lower (distal) end of the bone moves in a circle; it is a combination of flexion, extension, abduction and adduction.

Lateral flexion – Bending the head or trunk sideways.

Plantar flexion – Moving the foot downwards, away from the tibia.

Dorsiflexion – Moving the foot upwards, towards the tibia.

Supination – Facing the palm of the hand forwards (while in the anatomical position).

Pronation – Facing the palm of the hand backwards (while in the anatomical position).

Examples of the use of joints in some sporting techniques are shown in Table 4. Try and draw a similar table for each of the other types of synovial joint (condyloid, gliding, pivot and ball and socket).

Need to know more? For more information on joint movements, see Chapter 1, pages 11–14 in your Student Book.

EXAM TIP

The sports pages of a newspaper quite often contain action pictures of different sports. While you are reading through quickly do a simple joint movement analysis of each picture. It really becomes very easy with practice and will give you a lot of confidence for the exam.

MUSCLES

Although there are a lot of muscles to remember they are named according to things such as their location, size, shape, origin and insertion or number of heads or function. Knowing this might make it easier to learn the information.

Location: some muscles are named according to their position on the body, e.g. tibialis anterior, which is positioned on the front (anterior) of the tibia (tibialis).

Size: e.g. gluteus maximus, meaning large.

Origin and insertion: e.g. sternocleidomastoid. This muscle originates on the sternum and clavicle and inserts onto the mastoid process.

Number of heads: e.g. the <u>bi</u>ceps brachii has two heads (origins) whereas the <u>tri</u>ceps brachii has three.

Hinge joint	Flexion	Extension
ankle	(dorsiflexion) e.g. during the 'on your marks' phase of a sprint start	(plantar flexion) e.g. extending into the points position in ballet
knee	e.g. flexing the knee when the knee is lifted upwards when running	e.g. the position of the knee on the lead leg of a hurdler as they take off to jump the hurdle
elbow	e.g. when the elbow is flexed in preparation to throw a ball	e.g. when the elbow is extended when balancing in a handstand

Table 4 Joint movements – sport examples

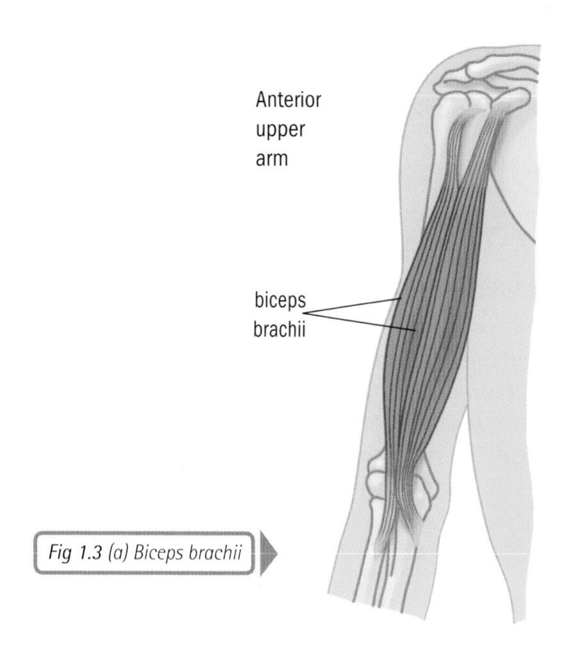

Fig 1.3 (a) Biceps brachii

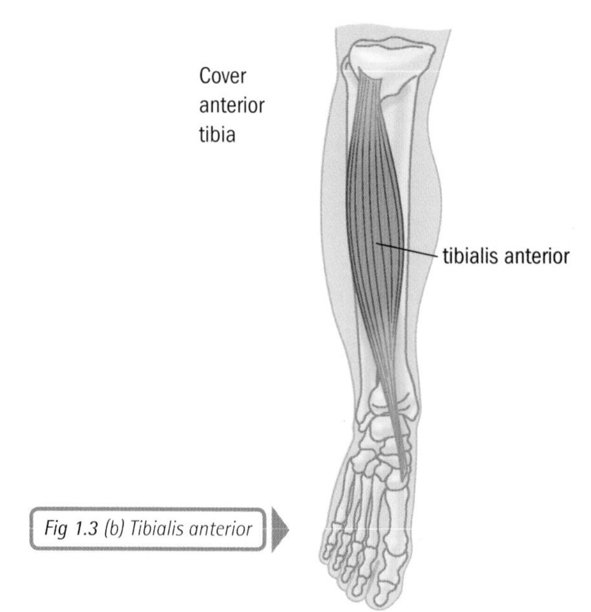

Fig 1.3 (b) Tibialis anterior

KEY TERMS

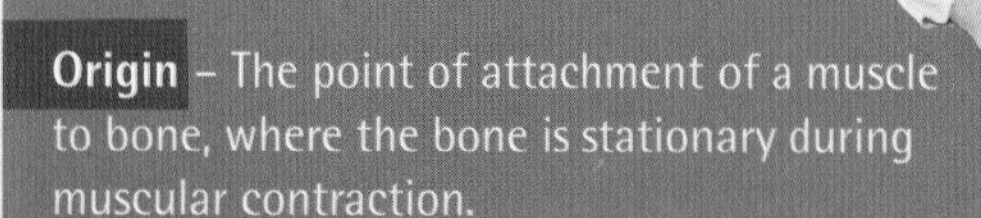

Origin – The point of attachment of a muscle to bone, where the bone is stationary during muscular contraction.

Insertion – The point of attachment of a muscle to bone, where the bone moves during muscular contraction.

Agonist muscle (prime mover) – The muscle that is directly responsible for the movement at a given joint.

Antagonist muscle – A muscle that works in conjunction with an agonist. As the agonist contracts the antagonist lengthens and returns to its original length.

It is easier to learn the muscles as an antagonistic pair, e.g. the biceps brachii flexes the elbow joint and the triceps brachii extends the elbow joint. The two muscles work together to produce co-ordinated movement of the elbow joint. Learn the muscles in bite-sized chunks so that you do not feel overwhelmed; learn the muscles for one particular joint before you move onto the next joint.

Try and identify the movement that each of the muscles in Fig 1.3 will produce when contracted. Check your answer on the muscle and joint summary table opposite.

Need to know more? For more information on the muscular system, see Chapter 1, page 15 in your Student Book.

EXAM TIP

Make sure that you give the full name for a particular muscle:

Biceps	✗	Biceps brachii	✓
Quadriceps medialis	✗	Rectus femoris, vastus lateralis, vastus intermedius and vastus	✓
Abdominals	✗	Rectus abdominus	✓

Joint	Joint type	Bones that articulate	Movement possible	Muscle acting as prime mover
wrist	condyloid	radius, ulna and carpal bones	flexion extension abduction/ adduction	flexors extensors
elbow	hinge	humerus radius ulna	flexion extension	biceps brachii triceps brachii
radioulnar	pivot	radius and ulna	pronation supination	pronator teres supinator muscle
shoulder	ball and socket	humerus and scapula (glenoid fossa)	flexion extension abduction adduction inward rotation outward rotation horizontal flexion horizontal extension	anterior deltoid latissimus dorsi middle deltoid and supraspinatus teres major subscapularis infraspinatus pectoralis major teres minor
shoulder girdle	gliding	scapula and clavicle	elevation of scapula upward rotation adduction depression	part I of trapezius part II of trapezius part III of trapezius part IV of trapezius
spine	cartilaginous gliding pivot	between individual vertebrae between the vertebral arches C1 and C2 (atlas & axis)	(of trunk only) flexion extension lateral flexion rotation to same side rotation to opposite side	 rectus abdominus erector spinae external/internal oblique internal oblique external oblique
hip	ball and socket	femur and pelvic bone (acetabulum)	flexion extension abduction adduction inward rotation outward rotation	iliopsoas gluteus maximus gluteus medius adductor longus/brevis/ magnus gluteus minimus gluteus maximus
knee	hinge	femur tibia	flexion extension	biceps femoris semitendinosus semimembranosus rectus femoris vastus lateralis vastus intermedius vastus medialis
ankle	hinge	talus tibia & fibula	plantarflexion dorsiflexion	soleus tibialis anterior

Table 5 Summary table: joints and muscles

Hinge joint	Flexion		Extension	
ankle	(dorsiflexion) e.g. during the 'on your marks' phase of a sprint start	tibialis anterior	(plantar flexion) e.g. extending into the points position in ballet	gastrocnemius
knee	e.g. flexing the knee when the knee is lifted upwards when running	biceps femoris	e.g. the position of the knee on the lead leg of a hurdler as they take off to jump the hurdle	rectus femoris
elbow	e.g. when the elbow is flexed in preparation to throw a ball	biceps brachii	e.g. when the elbow is extended when balancing in a handstand	triceps brachii

Table 6 Joint movements and muscles – sport examples

Table 4 (movement) from page 5 has been revisited and an appropriate muscle has been added for each movement. If you use this approach of gradually adding more information to your movement analysis it will make learning the information a lot easier and far less confusing.

Need to know more? For more information on muscular contraction, see Chapter 1, page 28 in your Student Book.

What type of contractions are taking place when a weight lifter lifts a weight above his head and then holds it there for three seconds before slowly lowering the weight back down onto the floor?

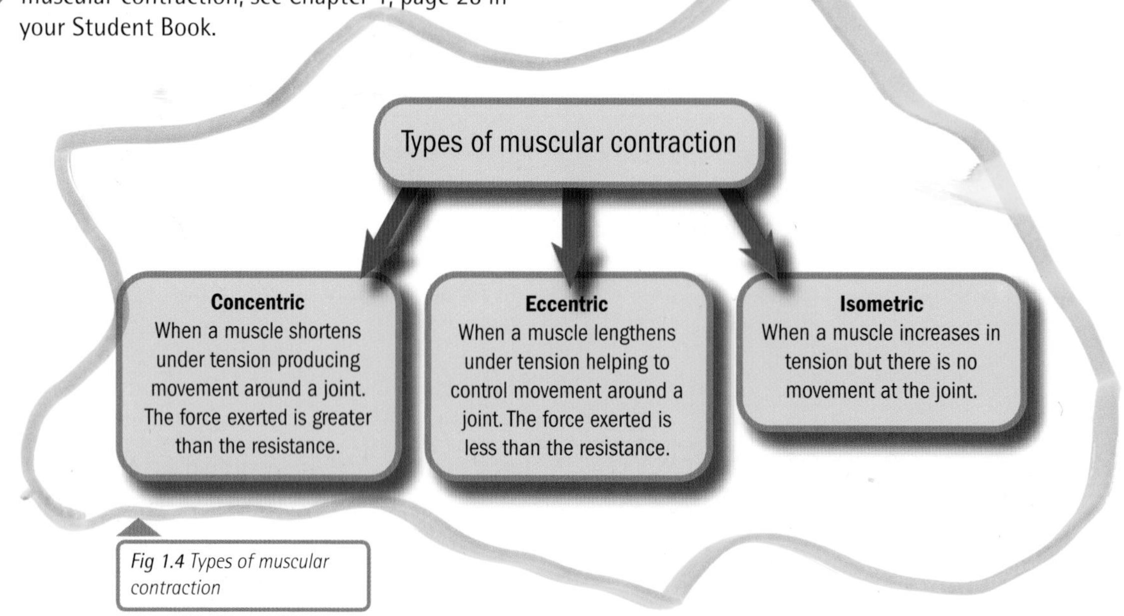

Fig 1.4 Types of muscular contraction

Most question papers include a movement analysis of a sporting action. Each analysis will require the following information:

Rugby goal kick – Jonny Wilkinson execution phase

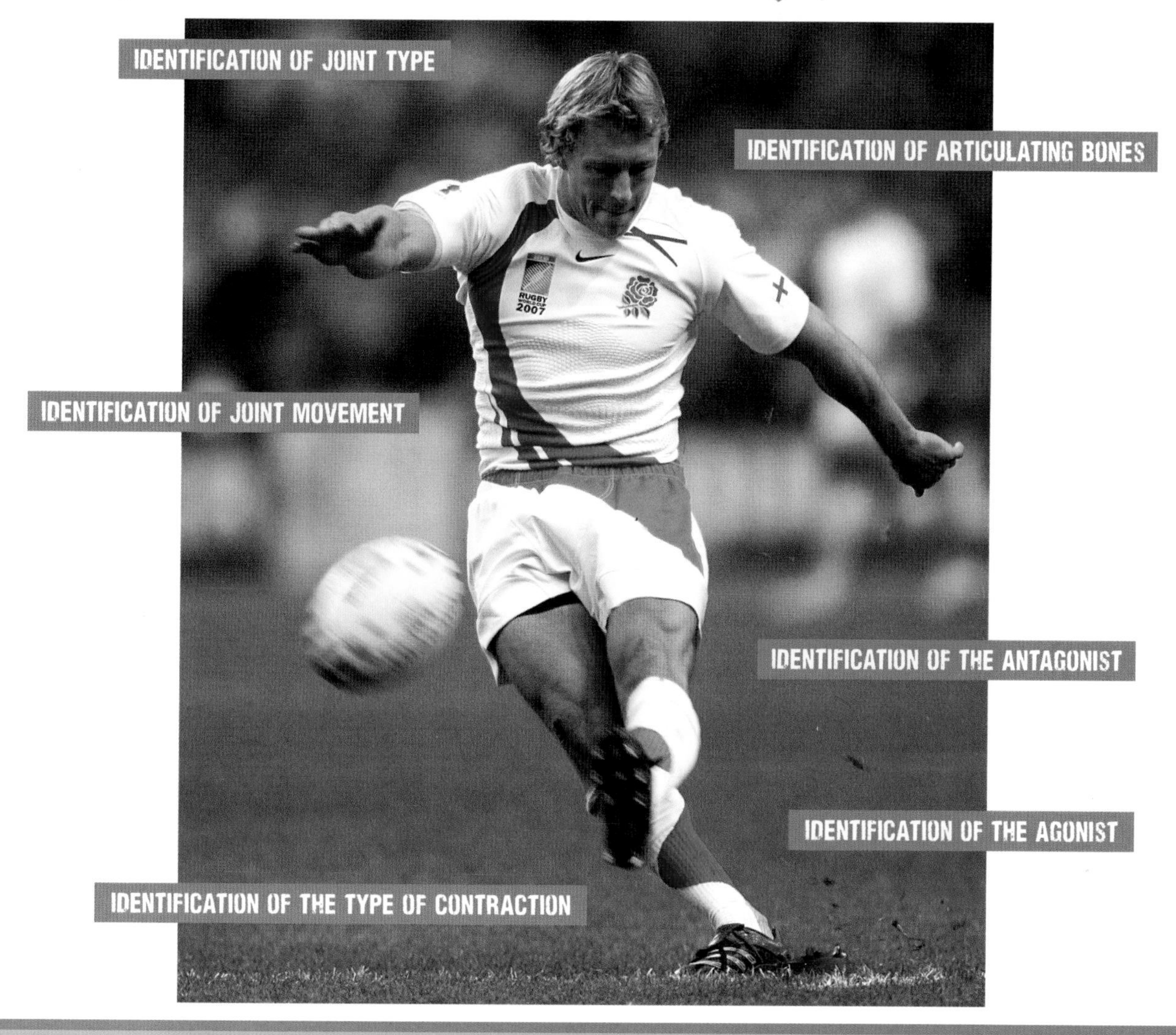

EXAM TIP

It is helpful to answer the movement analysis question in table format. It structures your answer and makes sure that you don't leave out any information by mistake.

Typical movements for analysis include a vertical jump, a bench press, a sit-up and a bicep curl.

In the upward phase of a vertical jump a movement analysis of the hip and knee would include the following information.

Joint	Joint type	Joint movement	Agonist	Agonist – contraction type	Antagonist
hip	ball and socket	extension	gluteus maximus	concentric	iliopsoas
knee	hinge	extension	rectus femoris	concentric	biceps femoris

Table 7 Movement analysis: vertical jump – upward phase

Try completing a similar table for another movement, e.g. the upward phase of a bench press.

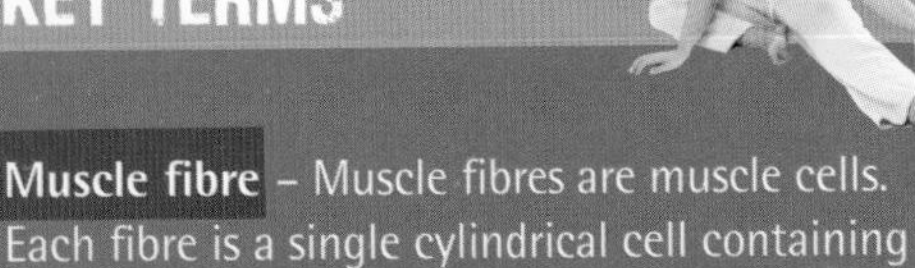

KEY TERMS

Muscle fibre – Muscle fibres are muscle cells. Each fibre is a single cylindrical cell containing several nuclei.

Slow twitch muscle fibre (slow oxidative fibre) – These fibres contract more slowly and do not produce as much force as fast twitch fibres. They are more suited to aerobic work as they contain more mitochondria and myoglobin.

Fast twitch muscle fibre – These fibres contract quicker and with more force than the slow twitch fibres. They are more suited to anaerobic work and therefore have a low resistance to fatigue. There are two types of fast twitch fibre, namely fast oxidative glycolytic (type 2a) and fast glycolytic (type 2b). Type 2b have the greatest anaerobic capacity, contracting with the most speed and force.

Aerobic exercise – Where aerobic respiration provides the majority of the energy needed for the activity. A good supply of oxygen is needed and exercise is sub-maximal.

Anaerobic exercise – Where anaerobic respiration provides the majority of the energy needed for the activity. Exercise intensity is maximal and the duration of the activity is short.

The percentage of each type of fibre in any given muscle is genetically determined. This makes some people far better suited to aerobic activities and other people more suited to anaerobic activities. As people tend to choose to take part in activities that they are good at, then their individual muscle composition will heavily influence their choice of activity.

Need to know more? For more information on muscle fibre types, see Chapter 1, page 32 in your Student Book.

Characteristics of muscle tissue

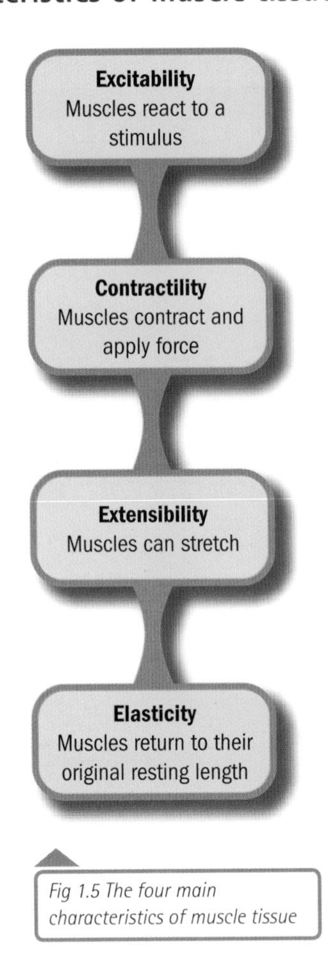

Fig 1.5 The four main characteristics of muscle tissue

Muscles contain **elastin**, a protein which, as the name suggests, has an elastic property. Elastin molecules look like tiny coiled springs and they are all interwoven with one another. This means that if you stretch muscle tissue it will return to its original length. If you play with an elastic band the band gets warmer and you will notice that it stretches further and recoils with greater force. In the same way muscle tissue is found to respond better after a warm-up.

Marathon runner (e.g. Paula Radcliffe)	**Sprinter** (e.g. Asafa Powell)
• They contain a lot of myoglobin, which is a structural characteristic of a type 1 fibre • They have a well-developed blood supply, which is a structural characteristic of a type 1 fibre • They have a high aerobic capacity, which is a functional characteristic of a type 1 fibre • They have a slow speed of contraction, which is a functional characteristic of a type 1 fibre	• They have few and small mitochondria, which is a structural characteristic of a type 2b fibre • They have more fibres per motor neurone, which is a structural characteristic of type 2b fibre • They fatigue relatively quickly, which is a functional characteristic of a type 2b fibre • They contract with a lot of force, which is a functional characteristic of a type 2b fibre

Table 8 Analysis of muscle fibres for two sports

Physiological effects of a warm-up and cool-down on skeletal muscle

Warming up, increasing the core temperature of the body:

i) Increased speed and force of contraction.

ii) Improved economy of movement, because of lower viscous resistance in a warm muscle.

iii) Haemoglobin releases oxygen in muscle tissue more readily.

iv) Increased flexibility.

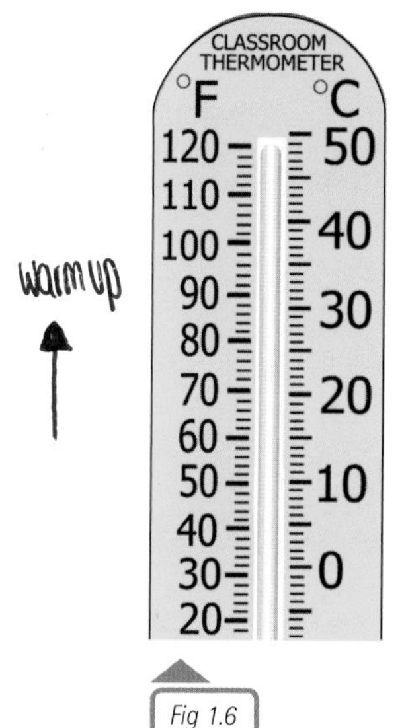

Fig 1.6

Cooling down, lowering the core temperature of the body:

i) Faster removal of lactic acid from fast twitch muscle fibre.

ii) Faster removal of carbon dioxide from muscle tissue.

iii) a reduction in the risk of delayed onset of muscle soreness (DOMS) caused by connective tissue damage.

LIFELONG PARTICIPATION IN AN ACTIVE LIFESTYLE AND ITS IMPACT ON BONE TISSUE

If you remember, as you get older bone tissue contains less collagen and bone tissue is less dense, resulting in brittle bones that are damaged quite easily. Participation in exercise can to some extent counteract this process. Growth is a good time for exercise to increase **bone mineral density** and therefore to **maximise peak bone mass.**

Continuing to follow an exercise programme will maintain bone mass and reduce age-related bone loss, reducing the risk of **osteoporosis**. Exercise will also preserve muscle strength and postural stability, reducing the risk of falling and possible bone fractures in later life. Bone tissue will become stronger and more dense as more physical demands are placed on the tissue.

Two types of exercise are important to bone health.

- **Weight-bearing activities** – where your body works against gravity and your legs and feet are carrying the weight of your body, for example walking and running.
- **Resistance activities** – when your muscles are working against a weight/resistance to improve the strength of the muscle, for example weight training. The body responds to exercise by depositing more calcium so that the bones can handle the weight and impact experienced during physical activity.

Growth plate injury

Not all participation in physical activity has a positive effect on bone tissue. In the exam you may be asked to identify a growth plate injury which has been caused by participation in a particular type of physical activity.

Sport	Growth plate injury	Possible reason
e.g. gymnastics	gymnast wrist	excessive force load with hyperextension of the wrist, e.g. during training for the vault or floor

Table 9 Growth plate injury

Other examples of sports where growth plate injuries occur are tennis and rugby.

You will need to be able to identify the injury, explain why it has occurred and suggest how the injury may be avoided.

EXAM TIP

A high-mark question at the end of the question paper will nearly always ask candidates to discuss both the positive **and** negative benefits of regular physical activity on at least one aspect of the musculoskeletal system.

Example: impact of exercise on the muscular and skeletal systems.

Positive impact

Increase in peak bone mass – exercise varies the line of stress and stimulates an increase in the amount of calcium salts deposited in the bone.

Reduces the risk of **osteoporosis.**

Increased joint stability because of strong ligaments, healthy cartilage and good muscle tone.

Good posture and alignment where stabilising muscles are strong. This helps the joints of the body cope with external forces as they are mechanically efficient.

Good core stability supports the lumbar spine and reduces the likelihood of lower back problems.

a)

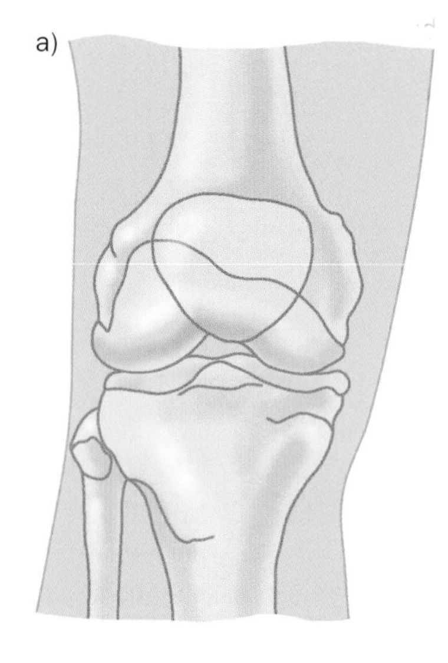

b)

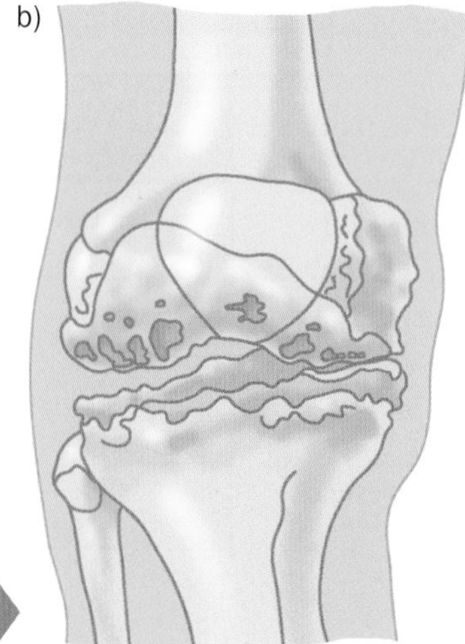

Fig 1.7

Negative impact

Joint dislocation occurs when the articulating bones are forced from their normal position and the joint ceases to function properly.

Osteoarthritis is when the articular cartilage is damaged and in some cases eventually wears away. This exposes the bone tissue and can lead to the formation of bone spurs. The joint becomes swollen and painful and movement is limited.

Joint sprain is a joint injury that stretches or tears a ligament. A ligament is strong connective tissue that joins one bone to another and provides joint stability. Constant wear and tear from physical activity can cause stretching of the ligament and reduced joint stability.

Growth plate injuries can result in abnormal growth of bone tissue (a decrease or accelerated bone growth) or a complete stop to bone growth.

Need to know more? For more information on positive and negative impacts, see Chapter 1, page 38 in your Student Book.

Choose one activity that you think has a positive impact on the muscular and skeletal systems and one activity that you think has a negative impact. Give both structural and functional points to support your answer.

CHECK

If you are satisfied with your knowledge and understanding, tick off the sections that you have revised so far. If you are not satisfied, then revisit those sections and refer to the pages in the 'Need to know more?' features.

- ☐ Understand, describe and give examples of the different types of joint found in the body.
- ☐ Use a variety of anatomical terms to describe a moving body during physical activity.
- ☐ Analyse a range of sporting techniques in terms of joint movements.
- ☐ Identify the major muscles associated with the main joints of the human body and explain their role as an agonist or an antagonist with reference to specific movements in physical activity.
- ☐ Carry out a full movement analysis of specific movements in physical activity.
- ☐ Understand the difference between concentric, eccentric and isometric muscular contraction.
- ☐ Distinguish between the three types of skeletal muscle fibre in the body and apply the characteristics to suggest reasons why certain individuals choose to take part in special types of physical activity.
- ☐ Recognise the considerable benefits of a warm-up and cool-down on skeletal muscle.
- ☐ Discuss the advantages of lifelong involvement in an active lifestyle in relation to both joint and muscle health and evaluate certain disorders of bones, joint and muscles that can result from participation in different types of physical activity.

EXAM PRACTICE

Q.1 Typically a tennis player will extend their shoulder joint when performing a serve.
Complete the following joint analysis for extension of the shoulder joint.

a) Joint type.
b) The articulating bones.
c) The muscle working as an agonist.
d) The type of contraction performed by the agonist.

4 marks

Q.2 The muscle fibre type that would be used during a maximal muscle contraction is the fast glycolytic (type 2b) fibre. Give two structural and two functional characteristics of this type of muscle fibre.

4 marks

Q.3 Identify **two** structures of the hip joint and describe the role of each during the performance of physical activity.

4 marks

Q.4 Identify:

a) the type of contraction occurring in the bicep brachii during the downward phase of a bicep curl
b) the muscle that is performing a similar contraction during the downward phase of a sit-up.

2 marks

See page 163 for answers.

CHAPTER 2

Basic concepts of biomechanics

LEARNING OBJECTIVES

By the end of this chapter you should be able to demonstrate knowledge and understanding of:

- The types of motion produced in different sporting techniques
- Sporting examples of linear, angular and general motion
- All three of Newton's Laws of Motion to a variety of sporting techniques
- The effect of size of force, direction of force and position of application of force on a body
- How centre of mass can increase or decrease stability in sporting techniques
- How to carry out a practical analysis of typical sporting actions.

MOTION

Motion is the process of changing place or position or, in other words, movement.

There are three types of motion.

- **Linear motion** – the straight line or curved progression of an object as a whole (e.g. *straight* – skiing straight down a hill; e.g. *curved* – a skier performing a curved turn down the slope).
- **Angular motion** – when an object acts as a radius and moves in a circular path about a fixed point. Most body segment motions are angular, e.g. the lower leg when kicking a rugby ball.
- **General motion** – a combination of linear and angular motion, e.g. running.

EXAM TIP

Remember that motion or movement will **only** take place when a force acts upon a body. How much force and where it makes contact with the body will determine the type of motion produced.

- For a body to move, the force that acts on it must be large enough to overcome the inertia of the body. A force acting on a tennis ball may cause the tennis ball to move but the same force may not be large enough to make a medicine ball move.
- Equally, if a body is in motion it will remain in motion until a force changes its state of motion.

- The inertia of a body in relation to linear motion is directly proportional to the mass of the body. So it will require more force to move a medicine ball than a tennis ball and equally once moving it will require more force to stop or slow down a medicine ball than a tennis ball.

EXAM TIP

When reading through any biomechanics text or question the notion of a 'body' is referring to any object, e.g. a ball, a bat, a person.

Need to know more? For more information on force, see Chapter 2, page 50 in your Student Book.

KEY TERMS

Inertia – The resistance a body has to a change in its state of motion.

Force – Is often described as pushes or pulls on a body.

Mass – The quantity of matter that a body contains. The weight of an object is proportional to its mass.

Centre of mass – The point where the mass of an object is concentrated. It is the object's point of balance.

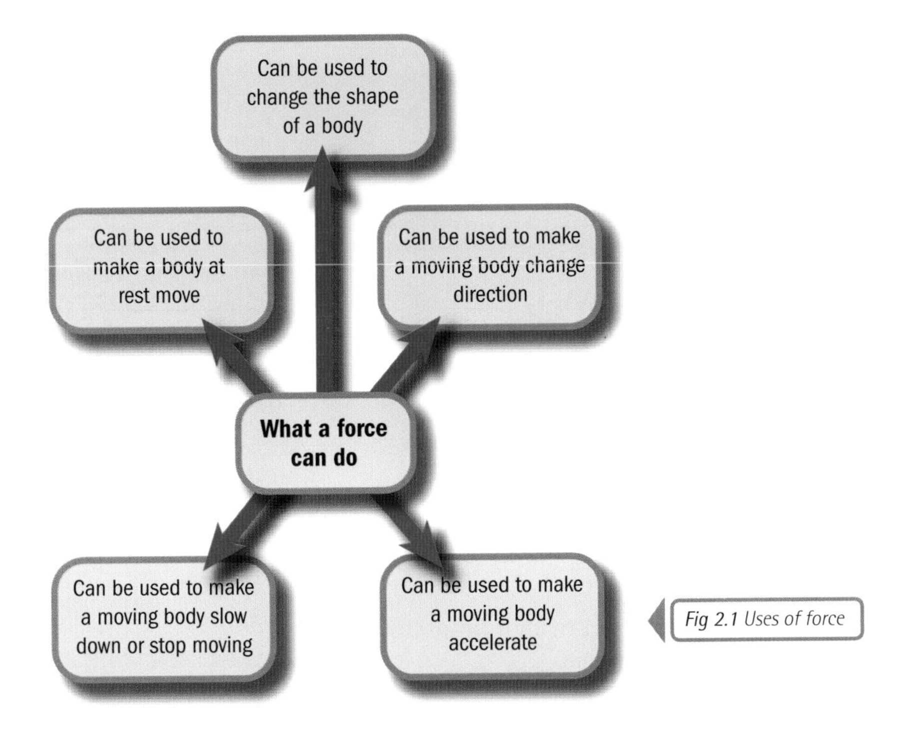

Fig 2.1 Uses of force

Move it	Change it	Shape it	Slow it/stop it	Accelerate it
A snooker ball will remain still on the table until it is struck with the snooker cue.	In tennis the direction of the ball struck by a forehand drive will change as the opponent strikes the ball to return it over the net.	When a trampolinist lands on the trampoline bed, the bed changes shape.	When the fielder catches the ball in rounders the flight of the ball is stopped.	As the long jumper gets to the end of their run-up they apply more force on the ground to accelerate into the final few strides before hitting the board.

Table 1 Different forces

The effect of a force (S.A.D.)

1. Depends on the **Size** of the force. The size of a force refers to its weight, which is a product of its mass and the external force of gravity. The force that a muscle can exert is governed by the size and number of muscle fibres.
2. Depends on where you **Apply** the force. If you apply a force slightly off the centre of mass then the motion produced will be angular motion.
3. Depends on the **Direction** of the force. If a force is applied through its centre of mass then the body will move in the same direction as the force.

EXAM TIP

If you remember, there are more fibres per motor neurone in a motor unit containing fast glycolytic muscle fibres (type IIb) than a motor unit containing slow oxidative muscle fibres (type I). Therefore the fast glycolytic motor units produce more force.

NEWTON'S LAWS OF MOTION

Isaac Newton formulated three laws of motion and all three can be applied to sports performance.

Newton's First Law of Motion (Law of Inertia)

'A body continues in a state of rest or uniform velocity unless acted upon by an external force.'

- A golf ball will stay on the tee until the golfer strikes the ball with their club.
- The athlete will remain on the blocks until the athlete contracts their muscles to produce the force necessary to start the race.
- When a sky diver free-falls and then deploys their parachute the parachute produces a resistance force (opposite to the direction of motion) that slows down the descent of the sky diver.

Newton's Second Law of Motion (Law of Acceleration)

'The acceleration of an object is directly proportional to the force causing it and is inversely proportional to the mass of the object.' (F=ma)

- A hockey ball will travel with greater acceleration if the body of the ball is hit with greater force by the hockey player.
- A sprinter will accelerate at a quicker rate when more force is exerted by the muscles as the foot reacts with the ground.
- A tennis ball will accelerate at a quicker rate when a greater force is applied by the racket when striking the ball. A greater force is produced by moving the racket head faster towards the ball and when the string tension is high.

Newton's Third Law of Motion (Law of Reaction)

'For every action there is an equal and opposite reaction.'

When a body exerts a force on another body then there is an equal and opposite force exerted back.

- When a batsman in cricket hits a ball with their bat, the cricket ball exerts an equal but opposite force on the cricketer's bat.
- When a swimmer performs a tumble turn, the wall of the pool pushes against the swimmer with the same force as the swimmer pushes against the wall of the pool.
- When a weightlifter pushes against the ground, the ground pushes against the weightlifter with the same force.

EXAM TIP

Every time there is a push there has to be a push back.

EXAM TIP

For an entertaining interpretation of the three Laws of Motion visit 'YouTube'. A visual stimulus usually helps you to remember information better, particularly if it is novel and funny.

Need to know more? For more information on Newton's Laws of Motion, see Chapter 2, page 51 in your Student Book.

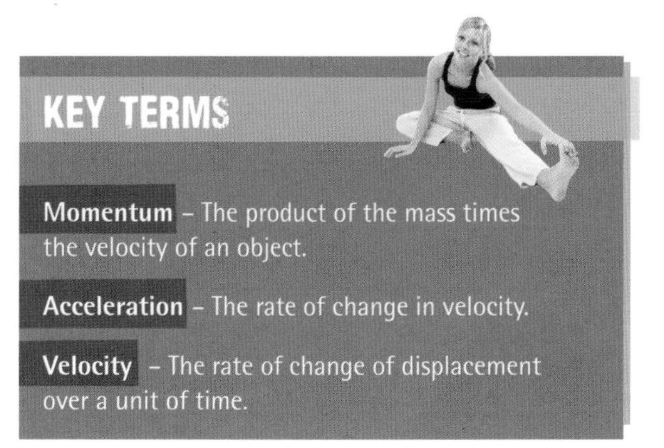

KEY TERMS

Momentum – The product of the mass times the velocity of an object.

Acceleration – The rate of change in velocity.

Velocity – The rate of change of displacement over a unit of time.

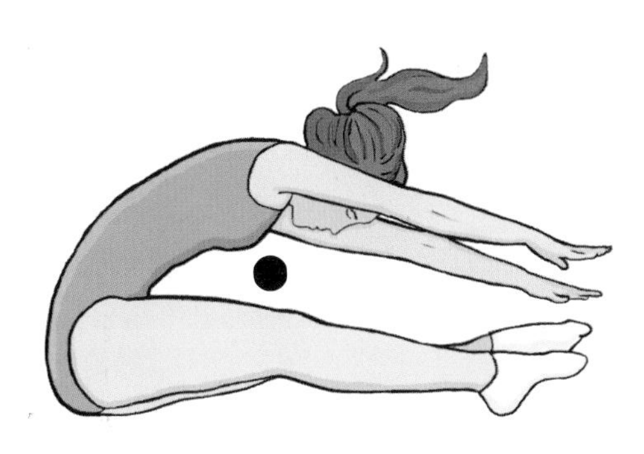

Fig 2.2 Centre of mass can move outside the body

CENTRE OF MASS

In a totally symmetrical body then the centre of mass will be located in the geometric centre of the body. People, however, come in all shapes and sizes and we are constantly changing the position of our bodies. Your centre of mass will be different if you are sitting rather than standing.

The centre of mass is not a fixed point and during the performance of some sporting techniques the centre of mass is located outside of the body.

- The development of the Fosbury Flop high jump technique was successful because the athlete's body shape means that during the jump their centre of mass remains below the bar.
- When performing a forward somersault on a trampoline the performer has to push their hips backwards and upwards to move their centre of mass forward. When they push off from the bed the force is acting slightly off centre, creating the angular motion needed to complete the technique.

KEY TERMS

Mass – The quantity of matter that a body contains. The weight of an object is proportional to its mass.

Centre of mass – The centre of mass of an object is the point where the mass of the object is concentrated. It is the object's point of balance.

Eccentric force – Applying a force that doesn't pass through the centre of mass will produce angular motion.

Need to know more? For more information on the centre of mass, see Chapter 2, page 52 in your Student Book.

EXAM TIP

Always make sure that you have prepared a practical example for all the key concepts. Trying to think of appropriate examples under exam conditions is stressful. It is better to adopt a Blue Peter style approach – here is one I did earlier.

Stability

If a performer can adopt a stable position they are more able to resist motion, which in some instances is a good thing. Consider the position that a sumo wrestler adopts at the start of a bout. In other techniques a performer deliberately alters their body position to create a less stable position in order to move into action more readily.

When an athlete moves from the 'take your marks' position into the 'get set' position during a sprint start they have effectively put themselves in a less stable position to enable a better start.

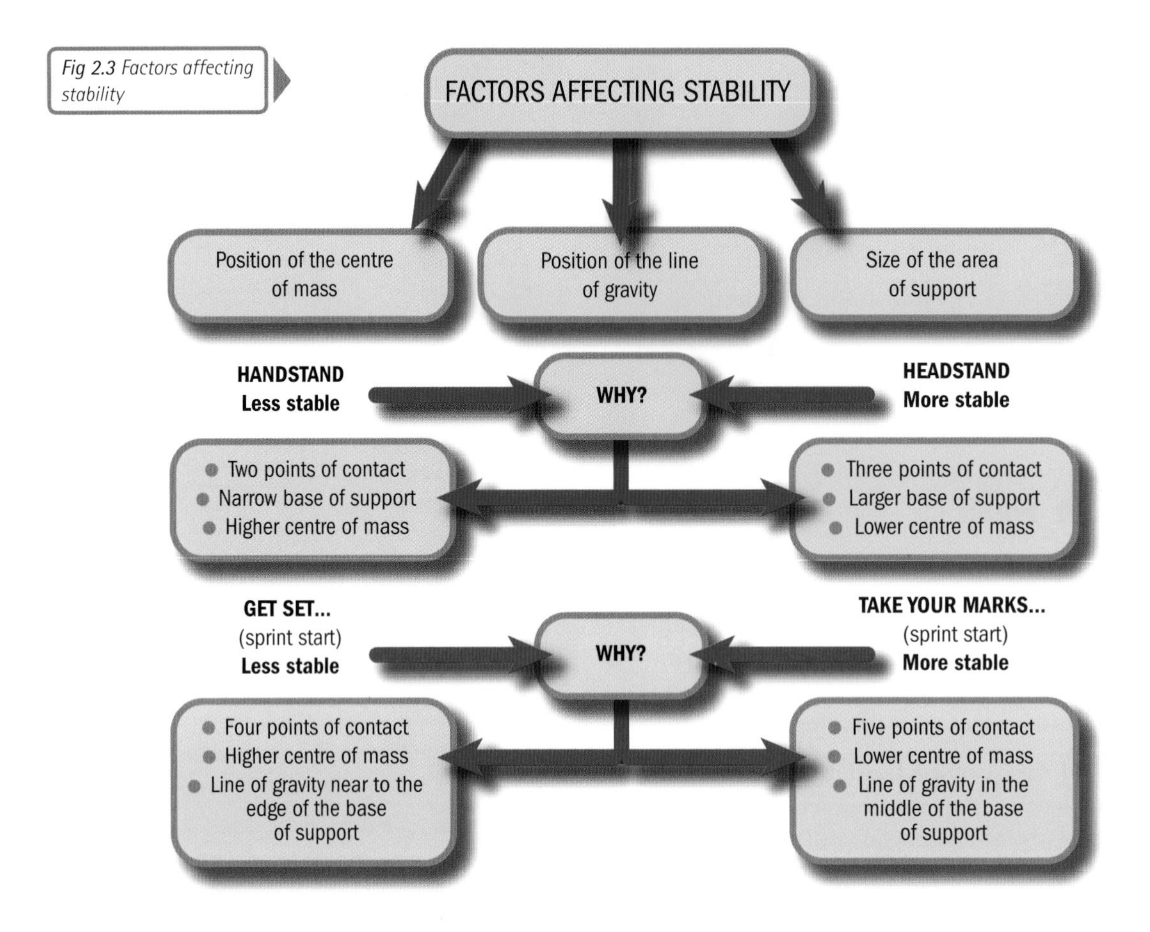

Fig 2.3 Factors affecting stability

CHECK

If you are satisfied with your knowledge and understanding, tick off the sections that you have revised so far. If you are not satisfied, then revisit those sections and refer to the pages in the 'Need to know more?' features.

- ☐ Understand the types of motion produced in different sporting techniques.
- ☐ Describe and give sporting examples of linear, angular and general motion.
- ☐ Apply all three of Newton's Laws of Motion to a variety of sporting techniques.
- ☐ Understand the effect of size of force, direction of force and position of application of force on a body.
- ☐ Apply your knowledge of centre of mass to increasing or decreasing stability in sporting techniques.
- ☐ Carry out a practical analysis of typical sporting actions.

EXAM PRACTICE

Q.1 When hitting a ball in table tennis, an understanding of force is important.

Explain how force can be exerted so that the ball:

i) moves straight.

ii) spins.

2 marks

Q.2 Describe how the position of the centre of mass can directly affect the balance of a performer.

3 marks

Q.3 Apply Newton's Three Laws of Motion to performing a weightlifting exercise.

3 marks

See page 164 for answers.

CHAPTER 3

The cardiovascular and respiratory systems

PART I

Response of the cardiovascular (heart) system to physical activity

LEARNING OBJECTIVES

Chapter 3 is divided into three parts. By the end of this part you should be able to demonstrate knowledge and understanding of:

- The link between the cardiac cycle and the conduction system of the heart
- The relationship between stroke volume, heart rate and cardiac output and resting values for each
- The changes that take place to stroke volume, heart rate and cardiac output during different intensities of physical activity
- The regulation of heart rate during physical activity.

REVIEW OF HEART STRUCTURE AND FUNCTION

'Aerobic work' refers to exercise that relies predominantly on the use of oxygen to supply the energy for prolonged performance. 'Aerobic system' refers to three distinct systems: the heart, vascular and respiratory systems, which closely interact to ensure a constant distribution of oxygen to the muscles during exercise.

EXAM TIP

Examination questions often require you to combine information from the three systems represented in Fig 3.1.2, particularly the heart and vascular systems.

KEY TERMS

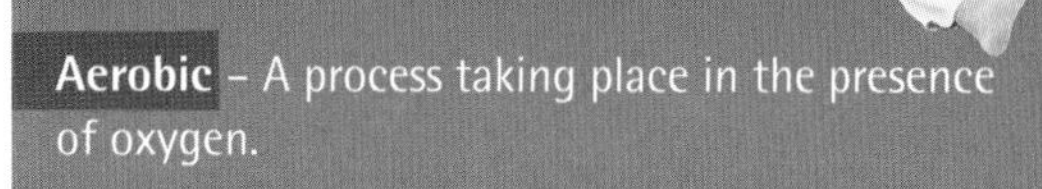

Aerobic – A process taking place in the presence of oxygen.

Anaerobic – A process taking place in the absence of oxygen.

Pulmonary – Linked to the lungs.

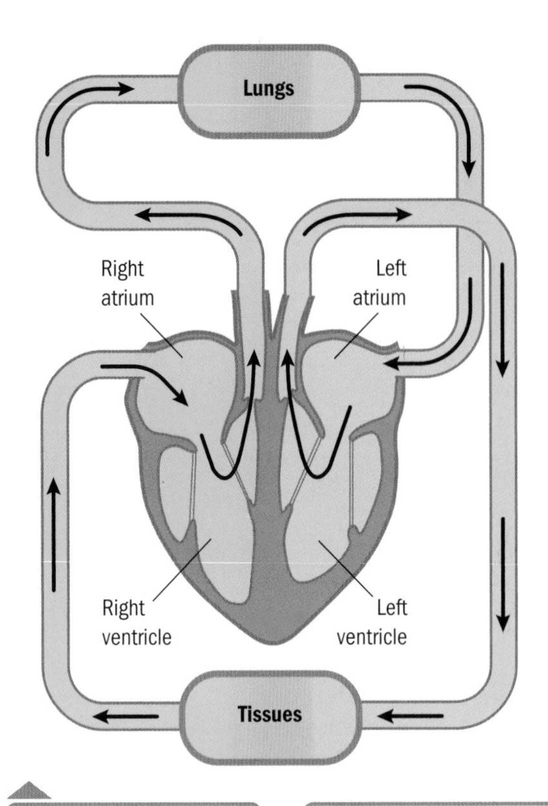

Fig: 3.1.1 The heart – a dual-action pump

Fig: 3.1.2 Interaction between heart, vascular and respiratory systems

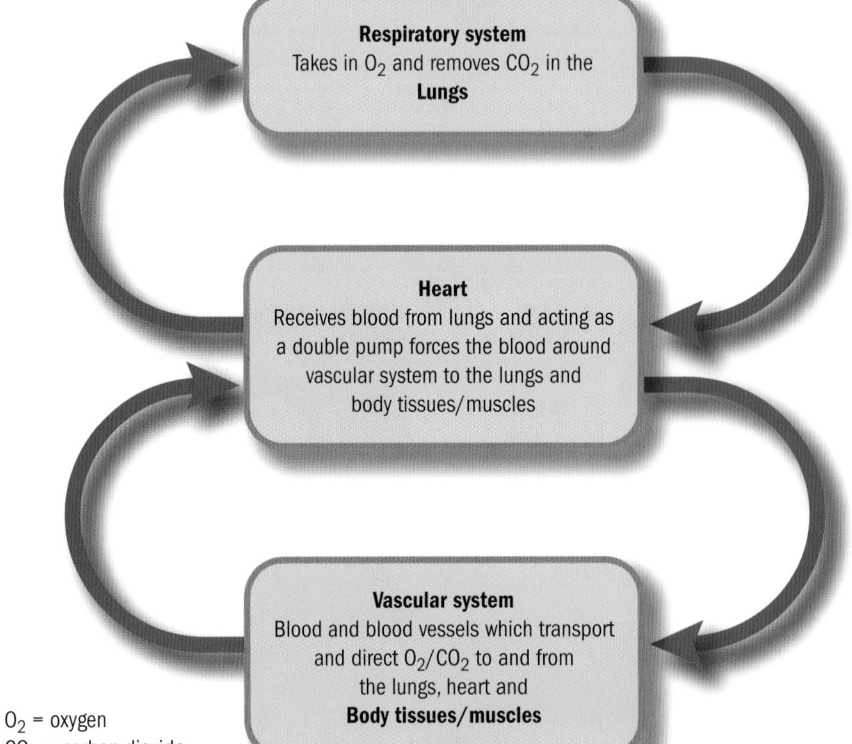

O_2 = oxygen
CO_2 = carbon dioxide

The marathon and long distance cycling are clear examples of aerobic exercise requiring a good supply of oxygen, but less obvious are sports with different positions/roles. The activities of midfield players in sports like football, hockey or the centre in netball to a lesser extent can be termed **aerobic** as they are required to run for prolonged periods, whereas forwards or a goalkeeper in the latter sports predominantly sprint or jump, activities which are dependent on energy supply with insufficient oxygen and conversely termed **anaerobic** work.

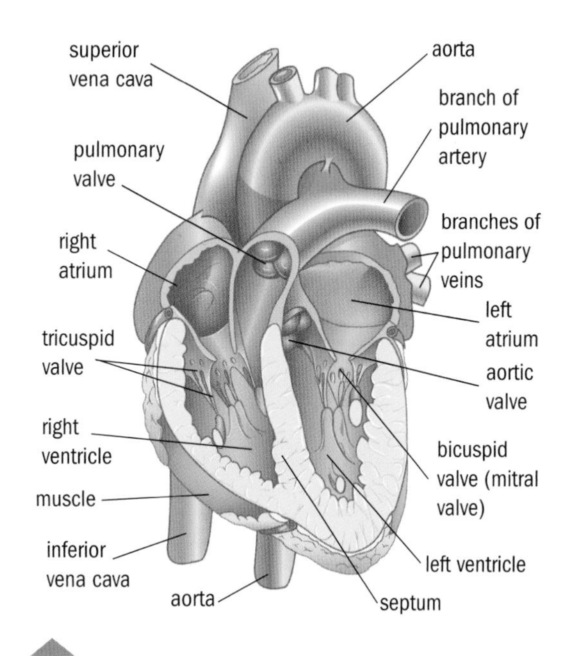

Fig 3.1.3 The internal/external structures of the heart

HEART'S CONDUCTION SYSTEM LINKED TO THE CARDIAC CYCLE

The heart has a dual-pump action with two separate pumps that work simultaneously to pump blood to two different destinations. The right side pumps **deoxygenated** blood (blood depleted of oxygen) towards the lungs and the left side pumps **oxygenated** blood (blood saturated/loaded with oxygen) towards the rest of the body.

Need to know more? For further information on the heart conduction system, see Chapter 3, Part I, pages 63–64 in your Student Book.

EXAM TIP

You will be required to sketch a diagram to summarise the structures and route of the cardiac impulse.

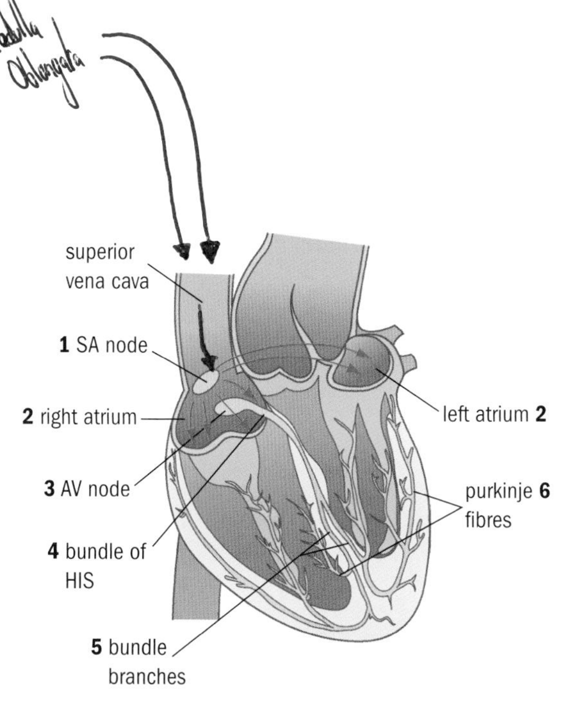

Fig 3.1.4 Structures involved in the conduction of the cardiac impulse

Conduction system

The heart is myogenic – it generates/controls its own electrical impulse called the cardiac impulse.

1. Cardiac impulse initiated from SA (sinoatrial) node (pacemaker) in right atrium.
2. Impulse passes through right and left atrium walls to AV node, causing both atria to contract; this is known as 'atrial systole'.

3 & 4. AV node conducts impulse down through bundle of HIS...

5. ...down through the left and right bundle branches to the apex of heart.
6. Impulse travels up around ventricle walls via purkinje fibres, causing both ventricles to contract; this is known as 'ventricular systole'.

Cycle continues. SA node initiates the next cardiac impulse.

The cardiac cycle

The cardiac cycle represents the mechanical events of one heartbeat. One complete cycle lasts approximately 0.8 seconds and consists of two phases (shown below) that represent the contraction and relaxation of the heart muscle.

EXAM TIP

You will be required to link the conduction system to events of the cardiac cycle.

REMEMBER IT!

The events during the cardiac cycle occur **simultaneously** – what takes place on the right is occurring at the same time on the left side of the heart.

Fig 3.1.5 Summary diagram of phases and sequence of events occurring during cardiac cycle

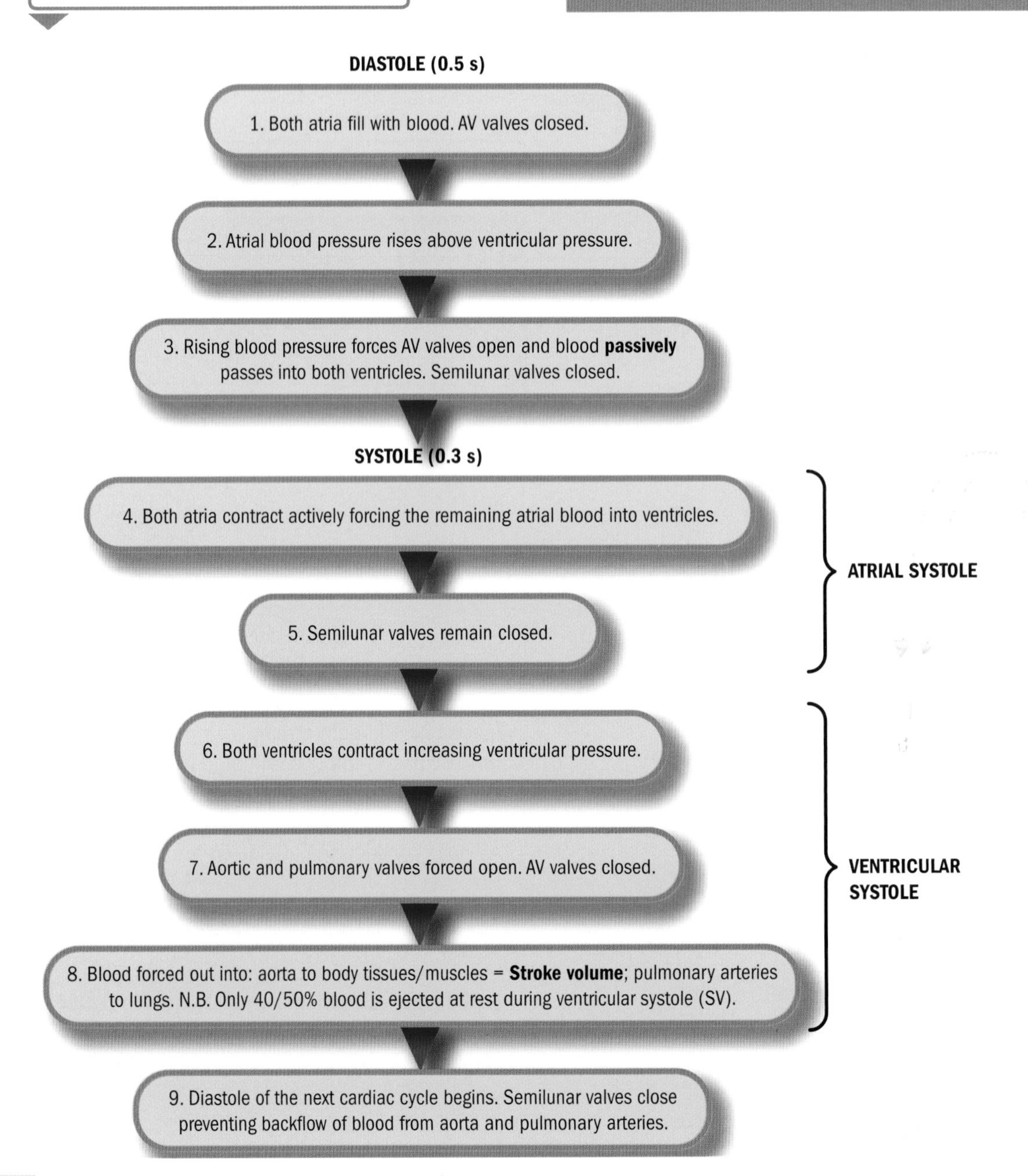

RELATIONSHIP BETWEEN, AND RESTING VALUES OF, HEART RATE, STROKE VOLUME AND CARDIAC OUTPUT

Heart rate (HR)

The heart rate (HR) represents the number of times the heart ventricles beat in one minute. The average resting heart rate is 70–72 beats per minute. Maximal heart rate is calculated using the following equation:

220 – Age = Max HR (for example 220 – 17 = 203).

Bradycardia is a resting heart rate below 60 beats per minute. It may indicate a high level of aerobic fitness. It may also be due to **hypertrophy** which is an increase in size/thickness of the heart muscle wall.

Stroke volume (SV)

The stroke volume (SV) is the volume of blood ejected by heart ventricles **per beat** or the difference in the volume of blood before and after each ventricle contraction. The average resting stroke volume is approximately 70 ml.

- The end diastolic volume (EDV), before contraction, is the volume of blood left in the ventricles at the end of the relaxation/filling stage of the cardiac cycle.
- The end systolic volume (ESV), after contraction, is the volume of blood left in the ventricles at the end of the contraction/emptying stage of the cardiac cycle.

To calculate SV: EDV – ESV = SV

REMEMBER IT!

When calculating blood volumes, always present figures from 1000 and above in litres (L/min), especially when referring to cardiac output, e.g.1000 ml = 1 l (litre).

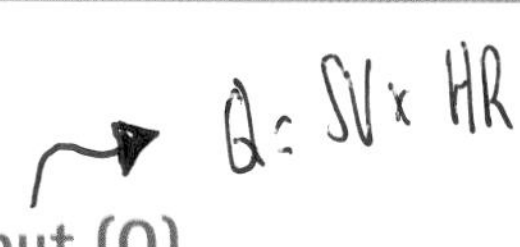

Cardiac output (Q)

This is the volume of blood ejected by heart ventricles in one minute.

	Q	=	SV	×	HR
Average	(Litres/min)	=	(ml/beat)	×	(bpm)
(rounded):	5 l/min	=	70 ml	×	72

The heart's response to exercise

	Exercise intensity		
	Resting	**Sub-maximal (moderate)**	**Maximal**
SV	60/80 ml	80/100 ml untrained 160/200 ml trained	100/120 ml untrained 160/200 ml trained
HR	70/72 bpm	Up to 100/130 bpm	220 – your age
Q	5 l/min	Up to 10 l/min	20–40 l/min

Table 1 Summary of SV, HR and Q values related to exercise intensity

KEY TERMS

Oxygen debt – Additional oxygen consumption during recovery, above that usually required when at rest.

Sub-maximal – Refers to exercise performed at an intensity below an athlete's maximal aerobic capacity, or max VO_2 – hence it represents aerobic work.

Before, during and after exercise HR is continually changing, but it may do any of the following depending upon the exercise undertaken. See Fig 3.1.7, which shows HR response to both sub-maximal and maximal exercise.

1. **Resting heart rate** – the average resting heart rate is 72, but if a question describes a young, fit aerobic athlete, it may be assumed they will have a resting heart rate below 60, known as bradycardia, due to an increase in stroke volume.
2. **Anticipatory rise** – the heart rate increases even before exercise begins due to the release of adrenalin from adrenal glands, which acts upon the SA node to increase heart rate and ventricle contraction to increase stroke volume (*hormonal control*).

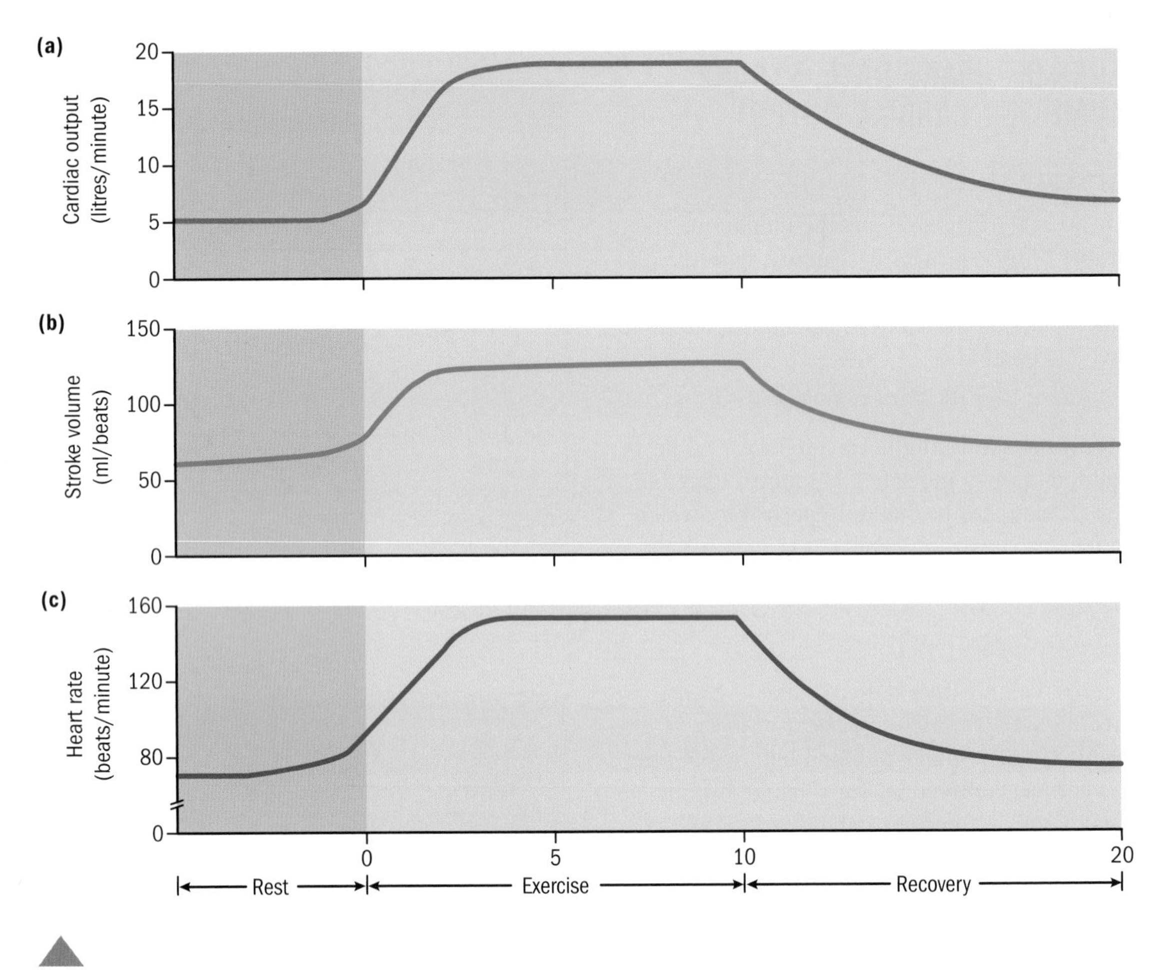

Fig 3.1.6 Response of heart rate (c) *and stroke volume* (b) *to control cardiac output* (a) *from rest, exercise and recovery*

Fig: 3.1.7 The typical HR response to sub-maximal and maximal work. Stages 1–7 show the significant changes that occur

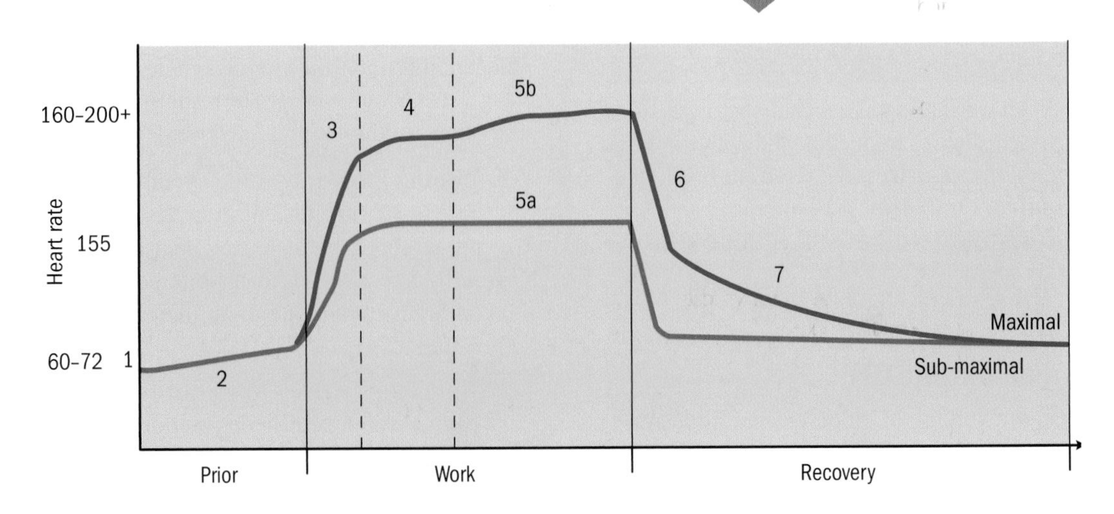

3. **Rapid increase in heart rate** at the start of exercise due to receptors.
   - Proprioreceptors (muscle and joint) relating to increased motor activity (*neural control*).
   - Chemoreceptors relating to increased CO_2/lactic acid (decreased pH) and decreased O_2 concentrations (*neural control*).
   - Continued/increased effect of **adrenalin** (*hormonal control*).

The above receptors stimulate the cardiac centre which stimulates the SA node to increase heart rate.

4. **Continued but slower increase in heart rate** due to:
   - continued effect of chemoreceptors and proprioreceptors (*neural control*)
   - increase in blood and heart temperature (*intrinsic control*)
   - increase in venous return (blood returning to the heart) (*intrinsic control*).

5a. **Slight fall/steady state plateau in the heart rate** (aerobic sub-maximal) due to:
   - oxygen supply equal to the demand of muscles
   - baroreceptors (blood pressure) (stretch receptors in blood vessels) slow down the heart rate to an optimal level to meet O_2 demands by stimulating the parasympathetic vagus nerve (*neural control*).

5b. **Continued rise in heart rate** (anaerobic maximal work) toward maximal values due to:
   - continued action of all factors listed in 2 and 3 above
   - anaerobic work where the supply of oxygen is below the muscle demand
   - continued anaerobic work increasing lactic acid to reduce pH, which inhibits enzyme action; this in turn stimulates pain receptors and ultimately causes muscle fatigue.

The maximal heart rate value can be calculated by subtracting the athlete's age from 220, but values above 180 bpm will be accepted as typical of maximal heart rate.

6. **Rapid fall in heart rate** as exercise stops due to decrease in stimulation of all the factors in 2, 3 and 4 above.

7. **Slower fall in heart rate** towards resting values. HR elevated above resting values to help repay **oxygen debt** (additional oxygen consumed during recovery, above that usually required when at rest in this time) and to remove the by-products of respiration, for example, lactic acid.

The more intense the exercise, the longer the elevated HR and recovery period due to the increase in by-products of respiration that need to be removed.

Stroke volume: response to exercise

Stroke volume increases from values around 60–80 ml per beat at rest to maximal values of around 120 ml per beat during exercise. SV increases due to:

- increased capacity of heart to fill. Increase in venous return (blood returning to the heart), which stretches ventricular walls and increases the filling capacity of the heart and hence the end diastole volume
- increased capacity of heart to empty. A greater EDV provides a greater stretch on the heart walls which increases the force of ventricular systole (contraction of ventricles). This increases ventricular contractility (the capacity of the heart ventricles to contract), which almost completely empties the blood from the ventricles, increasing SV.

Cardiac output: response to exercise

Cardiac output, being the product of stroke volume and heart rate ($Q = SV \times HR$), increases directly in line with exercise intensity from resting values of 5l/min up to maximal values of 20–40l/min, to supply the increased demand for oxygen from the working muscles.

Need to know more? For further information on heart rate and cardiac output response to exercise, see Chapter 3, Part I, pages 69–71 in your Student Book.

REGULATION OF HEART RATE DURING PHYSICAL ACTIVITY

Cardiac control centre (CCC)

The **medulla oblongata** in the brain contains the cardiac control centre (CCC), which is primarily responsible for regulating heart rate via the stimulation of the SA node.

The CCC is controlled by the **autonomic** nervous system (ANS), meaning that it is under involuntary control and consists of **sensory** and **motor** nerves from either the sympathetic or parasympathetic nervous system.

KEY TERMS

Receptors – Sensory receptors that detect changes in the body's status, e.g. chemo/proprioreceptors).

Sensory nerves – Transmit information detected by receptors **towards** the central nervous system (CNS), e.g. chemoreceptors about pp O_2 and pp CO_2. (pp = partial pressure)

Medulla oblongata – Part of the brain (CNS) responsible for regulating respiration, heart rate and blood vessels.

Autonomic nervous system – Controls the body's involuntary internal functions.

Motor nerves – Nerves from the central nervous system passing instructions to body parts, e.g. muscles, to contract.

The three main factors that affect the activity of the CCC are summarised in Fig 3.1.8.

- Neural control – primary control factor.
- Hormonal control.
- Intrinsic control.

In response to receptor stimulation via sensory nerves the CCC quite simply initiates the sympathetic or parasympathetic nervous systems to stimulate the SA node to either increase or decrease HR. **Sympathetic** nerves increase HR while **parasympathetic** nerves decrease HR. Fig 3.1.9 opposite summarises the sympathetic and parasympathetic control via motor nerves to the SA node.

Need to know more? For further information on heart rate regulation and control, see Chapter 3, Part I, pages 72–75 in your Student Book.

Fig 3.1.8 Summary of neural, hormonal and intrinsic factors affecting the activity of the CCC

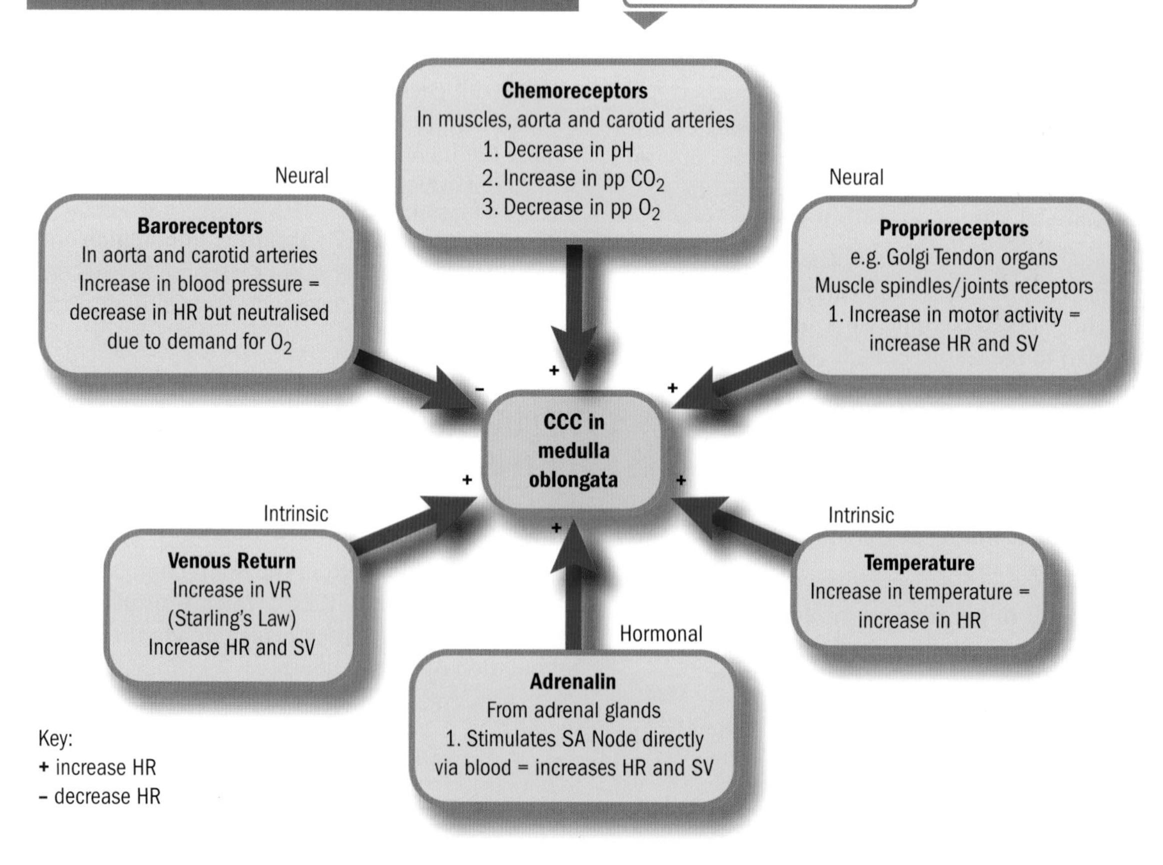

EXAM TIP

The stimulation of the vagus nerve is decreased simultaneously with the increased stimulation of the accelerator nerve. The effect is a much more rapid increase in heart rate than if just one of the above occurred.

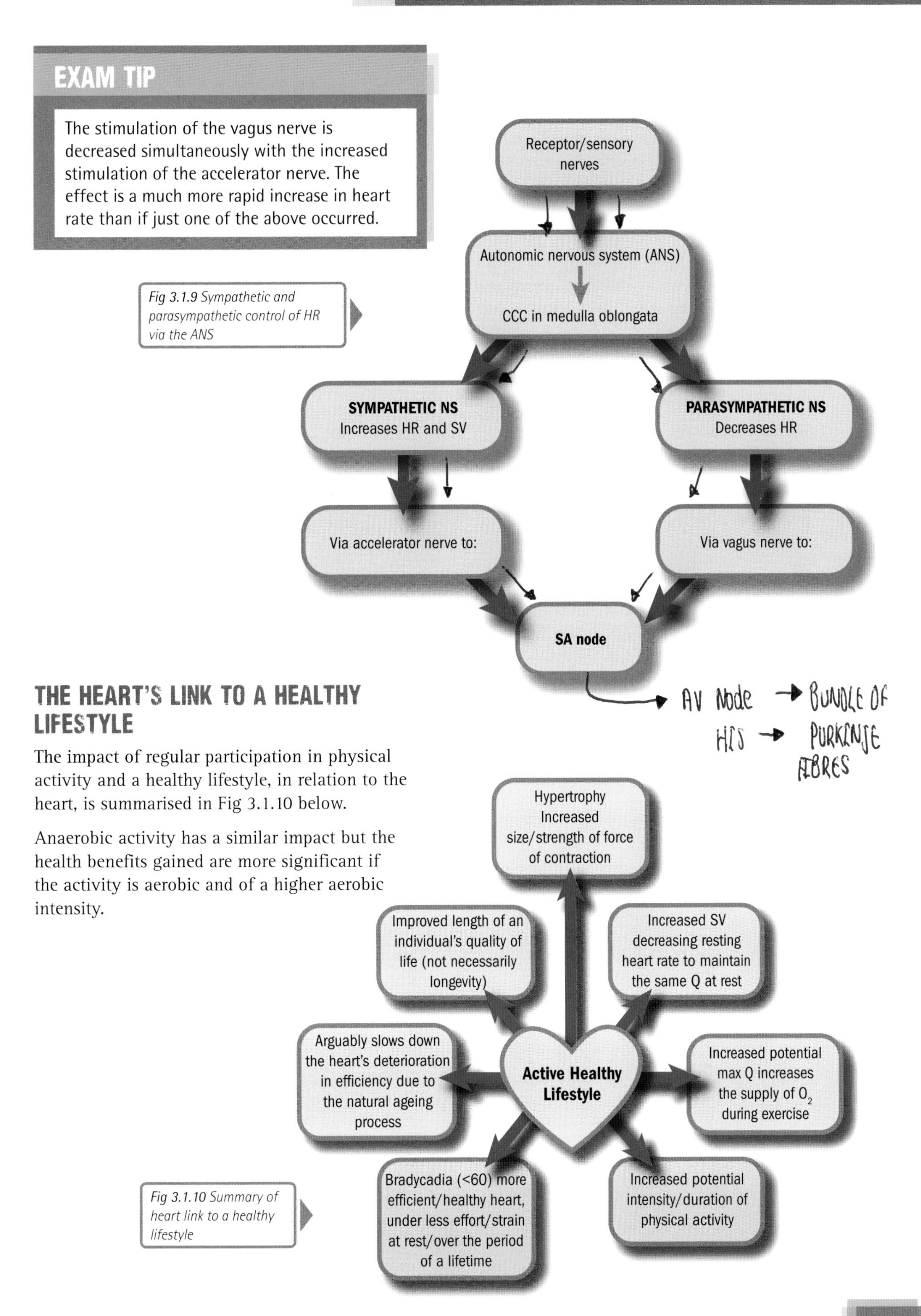

Fig 3.1.9 *Sympathetic and parasympathetic control of HR via the ANS*

THE HEART'S LINK TO A HEALTHY LIFESTYLE

The impact of regular participation in physical activity and a healthy lifestyle, in relation to the heart, is summarised in Fig 3.1.10 below.

Anaerobic activity has a similar impact but the health benefits gained are more significant if the activity is aerobic and of a higher aerobic intensity.

Fig 3.1.10 *Summary of heart link to a healthy lifestyle*

CHECK

If you are satisfied with your knowledge and understanding, tick off the sections that you have revised so far. If you are not satisfied, then revisit those sections and refer to the pages in the 'Need to know more?' features.

- ☐ Describe the link between the cardiac cycle and the conduction system of the heart.
- ☐ Describe the relationship between stroke volume, heart rate and cardiac output, and resting values for each.
- ☐ Explain the changes that take place to stroke volume, heart rate and cardiac output during different intensities of physical activity.
- ☐ Explain the regulation of heart rate during physical activity.

EXAM PRACTICE

Q.1 **a)** Taking part in physical activity is considered essential to maintaining a healthy lifestyle. Does the type of activity make a difference?

b) What are the positive impacts on the heart of participating in different types of physical activity?

5 marks

See page 165 for answers.

CHAPTER 3: PART II

Response of the cardiovascular (vascular) system to physical activity

LEARNING OBJECTIVES

By the end of this part you should be able to demonstrate knowledge and understanding of:

- Venous return: maintenance and impact on performance
- The distribution of cardiac output at rest and during exercise (the vascular shunt mechanism)
- The role of the vasomotor centre and the involvement of arterioles and precapillary sphincters
- O_2/CO_2 transport and the impacts of smoking
- Warm-up/cool-down effects on the vascular system
- Blood pressure: resting values and change due to exercise and hypertension
- The impact of physical activity on the cardiovascular system in reference to a lifelong involvement in an active lifestyle

THE VASCULAR SYSTEM

The vascular system controls blood supply. It consists of blood and blood vessels that transport and direct O_2 and CO_2 to and from the lungs, heart and body tissues/muscles.

- Cardiac output is distributed to the various organs/tissues of the body according to their need/demand for oxygen.
- The blood represents the substance that actually carries/transports the O_2 and CO_2.
- The vast system of blood vessels represents a system of tubing/plumbing that directs and delivers the flow of blood towards the body tissues/muscles.

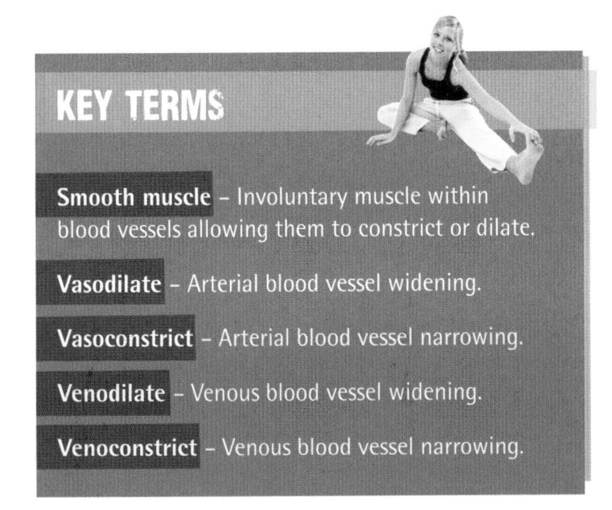

KEY TERMS

Smooth muscle – Involuntary muscle within blood vessels allowing them to constrict or dilate.

Vasodilate – Arterial blood vessel widening.

Vasoconstrict – Arterial blood vessel narrowing.

Venodilate – Venous blood vessel widening.

Venoconstrict – Venous blood vessel narrowing.

Circulatory networks

Blood vessel structure

- All blood vessels have three layers except for single-walled capillaries.
- Artery and arteriole walls have a large muscular middle layer of involuntary smooth muscle to allow them to vasodilate (widen) and vasoconstrict (narrow) to alter their shape/size to regulate blood flow.
- Arterioles have a ring of smooth muscle surrounding the entry to the capillaries into which they control the blood flow. Called precapillary sphincters, this ring of smooth muscle can vasodilate and vasoconstrict to alter their shape/size to regulate blood flow.
- Capillaries have a very thin, one-cell-thick layer to allow gaseous exchange to take place.

- Larger veins have pocket valves to prevent the back flow of blood and direct blood in one direction back to the heart.
- Venules and veins have a much thinner muscular layer, allowing them to venodilate (widen) and venoconstrict (narrow) to a lesser extent, and a thicker outer layer to help support the blood that sits within each valve.

Fig 3.2.1 Comparison of common structure of arteries, capillaries and veins

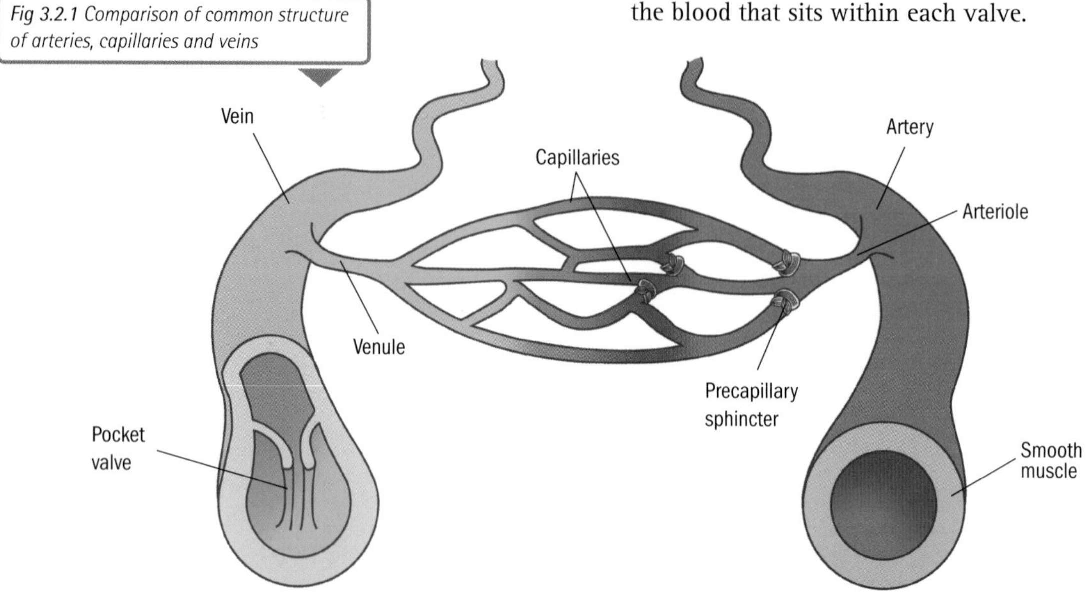

Fig 3.2.2 Double circulatory network: pulmonary and systemic circulation systems

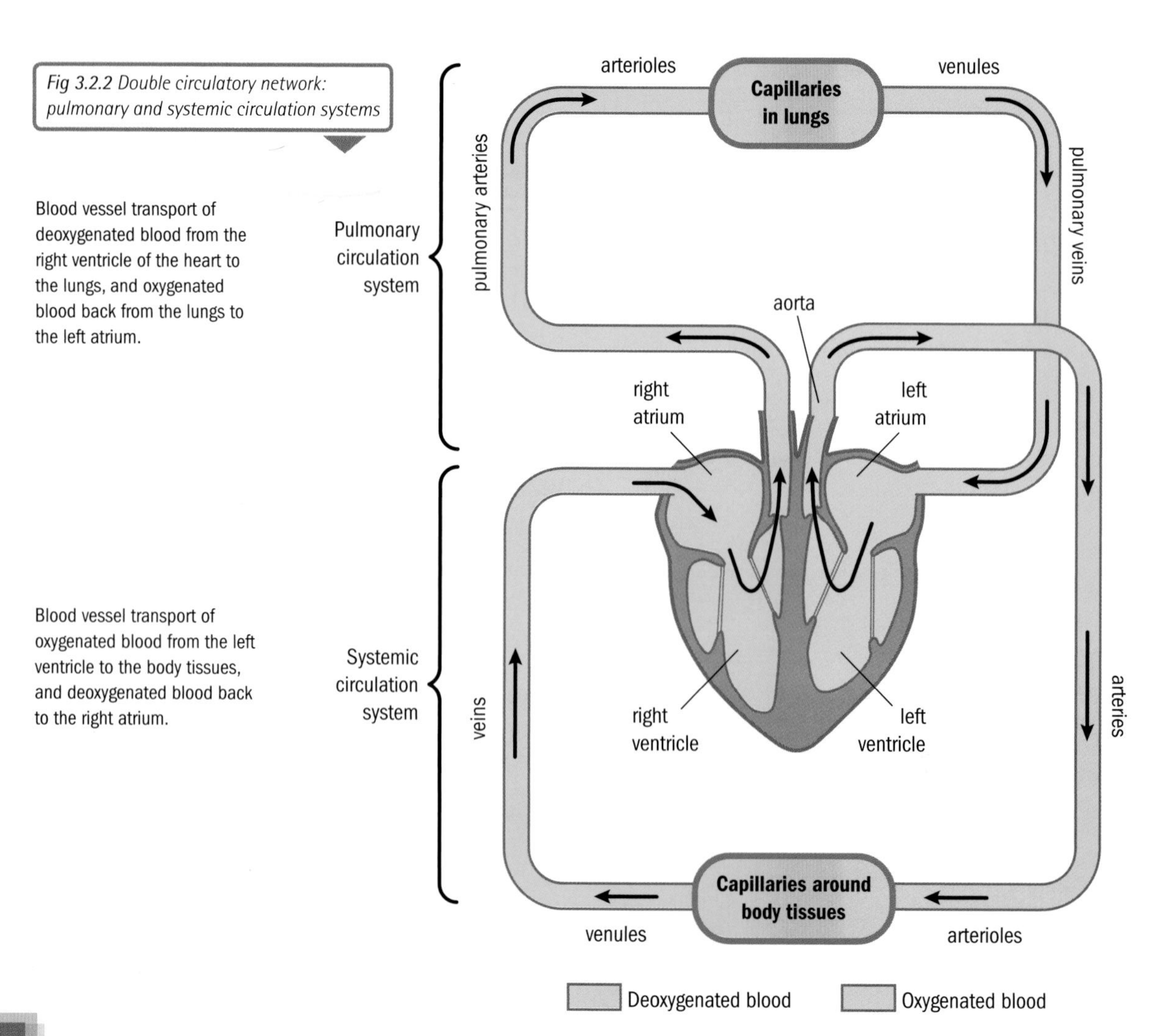

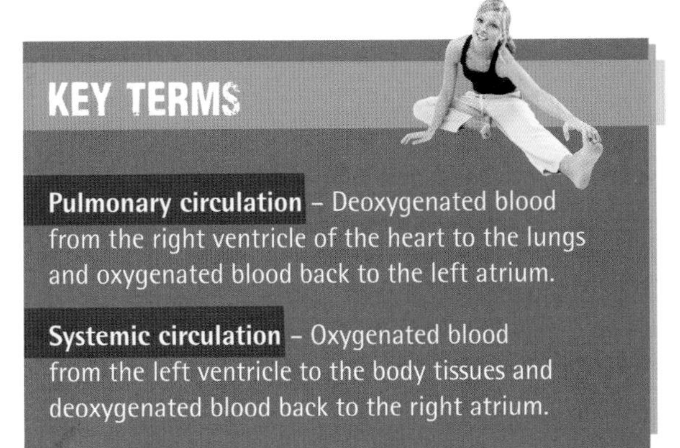

KEY TERMS

Pulmonary circulation – Deoxygenated blood from the right ventricle of the heart to the lungs and oxygenated blood back to the left atrium.

Systemic circulation – Oxygenated blood from the left ventricle to the body tissues and deoxygenated blood back to the right atrium.

REMEMBER IT!

Pulmonary arteries and veins do not carry blood normally associated with arteries and veins.

EXAM TIP

Exam questions often use the location of either the pulmonary artery or vein as a starting/reference point to test your knowledge of heart/vascular structure.

VENOUS RETURN MECHANISMS

Venous return

Venous return is the deoxygenated blood returning to the heart. Starling's Law of the heart states that 'Stroke volume is dependent upon venous return'. Hence, if VR increases, SV/Q increases and if VR decreases, SV/Q decreases.

Five venous return mechanisms help maintain/increase VR during exercise to ensure SV/Q are sufficient to supply the demand for oxygen during exercise.

1. Pocket valves (a).
2. Skeletal muscle pump (b).
3. Respiratory pump.
4. Smooth muscle (c).
5. Gravity.

Need to Know More? For further information on venous return mechanisms, see Chapter 3, Part II, page 83 in your Student Book.

REMEMBER IT!

SV directly affects cardiac output (Q), so if SV increases then Q increases. So VR is important because it determines SV and Q.

Blood pooling

VR requires a force to push blood back towards the heart. If there is insufficient pressure to push blood back towards the heart it causes blood pooling (blood that sits within pocket valves of veins) (Fig 3.2.4). An active cool-down prevents blood pooling after exercise by maintaining the muscle and respiratory pumps.

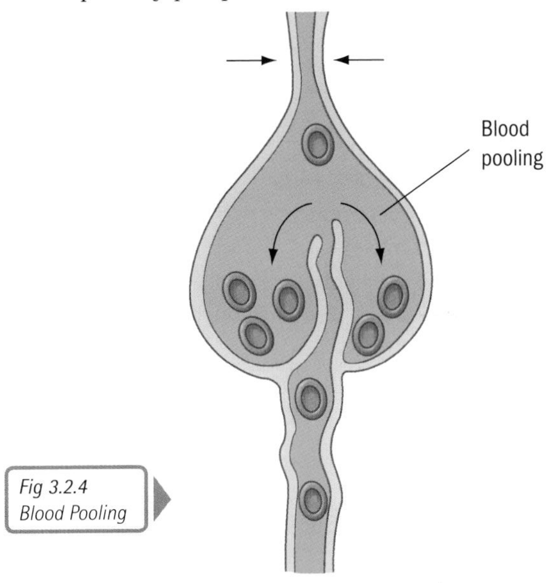

Fig 3.2.4 Blood Pooling

(a)

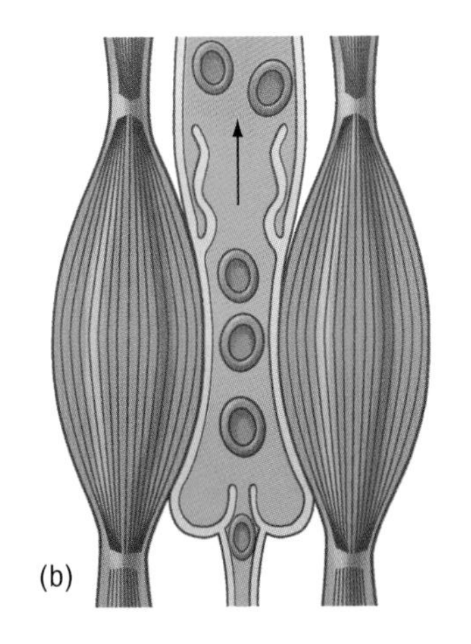

(b)

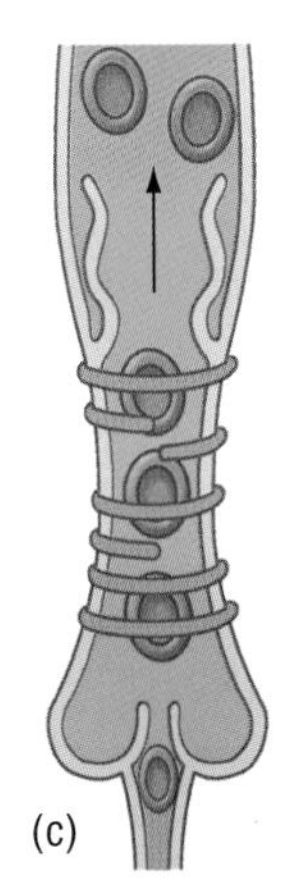

(c)

Fig 3.2.3 Venous return mechanisms

Venous return's impact on the quality of performance

VR determines SV and Q (Starling's Law). A reduction in SV/Q decreases oxygen transport to the working muscles, reducing their ability to contract/work aerobically.

Net effect: reduction in exercise intensity or muscles will work anaerobically and induce quicker muscle fatigue.

This is more significant in prolonged aerobic exercise dependent upon oxygen supply. It can also affect anaerobic activities in that a good VR will speed up recovery and therefore allow performers to work anaerobically for longer.

DISTRIBUTION OF CARDIAC OUTPUT (Q) AT REST AND DURING EXERCISE

Figure 3.2.5 summarises the redistribution of Q from rest to exercise conditions.

- At rest:
  - only 15–20 per cent of resting Q is supplied to the muscles
  - remaining 80–85 per cent Q is supplied to the body's organs.
- During exercise:
  - 80–85 per cent Q is supplied to the working muscles as exercise intensity increases
  - remaining 15–20 per cent of Q is supplied to the body's organs
  - blood supply to the brain is maintained.

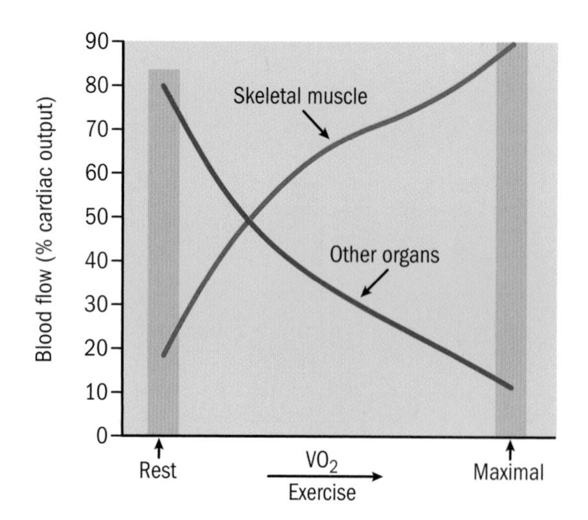

Fig 3.2.5 Redistribution of Q via vascular shunt mechanism

Vascular shunt mechanism

The process of redistributing cardiac output is called the vascular shunt mechanism.

- Skeletal muscle arterioles and precapillary sphincters vasodilate, increasing blood flow to working muscles.
- Organs' arterioles and precapillary sphincters vasoconstrict, decreasing blood flow to organs.

EXAM TIP

Up to four marks are available for explaining the vascular shunt mechanism: two marks are for vasodilation (one for arterioles or muscles, one for precapillary sphincters of muscles); two marks are for vasoconstriction (one for arterioles of organs, one for precapillary sphincters of organs).

Need to know more? For further information on redistribution of cardiac output between organs and muscles during exercise, see Chapter 3, Part II, page 85 in your Student Book.

EXAM TIP

Always link the redistribution of Q with the vascular shunt mechanism and vice versa.

VASOMOTOR CONTROL CENTRE

The vasomotor control centre (VCC) located in the medulla oblongata regulates the redistribution of Q by controlling the vascular shunt mechanism.

- Chemoreceptors and baroreceptors stimulate VCC.
- VCC increases or decreases stimulation via the sympathetic nervous system to either vasodilate or vasoconstrict the precapillary sphincters and arterioles supplying muscles and organs (vascular shunt mechanism) – see flow diagram, Fig 3.2.6.

Need To Know More? For further information on the vasomotor control centre, see Chapter 3, Part II, pages 87–88 in your Student Book.

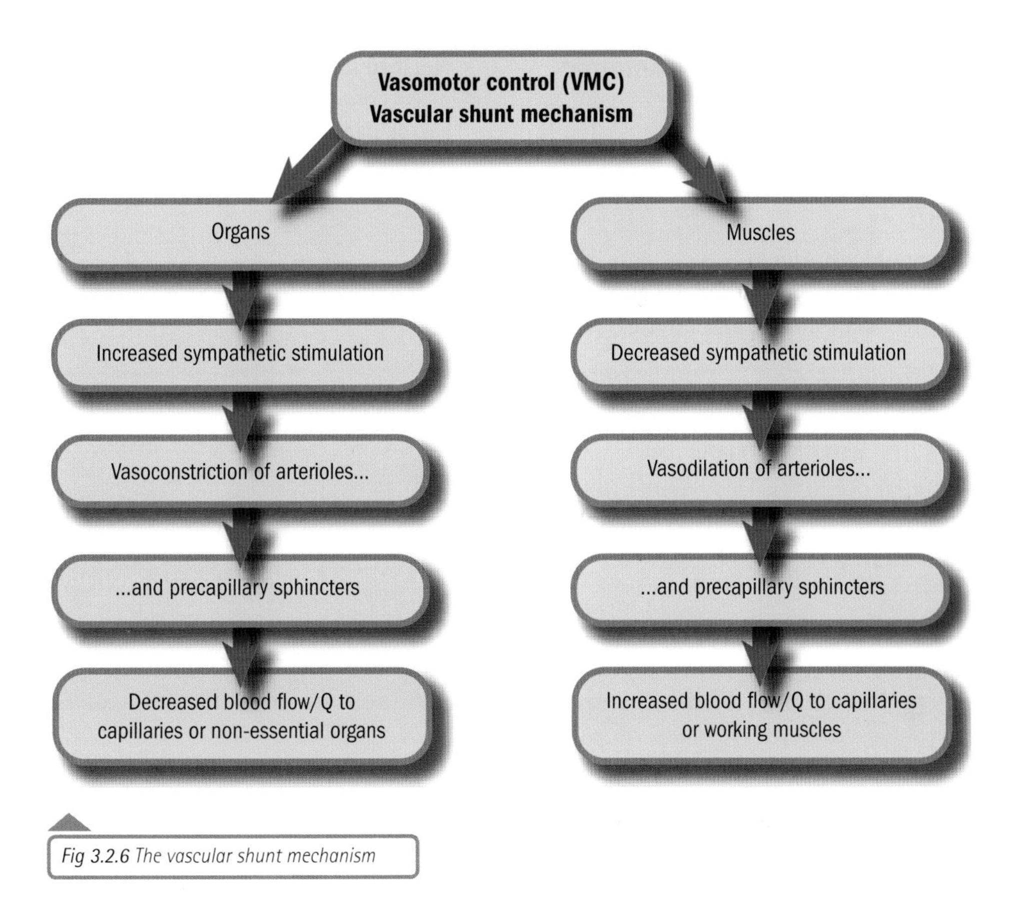

Fig 3.2.6 The vascular shunt mechanism

O_2 AND CO_2 TRANSPORT

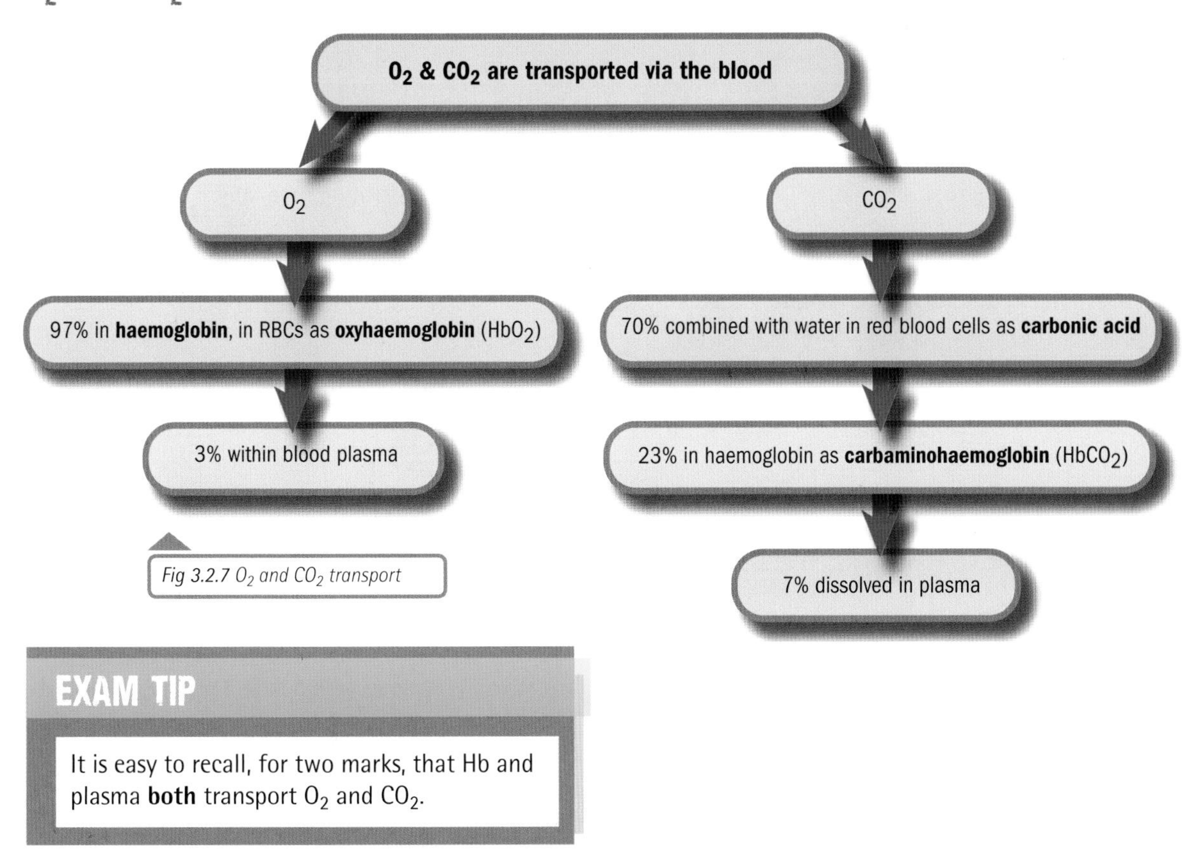

Fig 3.2.7 O_2 and CO_2 transport

EXAM TIP

It is easy to recall, for two marks, that Hb and plasma **both** transport O_2 and CO_2.

O_2/CO_2 – transport and performance

Efficient O_2 and CO_2 transport aids participation in physical activity in that it:

- prolongs duration of anaerobic and, especially, aerobic activity
- delays anaerobic threshold, which increases the possible intensity/work rate for the activity
- speeds up recovery during and after exercise.

Smoking's impacts on O_2 transportation

Tobacco smoke contains **carbon monoxide** (CO). Haemoglobin (Hb) within red blood cells combines with CO in preference to O_2. This reduces HbO_2 association in lungs and thus reduces maximal O_2 uptake. Blood O_2 transport/supply to the working muscles and lactate threshold are decreased.

Net effect: decreases optimal performance especially in aerobic activities. Hence, all the positive effects of efficient O_2 and CO_2 transport listed previously are reversed.

Need to Know more? For further information on O_2 and CO_2 transport, see Chapter 3, Part II, pages 87–88 in your Student Book.

Need to know more? For further information on effects of a warm-up and cool-down, see Chapter 3, Part II, pages 88–89 in your Student Book.

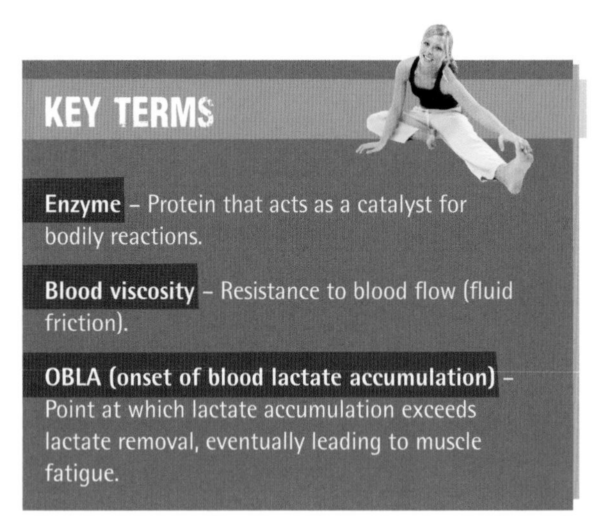

KEY TERMS

Enzyme – Protein that acts as a catalyst for bodily reactions.

Blood viscosity – Resistance to blood flow (fluid friction).

OBLA (onset of blood lactate accumulation) – Point at which lactate accumulation exceeds lactate removal, eventually leading to muscle fatigue.

WARM-UP/COOL-DOWN EFFECTS ON THE VASCULAR SYSTEM

Warm-up	Cool-down
Provides a gradual increase in blood flow/Q due to vascular shunt mechanism, via: • vasoconstriction of organ arterioles/precapillary sphincters, decreasing blood flow to organs • vasodilation of muscle arterioles/precapillary sphincters, increasing blood flow to muscles.	Keeps metabolic activity elevated, which decreases heart rate and respiration gradually.
Increases body/muscle temperature, increasing transport of **enzyme** activity required for energy and muscle contraction.	Maintains vasodilation of muscle arterioles/precapillary sphincters, which keeps capillaries dilated to flush muscles with oxygenated blood.
Increases body/muscle temperature which decreases blood viscosity, improving blood flow to working muscles, and increases dissociation of O_2 from haemoglobin.	Maintains respiratory/muscle pumps, which maintains venous return, which: • prevents blood pooling in veins • maintains blood flow (SV and Q) to supply O_2, which maintains blood pressure.
Decreases **OBLA** (onset of blood lactate accumulation) due to the onset of anaerobic work without a warm-up.	Increases the removal of blood and muscle lactic acid and CO_2.

Table 1 Warm-up and cool-down effects on vascular system

BLOOD PRESSURE (Bp)

- Blood pressure is the pressure exerted by the blood against the (arterial) blood vessel walls.
- Bp is normally expressed as: $\frac{\text{Systolic}}{\text{Diastolic}}$
- **Systolic** Bp represents ventricular systole and **Diastolic** Bp represents the ventricular diastole.
- The average resting Bp is $\frac{120 \text{ mmHg (in the aorta)}}{80 \text{ mmHg}}$ (mmHg = millimetres of mercury)
- Blood pressure is also expressed as: blood flow (Q) × resistance
- Bp is measured using a sphygmomanometer.

Bp changes during physical activity

Endurance (aerobic) training

- Systolic.
  - **Sub-maximal**: Systolic Bp increases in line with exercise intensity and may plateau during sub-maximal exercise (around 140–160 mmHg).
  - May decrease gradually if this sub-maximal intensity is prolonged.
  - **Maximal**: Systolic Bp continues to increase in line with intensity, from 120 mmHg to above 200 mmHg during exhaustive exercise intensity.
- Diastolic.
  - **Sub-maximal**: Diastolic Bp changes little during sub-maximal exercise.
  - During gross muscle activities like rowing/running **localised** muscular diastolic Bp may fall to around 60–70 mmHg.
  - **Maximal**: Diastolic Bp may increase a little (max 12%/>10 mmHg) as exercise intensity reaches maximum levels.

It is recommended that exercise should stop if diastolic Bp increases by 15 mmHg. (An athlete running may have a typical Bp of 200/60.)

Isometric (resistance) training

- Heavy weight-training involving isometric contractions causes a marked increase in both systolic and diastolic Bp which can exceed 480/350 mmHg.
- Resting Bp after resistance training tends to not change and may decrease.

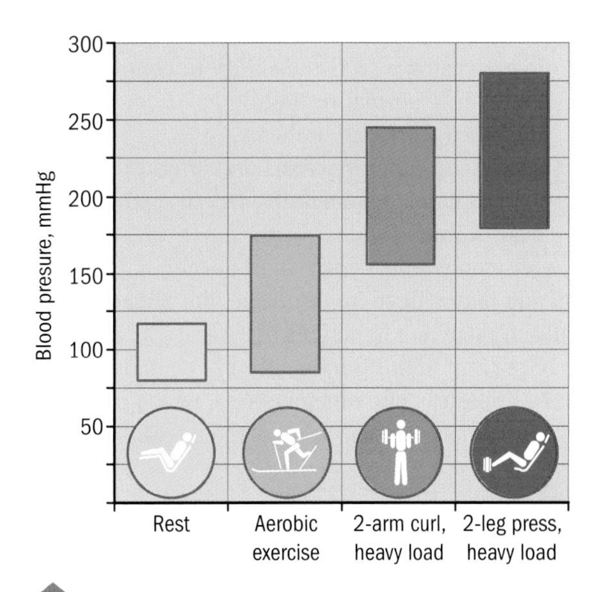

Fig 3.2.8 Blood pressure response to varying intensities of exercise

Post-exercise recovery

- Systolic Bp decreases temporarily below pre-exercise levels for up to 12 hours.
- Diastolic Bp also remains low/below normal resting levels for hours afterwards.

Long-term effects

- It is thought by some that resting Bp may decrease with continued endurance training.
- Resting Bp is generally lowered in people who already have mild/moderate hypertension.
- Endurance training can reduce the risk of developing high Bp.
- Bp changes little during sub-maximal or maximal work rates.
- Although resistance/isometric training significantly increases both systolic and diastolic Bp it does not increase resting Bp.
- There are little or no changes to those who are already max hypertensive.

Hypertension and Bp

Hypertension is long-term, enduring high Bp. Treatment is normally provided if Bp exceeds 140 mmHg over 90 mmHg, but 160 over 95 is more commonly regarded as real hypertension.

Effects:

- hypertension affects the ability to control/maintain a normal resting Bp
- increased workload on heart
- accelerates atherosclerosis and arteriosclerosis
- arterial damage, increasing risk of a stroke and heart failure.

Exercise may reduce the risk of developing high Bp and may reduce Bp in people that already have mild to moderate hypertension. An active lifestyle may prevent high Bp indirectly by reducing the risk of obesity and reducing stress, which may help to keep blood pressure at moderate levels.

Need to Know more? For further information on Blood Pressure, see Chapter 3, Part II pages 89–93 in your Student Book.

IMPACT OF PHYSICAL ACTIVITY ON THE CARDIOVASCULAR SYSTEM IN REFERENCE TO A LIFELONG INVOLVEMENT IN AN ACTIVE LIFESTYLE

Coronary heart disease (CHD)

Coronary heart disease (CHD) is the single largest cause of death in the Western world and is linked to a more sedentary lifestyle. There is a cause-and-effect relationship where the two blood vessel diseases lead to the two heart related diseases (Fig 3.2.9).

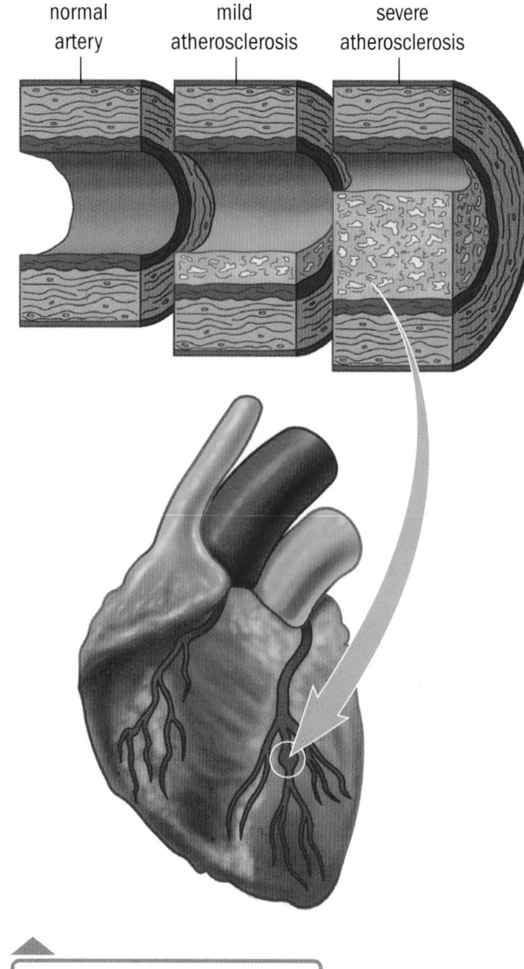

Fig 3.2.10 Development of atherosclerosis in a coronary artery

Blood Vessels (CHD)

Arteriosclerosis: Hardening of the arterial walls reducing their efficiency to vasodilate/constrict and regulate Bp and the vascular shunt mechanism.

Atherosclerosis: A progressive narrowing (of the diameter) of the arterial blood vessel walls from fatty deposits, restricting blood flow and increasing Bp and the formation of blood clots.

cause & effect

Heart (CHD)

Angina: Partial blockage of the coronary artery causing intense chest pain due to an inadequate O_2 supply to the heart muscle wall, normally to a smaller area of the heart.

Heart Attack: A more severe/sudden or total restriction in O_2 supply to part of the heart muscle wall usually causing permanent damage/death.

Fig 3.2.9 Effects of CHD on blood vessels and heart

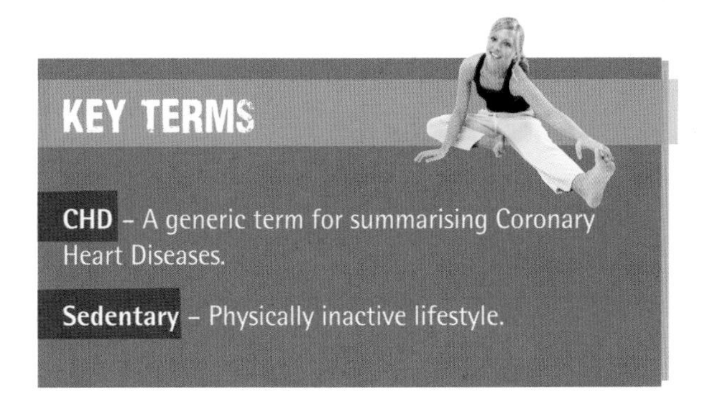

KEY TERMS

CHD – A generic term for summarising Coronary Heart Diseases.

Sedentary – Physically inactive lifestyle.

CHD risk factors

Five primary risk factors are associated with developing CHD.

1. Physical inactivity.
2. High blood pressure.
3. Smoking.
4. High blood lipids (diet).
5. Obesity (body mass index – BMI).

CHD is two or three times more likely in inactive sedentary individuals. Inactivity is a major risk factor for CHD, doubling the risk of a heart attack. There is a cause-and-effect relationship between physical inactivity and CHD. Lifelong involvement in an active lifestyle will help maintain significant protection from CHD.

Lessening the risk

Physical activity:

- improves heart efficiency: hypertrophy, pumping capacity and circulation
- improves vascular efficiency: vascularisation, capacity/size of coronary circulation
- decreases blood lipids, reducing athero/arteriosclerosis.

Net effect: reduces arterial disease thus reducing risk of angina/heart attack – and:

- may reduce Bp and risk of developing hypertension
- alleviates tension/stress helping reduce hypertension
- reduces obesity
- acts as a stimulus for a healthier lifestyle – to stop smoking and improve diet.

Regular physical activity and weight control by means of good nutrition/diet offer the greatest protection against developing CHD. Physical activity has an all encompassing effect on nearly all the CHD risk factors that cannot be achieved by modifying any other single risk factor in isolation.

Recommendations for physical activity

The health benefits to protect against CHD do not require high intensity exercise; the level of activity required is generally low. Walking, low-intensity jogging/cycling and similar activities provide adequate protection against CHD. However, higher intensity exercise will provide even greater protection.

The American College of Sports Medicine (ACSM) has outlined three guidelines in relation to physical activity which summarise the general recommendations found among health organisations across the world.

1. People should engage in moderate activity for at least 30 minutes most or, preferably, every day of the week.
2. People with or at risk of heart disease may need to:
   - improve cardiorespiratory fitness, approximately 3–4 hours of regular physical exercise per week
   - halt the progression of fatty plaques in the arteries, approximately 4–5 hours of regular physical exercise per week
     - for regression of fatty plaques, approximately 5–6 hours of regular physical exercise per week.
3. Activity does not need to be done in continuous blocks; accumulation of activity throughout the day may bring about an equivalent effect to that obtained from a single longer session.

The important thing to remember is that a healthier diet and a sustained programme of physical activity can chip away at fatty deposits which block precious oxygen from getting to your heart and lead to a lifelong involvement in an active and healthy lifestyle.

CHECK

If you are satisfied with your knowledge and understanding, tick off the sections that you have revised so far. If you are not satisfied, then revisit those sections and refer to the pages in the 'Need to know more?' features.

- ☐ Venous return: maintenance and impact on performance.
- ☐ The distribution of cardiac output at rest and during exercise (the vascular shunt mechanism).
- ☐ The role of the vasomotor centre and the involvement of arterioles and precapillary sphincters.
- ☐ O_2/CO_2 transport and the impacts of smoking.
- ☐ Warm-up/Cool-down effects on the vascular system.
- ☐ Blood pressure: resting values and change due to exercise and hypertension.
- ☐ Impact of physical activity on the cardiovascular system in reference to a lifelong involvement in an active lifestyle.

EXAM PRACTICE

Q.1 Blood pressure is essential to apply the force needed to circulate the blood around the body to supply oxygen to the working muscles.

a) Explain the difference between blood pressure and hypertension.

b) What changes occur to blood pressure during physical activity?

5 marks

See page 165 for answers.

CHAPTER 3: PART III

Response of the cardiovascular (respiratory) system to physical activity

LEARNING OBJECTIVES

By the end of this part you should be able to demonstrate knowledge and understanding of:

- The mechanics of breathing at rest and during exercise
- Respiratory volumes at rest and during exercise
- Resting: gaseous exchange during internal and external respiration
- Exercise: gaseous exchange, diffusion gradient and dissociation of oxyhaemoglobin
- Ventilatory response/regulation of breathing via neural/chemical control during exercise
- Altitude effects on the respiratory system and influences on performance
- The impact of physical activity, asthma and smoking on the respiratory system with reference to lifelong involvement in an active lifestyle
- Cardio-respiratory control.

REVIEW OF RESPIRATORY STRUCTURES

There are three main respiratory processes:

1. Pulmonary ventilation – the breathing of air in and out of the lungs.
2. External respiration – exchange of O_2 and CO_2 between the lungs and blood.
3. Internal respiration – exchange of O_2 and CO_2 between the blood and muscle tissues.

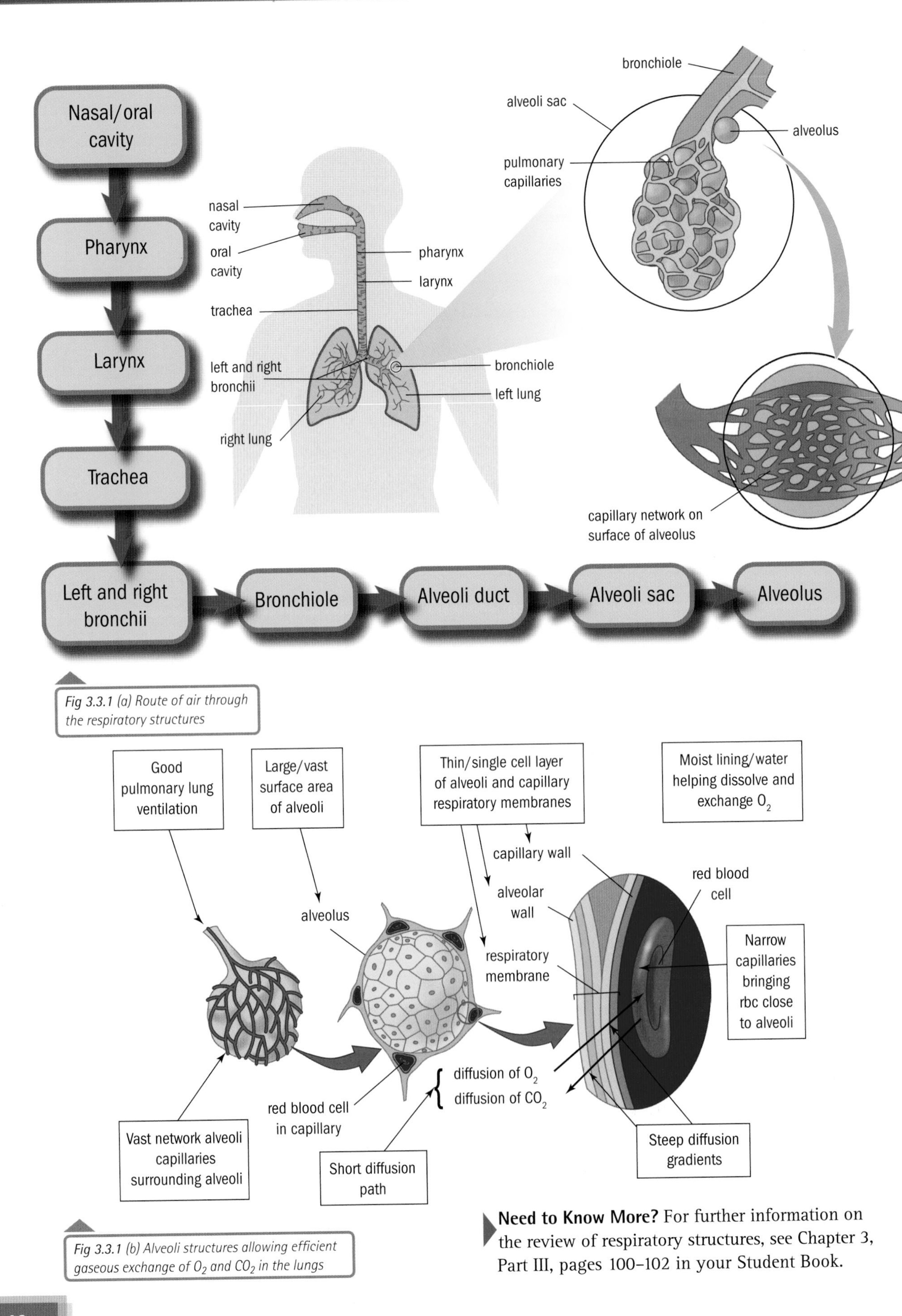

Fig 3.3.1 (a) Route of air through the respiratory structures

Fig 3.3.1 (b) Alveoli structures allowing efficient gaseous exchange of O_2 and CO_2 in the lungs

Need to Know More? For further information on the review of respiratory structures, see Chapter 3, Part III, pages 100–102 in your Student Book.

MECHANICS OF BREATHING AT REST AND DURING EXERCISE

Muscles apply the force to initiate the mechanics of breathing at rest and during exercise.

RESTING

Inspiration (active)	Expiration (passive)
1 Diaphragm contracts (**active**) External intercostals contract (**active**)	1 Diaphragm relaxes (**passive**) External intercostals relax (**passive**)
2 Diaphragm flattens/ pushed down Ribs/sternum move up and out	2 Diaphragm pushed upward Ribs/sternum move in and down
3 Thoracic cavity volume increases	3 Thoracic cavity volume decreases
4 Lung air pressure decreases below atmospheric air (outside)	4 Lung air pressure increases above atmospheric air (outside)
5 Air rushes into lungs	5 Air rushes out of lungs

Table 1 Mechanics of breathing at rest

EXERCISE

Inspiration (active)	Expiration (passive)
1 Diaphragm contracts External intercostals contract (**active**) ***Sternocleidomastoid*** contracts (**active**) ***Scalenes*** contract ***Pectoralis minor*** contracts (**active**)	1 Diaphragm relaxes External intercostals relax ***Internal intercostals*** contract (**active**) ***Rectus abdominus/ Obliques*** contract (**active**)
2 Diaphragm flattens with more force Increased lifting of ribs and sternum	2 Diaphragm pushed up harder with more force Ribs/sternum pulled in and down
3 Increased thoracic cavity volume	3 Greater decrease in thoracic cavity volume
4 Lower air pressure in lungs	4 Higher air pressure in lungs
5 More air rushes into lungs	5 More air pushed out of the lungs

Table 2 Mechanics of breathing during exercise

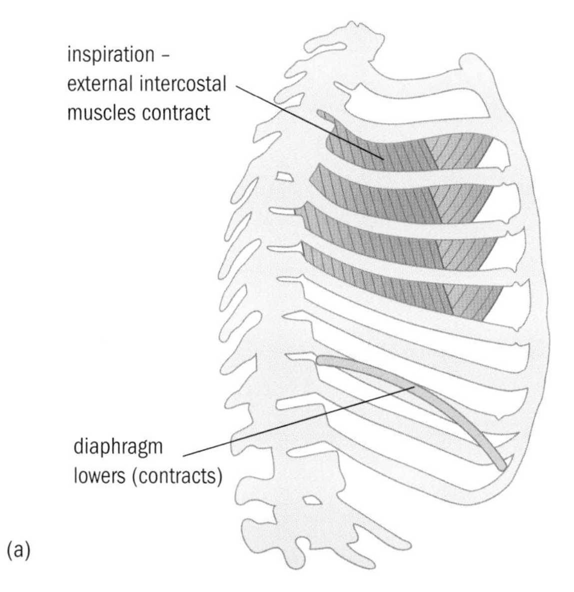

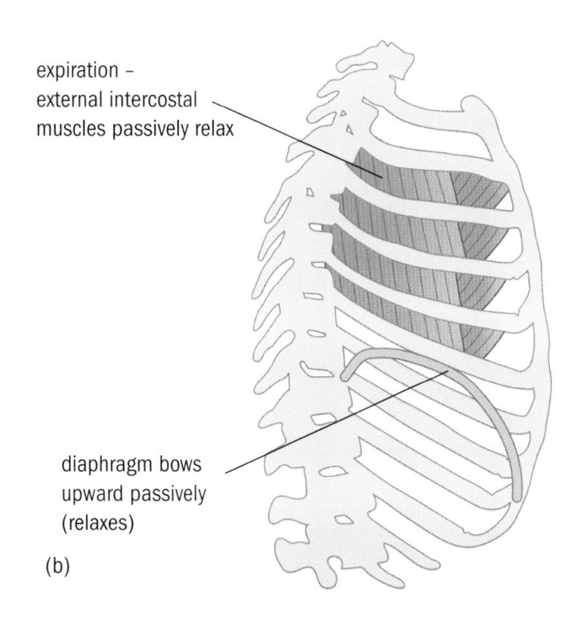

Fig 3.3.2 Active inspiration (a), and passive expiration (b) at rest

During exercise the demand for O_2 by the working muscles increases and it is the additional respiratory muscles that increase the depth and rate of breathing.

EXAM TIP

Respiratory muscles initiate breathing by increasing and decreasing the volume of the lung cavity and therefore lung pressures. Do not make the mistake of thinking the lungs or pressure differences themselves initiate breathing.

Need to Know More? For further information on mechanics of breathing, see Chapter 3, Part III, pages 103–104 in your Student Book.

RESPIRATORY VOLUMES

The link between tidal volume (TV), breathing frequency (f) and ventilation (VE) is shown by the following equation:

$$VE = TV \times f$$
$$= 500\,ml \times 15$$
$$= 7500\,ml/min$$
$$= 7.5\,l/min$$

EXAM TIP

Remember the close similarity between the heart and respiratory equations and don't confuse them when answering heart/respiratory volume questions.

Remember respiratory refers to air and heart refers to blood.

GASEOUS EXCHANGE: RESTING

- Gaseous exchange is the exchange of O_2 and CO_2 by the process of diffusion.
- Diffusion is the movement of a gas from an area of high pressure to an area of low pressure.
- The difference between the high and low pressure is called the **diffusion gradient**; the larger the gradient, the larger the diffusion/gaseous exchange that takes place.
- Partial pressure is the pressure a gas exerts within a mixture of gases.

KEY TERM

Myoglobin – Red pigment in muscles that stores and transports O_2 to mitochondria within muscles.

EXAM TIP

You will not be required to know actual partial pressures – only whether the pp is higher/lower and the reasons why.

Lung volume	Definition	Resting volume	Change due to exercise
tidal volume X	volume of air inhaled/exhaled per breath during rest	500 ml per breath	increases: up to around 3–4 litres
frequency = VE	number of breaths in one minute	12–15	increase: 40–60
minute ventilation	volume of air inspired/expired in one minute	6–7.5 l/min	increase: values up to 120 l/min in smaller individuals and up to 180+ l/min in larger aerobic trained athletes

Table 3 Lung volume changes during exercise

	External respiration	Internal respiration
where?	alveolar–capillary membrane, between alveoli air and blood in alveolar capillaries	tissue–capillary membrane, between the blood in the capillaries and the tissue (muscle) cells walls
movement	O_2 in alveoli diffuses to blood; CO_2 in blood diffuses to alveoli	O_2 in blood diffuses to tissue; CO_2 in tissue diffuses to blood
why? – O_2	pp of O_2 in alveoli higher than the pp of O_2 in the blood so O_2 diffuses into the blood	pp of O_2 in blood is higher than the pp of O_2 in the tissue so O_2 diffuses into the myoglobin within tissues
why? – CO_2	pp of CO_2 in the blood is higher than the pp of CO_2 in the alveoli so CO_2 diffuses into the alveoli	pp of CO_2 in the tissue is higher than the pp of CO_2 in the blood so CO_2 diffuses into the capillary blood

Table 4 Gaseous exchange during external and internal respiration

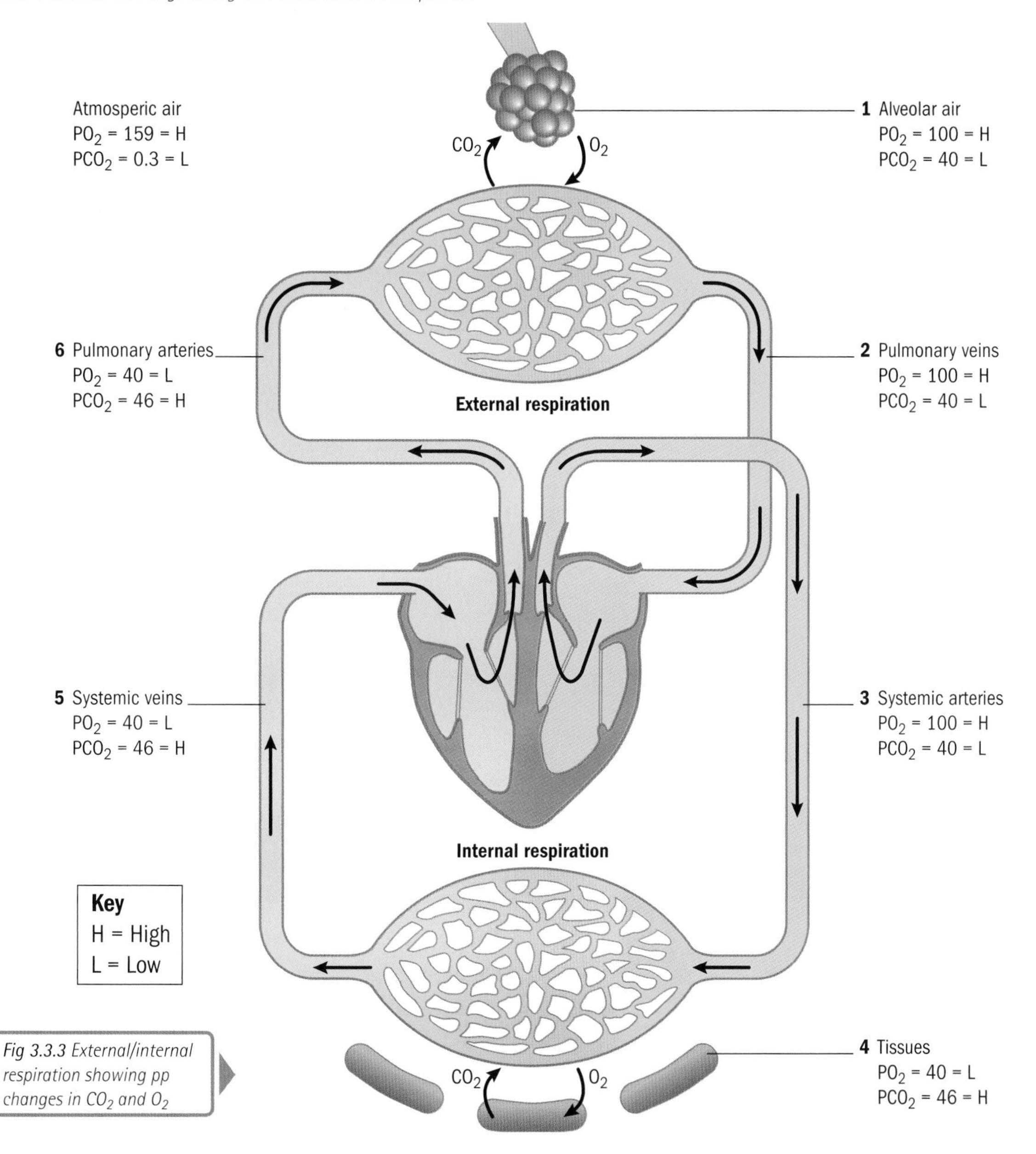

Fig 3.3.3 External/internal respiration showing pp changes in CO_2 and O_2

The simplest way to remember whether blood has a high or low pp of CO_2 or O_2 is to think back to the terms 'oxygenated' and 'deoxygenated'. If the blood is oxygenated, it has a high pp of O_2 and a low pp of CO_2. Deoxygenated blood has the opposite. Similarly, in the tissues/muscles and alveoli pp of O_2 and CO_2 are the opposite to that of the pp of blood within the vessels of the vascular system.

Need to know more? For further information on resting gaseous exchange see Chapter 3, Part III, pages 105–108 in your Student Book.

GASEOUS EXCHANGE: EXERCISE

An oxygen–haemoglobin dissociation curve informs us of the amount of haemoglobin associated/saturated with O_2.

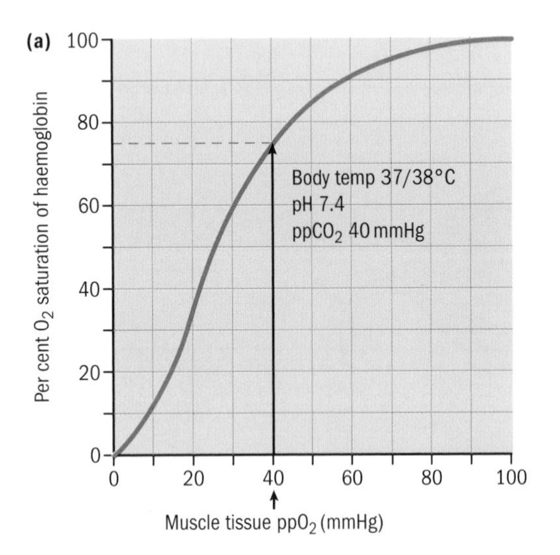

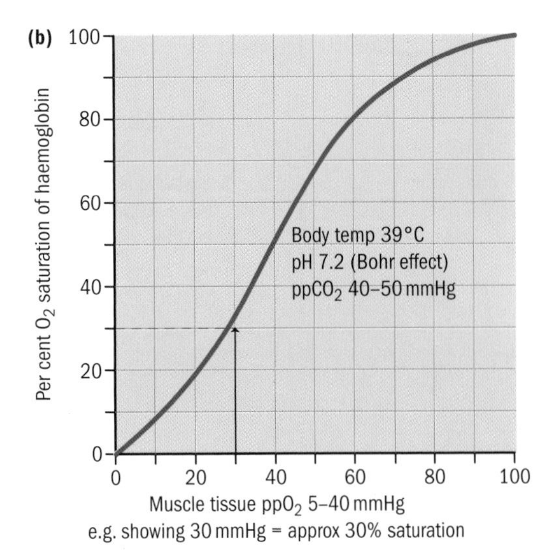

Fig 3.3.4 Comparison of oxygen–haemoglobin dissociation curves (a) at rest and (b) during exercise

REMEMBER IT!

The exchange of oxygen and carbon dioxide takes place in the lungs and tissues and is called external and internal respiration respectively.

Oxyhaemoglobin saturation (HbO_2) and diffusion gradients

Internal respiration

During exercise, four factors shift the dissociation curve to the right.

1. Increase in pp of CO_2 increasing O_2 diffusion gradient.
2. Decrease in pp of O_2 within muscle increasing O_2 diffusion gradient.
3. Increase in blood and muscle temperature.
4. Bohr effect – increase in acidity (lower pH).

These factors increase O_2/CO_2 diffusion gradients between blood capillaries/muscle tissue which therefore increase the dissociation of oxygen from Hb and the supply of O_2 to the working muscles.

Recall from Part II (see page 33) that oxygen is transported within the haemoglobin of the red blood cells (97 per cent) and blood plasma (3 per cent).

External respiration

Deoxygenated venous blood returning to the lungs has a higher pp of CO_2 and lower pp of O_2 than at rest. This increases the **diffusion gradient** for both O_2 and CO_2 across the alveoli-capillary membrane, resulting in both a quicker and greater amount of gaseous exchange. This ensures haemoglobin is almost fully saturated with oxygen.

Need to Know More? For further information on changes to gaseous exchange due to exercise, see Chapter 3, Part III, pages 108–111 in your Student Book.

VENTILATORY RESPONSE TO EXERCISE

Like heart rate, pulmonary ventilation (VE) changes in response to sub-maximal to maximal exercise. The following stages can be observed.

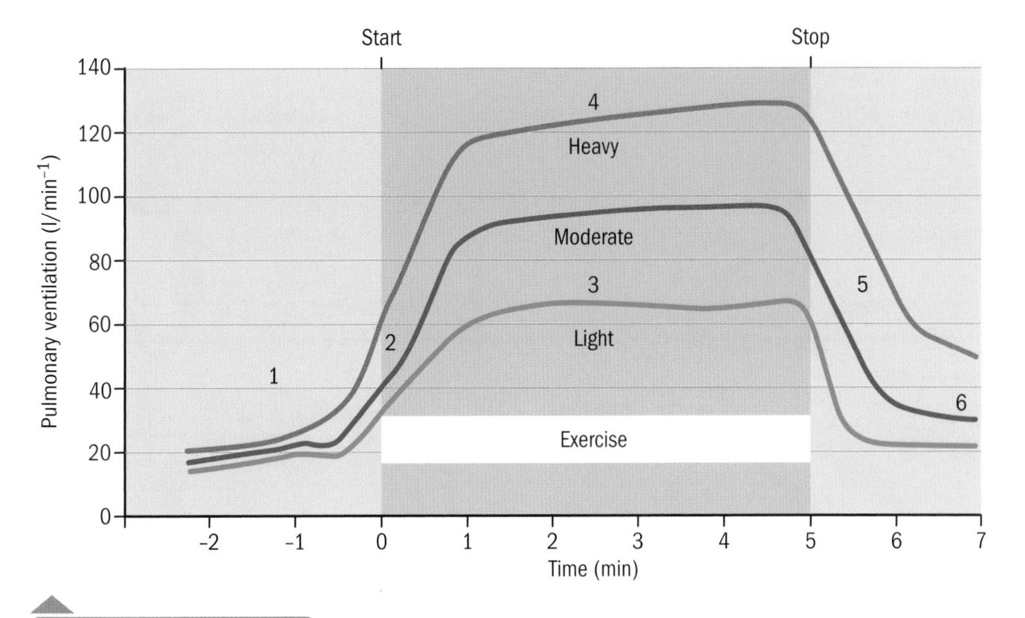

Fig 3.3.5 Ventilatory response to various intensities of exercise

EXAM TIP

You will be required to describe and explain the changes in VE from resting to sub-maximal and maximal workloads.

1. **Anticipatory rise** prior to exercise in all three work intensities in Fig 3.3.5 due to release of hormones and adrenalin, which stimulate the respiratory control centre (RCC).
2. **Rapid rise** in VE at the start of exercise due to neural stimulation of RCC by muscle/joint proprioreceptors.
3. **Slower increase/plateau** in sub-maximal exercise due to continued stimulation of RCC by proprioreceptors, but with additional stimulation from temperature and chemoreceptors (increase in temperature, CO_2 and lactic acid levels and a decrease in blood O_2). Plateau represents a steady state where the demands for oxygen by the muscles are being met by oxygen supply.
4. **Continued but slower increase** in heart rate towards maximal values during maximal work due to continued stimulation from the receptors above and increasing chemoreceptor stimulation due to increasing CO_2 and lactic acid accumulation.
5. **Rapid decrease** in VE once exercise stops due to the cessation of proprioreceptor and decreasing chemoreceptor stimulation.
6. **Slower decrease** towards resting VE values.

The more intense the exercise period, the longer the elevated level of respiration required to help remove the increased by-products of exercise – for example, lactic acid.

Need to Know More? For further information on ventilatory response to exercise, see Chapter 3, Part III, pages 111–112 in your Student Book.

Regulation of breathing via neural/ chemical control

The respiratory control centre (RCC) is located in the medulla oblongata of the brain and regulates breathing. It controls breathing via the respiratory muscles. The respiratory muscles are under involuntary neural control from the inspiratory and expiratory centres, which stimulate the respiratory muscles both at rest and during exercise.

Figs 3.3.6 and 3.3.7 summarise the factors affecting the RCC and respiratory control at rest and during exercise.

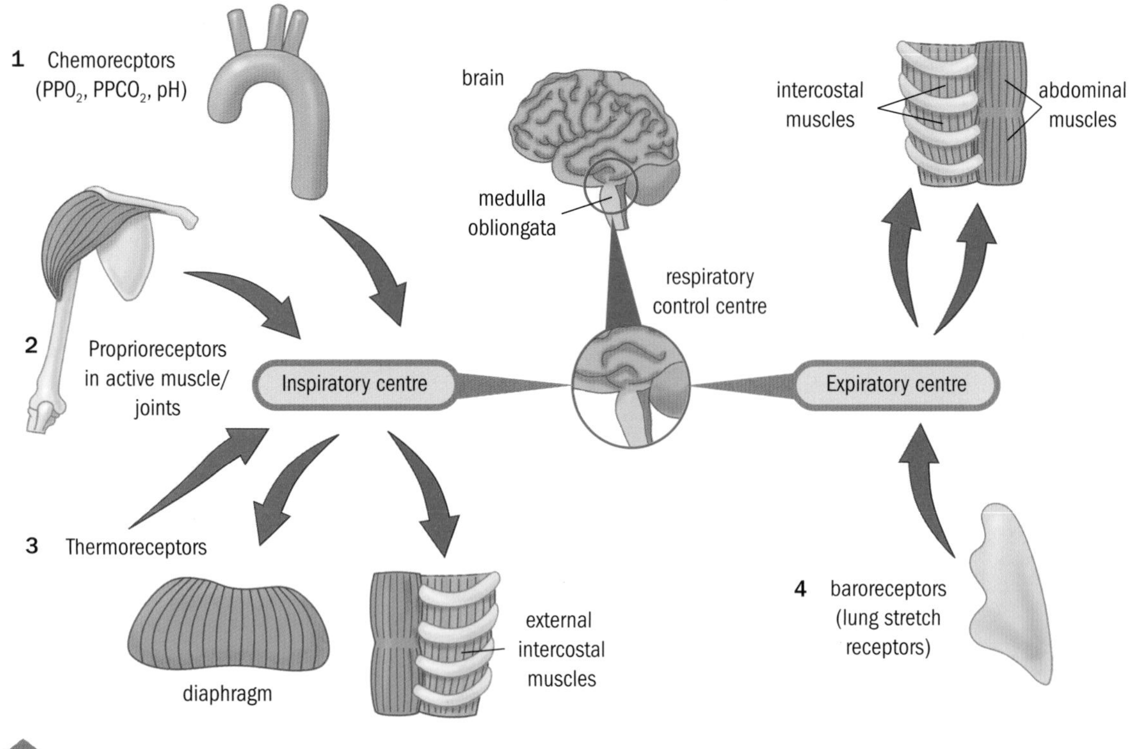

Fig 3.3.6 Factors affecting activity of the inspiratory and expiratory centres in the RCC

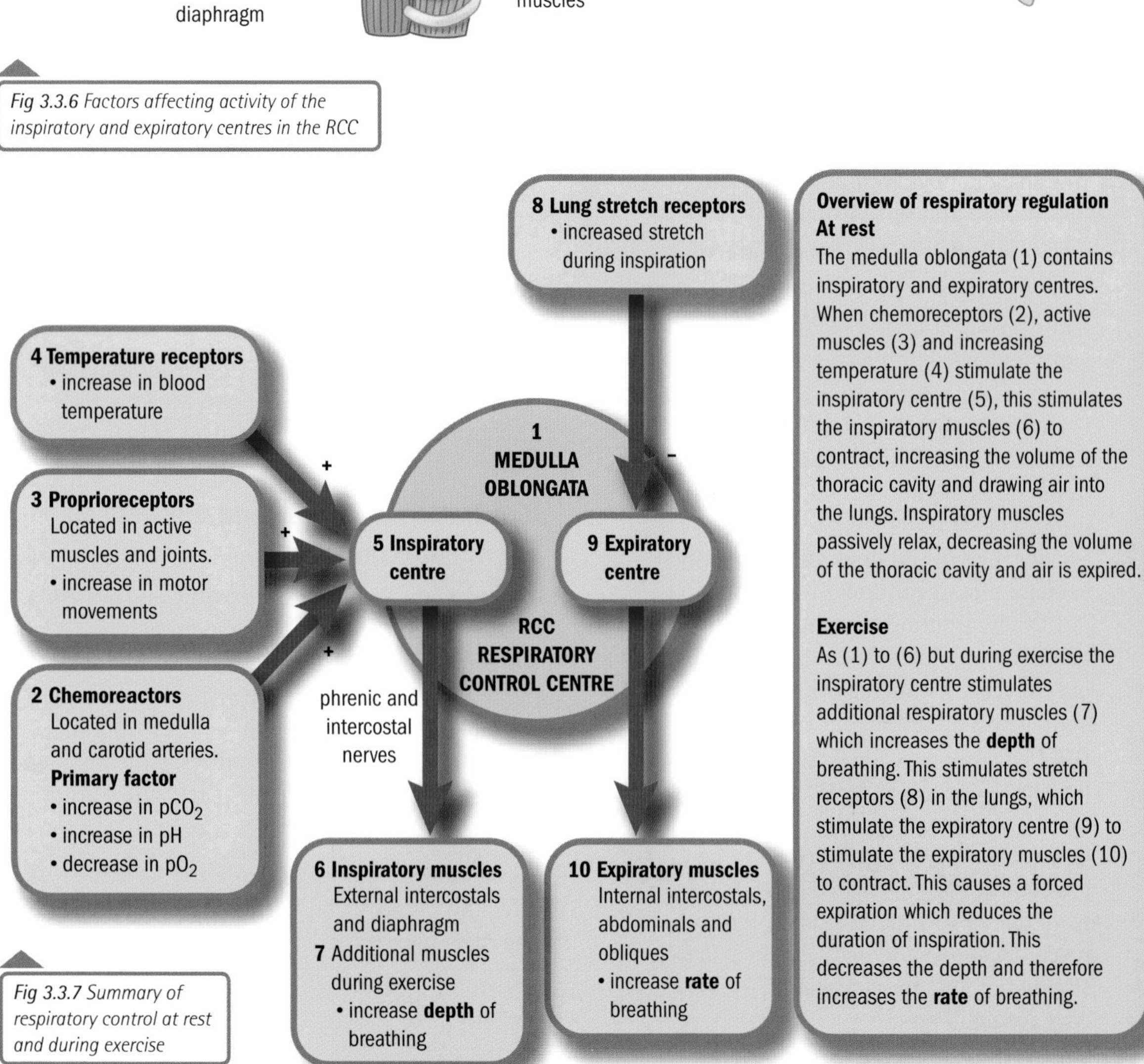

Fig 3.3.7 Summary of respiratory control at rest and during exercise

ALTITUDE EFFECTS ON THE RESPIRATORY SYSTEM

- Exposure to high altitude has a significant effect upon performance and is a recognised ergogenic training aid.
- At high altitude (above 1500 metres) the pp of oxygen decreases (hypoxic) and this has a series of knock-on effects which decrease the efficiency of the respiratory processes; these are summarised in Fig 3.3.8 below.

KEY TERM

Ergogenic – Anything that improves performance.

Performance at altitude leads to decreased power outputs, e.g. slower running and cycling speeds especially in aerobic events dependent upon O_2 supply.

Conversely, short anaerobic activities, e.g. 100/200 m sprints, long/triple/high jump, javelin/discus, are all events that may improve as a result of performance at altitude.

Need to Know More? For further information on effects of altitude on the respiratory system, see Chapter 3, Part III, pages 115–116 in your Student Book.

IMPACT OF PHYSICAL ACTIVITY ON THE RESPIRATORY SYSTEM WITH REFERENCE TO LIFELONG INVOLVEMENT IN AN ACTIVE LIFESTYLE

Respiratory adaptations to physical activity

The net training effect upon the respiratory system is to increase its efficiency to supply O_2 to the working muscles during higher intensities of physical activity, primarily due to an increase in efficiency of:

- respiratory structures
- breathing mechanics
- respiratory volumes
- gaseous exchange/diffusion.

Fig 3.3.8 Effects of altitude on the respiratory system

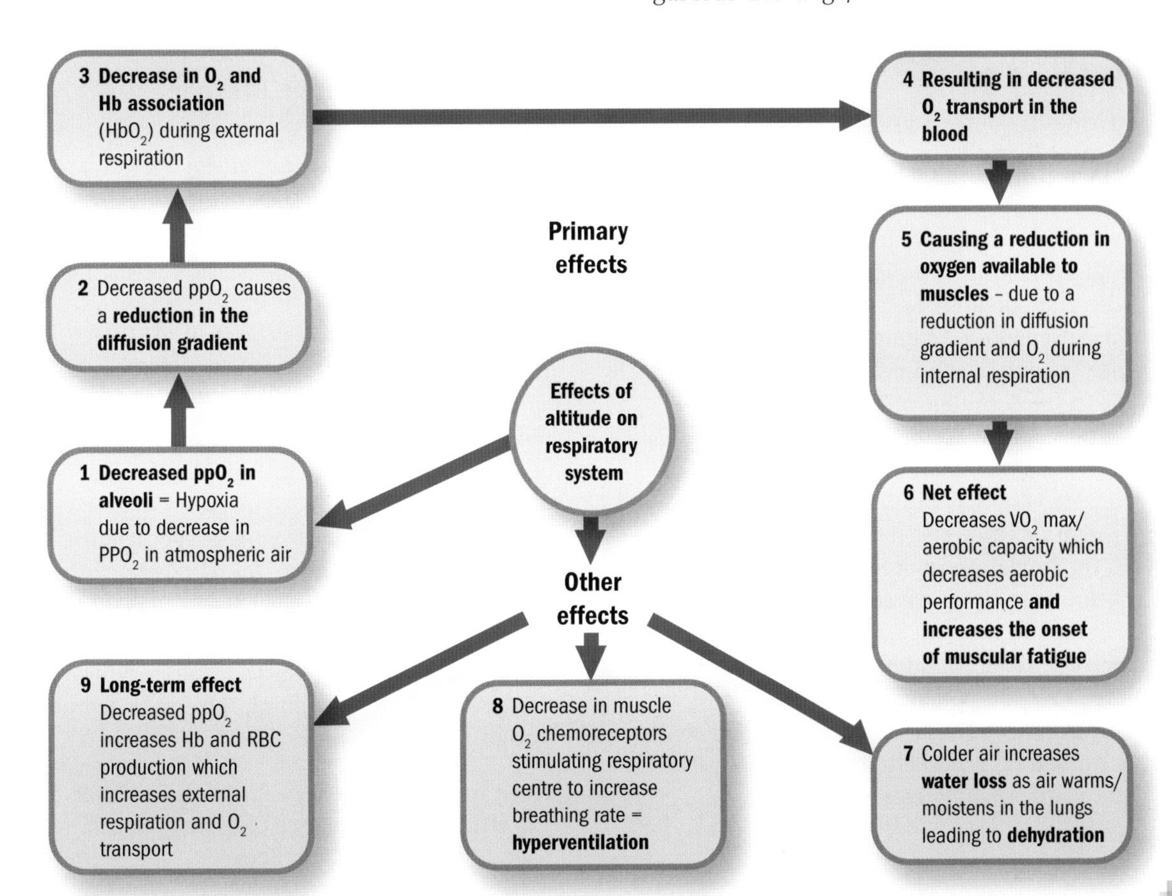

The net effect of all the above efficiency improvements is that **VO_2 max** and the **lactate threshold** increase, both of which improve performance, giving the following benefits.

- Aerobic performance during higher/maximal work rates is both increased and prolonged.
- The effort of sub-max work is reduced therefore increasing potential duration of performance.
- Greater effect on aerobic endurance activity – which is dependent more upon O_2 – although it will delay the anaerobic threshold and therefore delay fatigue during anaerobic activity.

If an athlete increases their lactate threshold they can run, swim or cycle faster aerobically, at an intensity that would previously have been anaerobic and caused an accumulation of lactate levels causing fatigue.

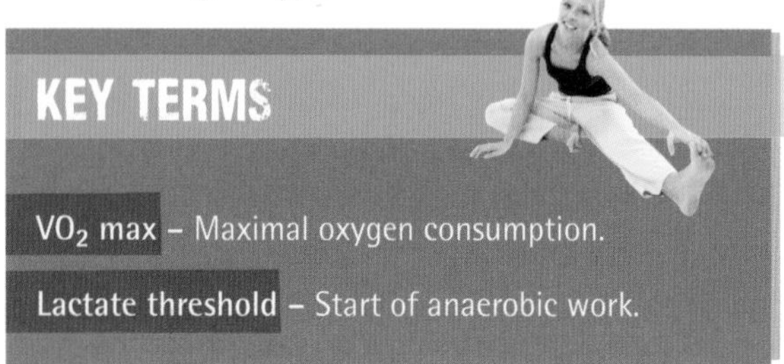

KEY TERMS

VO_2 max – Maximal oxygen consumption.

Lactate threshold – Start of anaerobic work.

Need to Know More? For further information on the impact of activity on the respiratory system and inspiratory muscle training (IMT), see Chapter 3, Part III, pages 116–118 in your Student Book.

Respiratory system and an active lifestyle

Asthma and an active lifestyle

- **Symptoms** – Asthma is the reversible narrowing of airways leading to: hyperirritability of airways, coughing, wheezing, breathlessness or mucus production.
- **Measurement** – Asthma is measured by inhaling into a spirometer and measuring the exhaled volume of air. If an individual improves their expiratory volumes after inhaling bronchodilator treatments they are considered to have asthma.
- **Triggers** – Drying of the airways causing an inflammatory response which constricts/narrows airways, termed bronchoconstriction. Common triggers include: exercise, known as 'exercise induced asthma' (EIA); exhaust fumes; dust; hair and pollens.
- **Performance effects** – Asthma can reduce performance, especially in elite aerobic athletes, and is increasingly common in athletes.
- **Management**
  - Medical treatments – treated by inhaled medication, bronchodilators.
    - '*Reliever*' (blue) relaxes muscles around airways and is normally taken before exercise or in response to symptoms.
    - '*Preventer*' (non-blue) suppresses the chronic inflammation/sensitivity of the airway structures and is normally taken daily.
  - Non-medical treatments.
    - A warm-up helps provide a 'refractory period' (asthma-free period) for up to two hours, avoiding EIA.
    - Caffeine is also a bronchodilator so pre-exercise caffeine drinks may be of use.
    - IMT increases strength of respiratory muscles, increases airflow and alleviates breathlessness, allowing improved performance. This is now a well established drug-free method of managing asthma for athletes.
    - Other strategies: stop conditions acting as triggers; refrain from training with respiratory infections or exercising in cold (winter)/dry air conditions.

Need to Know More? For further information on asthma and respiration, see Chapter 3, Part III, pages 118–120 in your Student Book.

Smoking and an active lifestyle

Smoking effects.

- Impairs lung function and diffusion rates.
- Increases damage and risk of respiratory diseases, infections and symptoms.
  - Irritates/damages/constricts/reduces elasticity of respiratory structures.
  - Triggers asthma, shortness of breath, coughing/wheezing, mucus/phlegm.

Performance effects.

- Smoking decreases the efficiency of the respiratory system to take in (VO_2 max) and supply O_2 to our working muscles.
- Smoking impairs performance, even among highly trained athletes.
- Mostly affects endurance based exercise, especially high-intensity maximal activity like the triathlon, but it reduces respiratory health in general so even walking the dog or a round of golf are impaired.

Need to Know More? For further information on the effects of smoking, see Chapter 3, Part III, page 127 in your Student Book.

CARDIO-RESPIRATORY CONTROL

It is easier to learn and understand the control mechanisms of the heart, vascular and respiratory systems as one. Fig 3.3.9 shows that many of the factors affecting the CCC, VCC and RCC are the same, and stimulate the control centres to respond at exactly the same time.

Fig 3.3.9 Summary of cardio-respiratory control during exercise

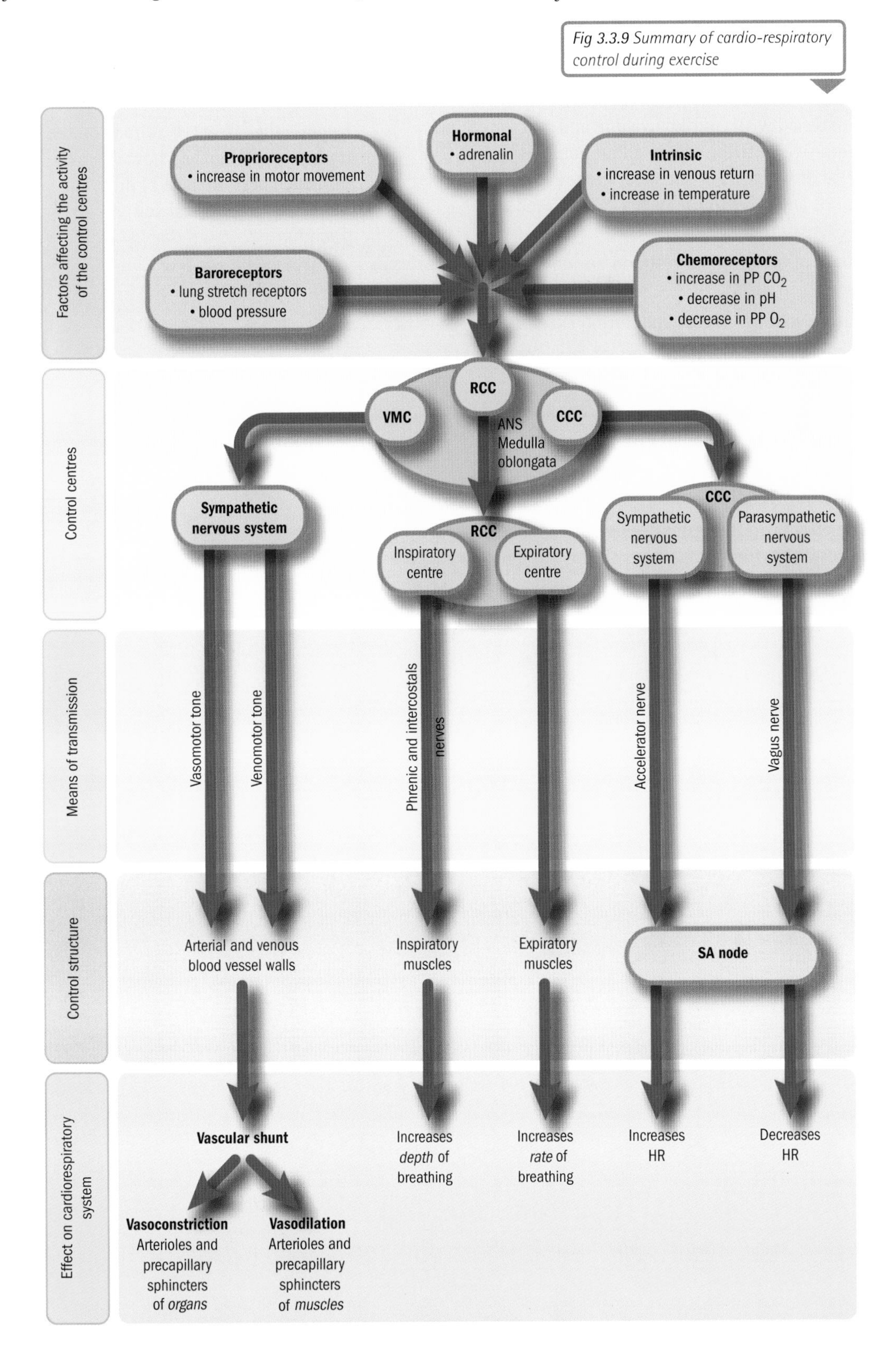

All exam questions on 'control' are incorporated within Fig 3.3.9. Practise and learn to identify question requirements, and which parts of this figure to include or leave out.

CHECK

If you are satisfied with your knowledge and understanding, tick off the sections that you have revised so far. If you are not satisfied, then revisit those sections and refer to the pages in the 'Need to know more?' features.

- ☐ Mechanics of breathing at rest and during exercise.
- ☐ Respiratory volumes at rest and during exercise.
- ☐ Resting: gaseous exchange during internal and external respiration.
- ☐ Exercise: gaseous exchange, diffusion gradient and dissociation of oxyhaemoglobin.
- ☐ Ventilatory response/regulation of breathing via neural/chemical control during exercise.
- ☐ Altitude effects on the respiratory system and influences on performance.
- ☐ Impact of physical activity, asthma and smoking on the respiratory system with reference to lifelong involvement in an active lifestyle.
- ☐ Cardio-respiratory control: summary.

EXAM PRACTICE

Q.1 In the 1968 Olympics held in Mexico at an altitude over 2300 m there were new world records established in the throw/jump and sprint events but none in any of the distance events.

Explain the effects of altitude on the repiratory system and how this may influence performance of different intensities of physical activity.
5 marks

See page 166 for answers.

CHAPTER 4

Classification of motor skills and abilities

LEARNING OBJECTIVES

By the end of this chapter you should be able to demonstrate knowledge and understanding of:

- The classification of movement skills by placing them on a variety of continua
- Methods of manipulating skills practice to facilitate learning and improve performance
- How to evaluate critically these methods and their effectiiveness in the learning of movement skills
- The characteristics of gross motor abilities and psychomotor abilities.

ANALYSING MOVEMENT SKILLS

We use a continuum (plural continua) to analyse a movement skill. Continua are on imaginary scales between two extremes that show a gradual increase/decrease in a number of characteristics.

We use continua to classify movement skills because:

- it is difficult to be specific as skills have elements of all characteristics to a greater or lesser extent
- these characteristics can change depending on the situation in which they are performed.

KEY TERM

Continuum (pl. continua) – An imaginary scale between two extremes that shows a gradual increase/decrease in a number of characteristics.

EXAM TIP

Make sure that you can explain why we use continua to classify skills.

CLASSIFYING MOVEMENT SKILLS

There are six continua that you need to be able to use to classify skills:

1. Muscular involvement: Gross – Fine
2. Environmental influence: Open – Closed
3. Continuity: Discrete – Serial – Continuous
4. Pacing: Self (internally) paced – Externally paced
5. Difficulty: Simple – Complex
6. Organisation: Low – High.

Let's now look at these in a little more detail.

1. **Muscular involvement**

   Gross ________________ Fine

   Gross

   Involves large muscle movements where there is little concern for precision. For example, hammer throwing is a gross skill.

   Fine

   Involves intricate movements using small muscle groups and emphasises hand–eye co-ordination. Usually involves accuracy. For example, the wrist and finger action of a spin bowler.

2. **Environmental involvement**

   Open ________________ Closed

   Open

   Movements that are affected by: the environment; team mates; opponents; playing surface. Lots of decisions to be made. They are usually externally paced. For example, shooting in basketball/netball.

   Closed

   Not affected by the environment, they are habitual. Follows a technical model. They are usually self-paced. For example, a gymnastic vault.

3. **Continuity**

   Discrete ______ Serial ______ Continuous

   Discrete

   Have a clear beginning and end. To be repeated this single skill must be started again. For example, a gymnastic through vault.

   Serial

   Skills that have a number of discrete elements put together in a definite order to make a movement or sequence. For example, a trampolining sequence or the triple jump.

   Continuous

   Have no definite beginning or end. The end of one cycle of the movement is the start of the next. For example, cycling or breast stroke.

4. **Pacing**

   Self (internally) paced ______ Externally paced

   Self (internally) paced

   The performer is in control and determines when the movement starts and the rate at which it proceeds. For example, a javelin throw.

   Externally paced

   The control of the movement is not determined by the performer but by the environment (often the opponent). For example, receiving a pass in football or hockey or receiving a serve in tennis or badminton.

5. **Difficulty**

   Simple ________________ Complex

   Simple

   Little information to process and few decisions to make. A small number of sub-routines involved where speed and timing are not critical. The use of feedback is not significant. For example, sprinting.

   Difficult

   Have a high perceptual load leading to many decisions having to be made. The skill will have many sub-routines where speed and timing are critical, together with the significant use of feedback. For example, a tennis serve.

6. **Organisation**

   Low ________________ High

   Low

   Made up of sub-routines that are easily separated and practised by themselves. For example, swimming strokes.

   High

   Movement skills where the sub-routines are very closely linked together and are very difficult to separate without disrupting the skill. For example, the golf swing.

Movement skills usually comprise several parts that are referred to as sub-routines; for example, breast stroke consists of body position, arm action, leg action and breathing. These sub-routines together make up the movement skill.

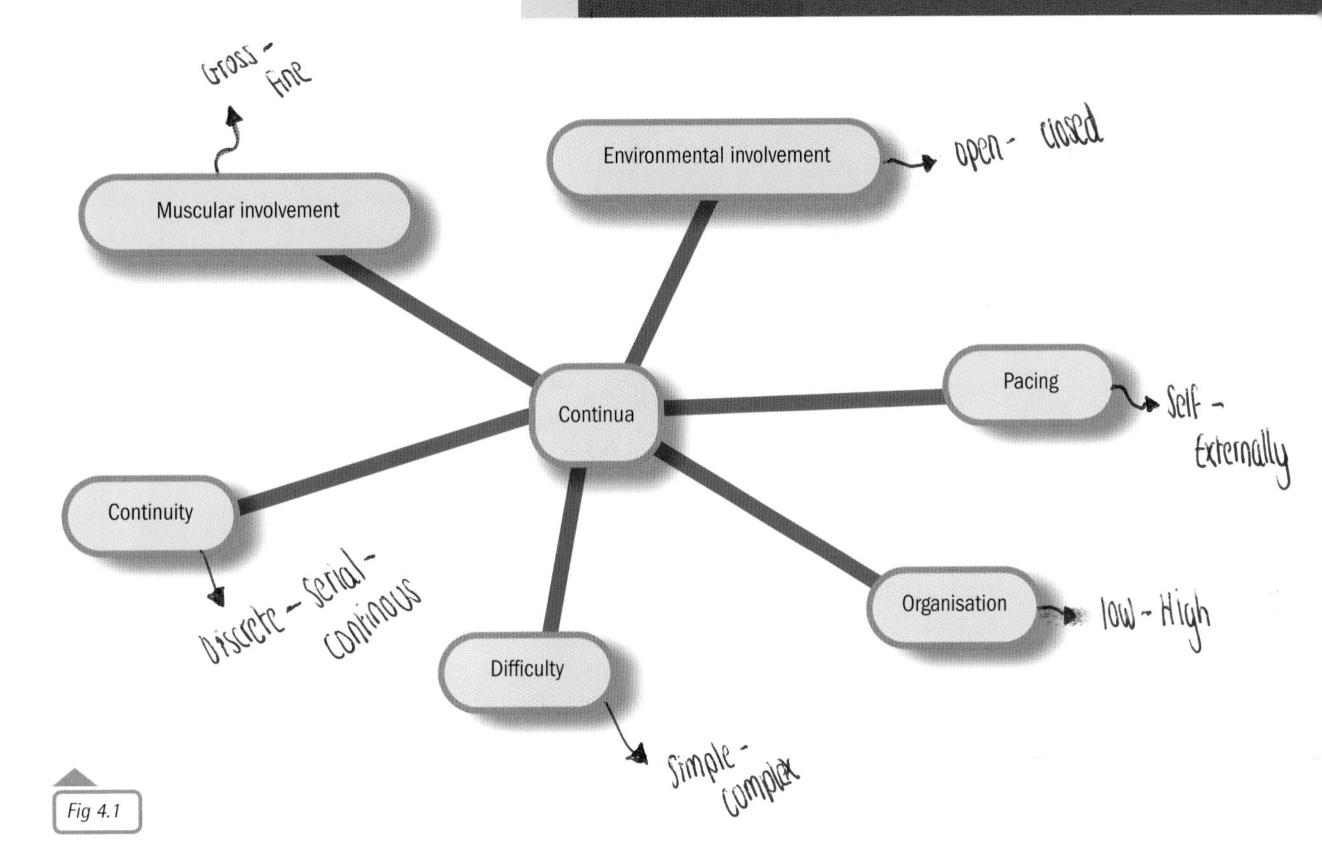

Fig 4.1

The application of classification to the organisation and determination of practice

We classify skills because it tells us:

- how to teach skills
- how we can improve skills
- how we can practise skills.

The conditions in which a skill is learned and practised should:

- be the same as those in which it is normally performed
- be determined by the nature of the skill
- ensure that positive transfer will occur.

Practice conditions are determined by the nature of the skill and in order to establish this several aspects need to be considered. This is called task analysis.

EXAM TIP

Whenever you are asked to classify a skill, you also need to be able to explain or justify how you have arrived at your decision. This is because the skill will be different depending on the situation it is performed in. You have to explain the situation the skill is being performed in together with the characteristics it has of the classification you are examining.

KEY TERM

Positive transfer – One skill helps the learning and performance of another.

Using the classification continua will tell us which practice method to use.

Classification type	Characteristics	Practice
continuous	end of one movement is the beginning of the next, cyclic	whole
discrete	single integrated action, specific skill, clear end and beginning	whole or part dependent on the skill
serial	several integrated actions, several discrete skills put together in a definite order	part method, progressive
low in organisation	skills that can easily be broken down into separate parts and practised by themselves	part method, progressive part method
high in organisation	skills that cannot easily be broken down into separate parts, without disrupting the skill	whole method
low in complexity	gross, habitual skills, low perceptual and decision-making aspects, few sub-routines to organise	whole method
high in complexity	intricate, highly perceptual with many decisions to be made and many sub-routines to be organised	part practice and simplification method

Table 1 Classification of skills

Need to know more? For further information on application of classification in determining practice methods, see Chapter 4, pages 125–129 in your Student Book.

USING SKILLS PRACTICE TO HELP LEARNING AND TO IMPROVE PERFORMANCE

Table 2 below identifies different types of practice and their characteristics.

Practice type	Characteristics	Example	Advantages	Disadvantages	Additional information
part practice	working on and perfecting isolated sub-routines; once the sub-routines are perfected they are put back together	practising body position, leg action and breathing of swimming strokes, and then putting them all together	• reduces the information to be processed and therefore reduces the possibility of overload • reduces the complexity and if the skill is dangerous reduces the risk and fear • success in the parts of the skill motivates the learner and gives confidence • good for learning serial skills and skills low in organisation	• takes longer than other methods • transferring the parts back into the whole can sometimes be difficult • learners can lose kinaesthetic sense and flow of the skill	• sub-routines must be divided into meaningful parts • learner must see the whole skill demonstrated prior to learning so they have an image of what they are learning

continued ▶

Practice type	Characteristics	Example	Advantages	Disadvantages	Additional information
whole practice	the skill is learned in its complete form without being broken down into sub-routines or parts	basketball dribble, cartwheel, golf swing, sprinting	• good for skills high in organisation or continuous; good for skills low in complexity • allows the learner to get the flow and timing (kinaesthesis) of the skill • helps the learner understand the movement • also can be quicker than other methods • good for ballistic skills	not suitable for complex or dangerous skills	ideally all skills should be taught by this method
progressive practices	parts of a complex skill are practised in isolation; they are then linked together to form larger and larger parts before finally becoming the whole skill: 1. Learn part 1 – perform part 1 2. Learn part 2 – perform parts 1 & 2 3. Learn part 3 – perform parts 1, 2 & 3 4. Learn part 4 – perform parts 1, 2, 3 & 4	gymnastic floor routine, triple jump, lay-up shot in basketball	• good for complex skills as it reduces the information load • good for skills low in organisation • good for serial skills • helps the flow of the skill and can also help the transfer of sub-routines into the whole skill	not suitable for skills high in organisation	sometimes known as chaining

continued ▶

Practice type	Characteristics	Example	Advantages	Disadvantages	Additional information
whole/part-whole	1. learner tries the whole skill first to get the feel of the performance 2. teacher identifies the weak parts of the skill and these are practised in isolation 3. once the weak parts are perfected the whole skill is tried again	tennis serve: coach identifies that the ball is not being tossed up high enough and practises and perfects this before returning to the whole serve	learner gets the feel for the skill and the flow; this method can be quicker than the part method as only the parts which the learner has difficulty with are practised	not suitable for highly organised or dangerous skills	

Table 2 Practice types

Need to know more? For further information on practice types, see Chapter 4, pages 130–134 in your Student Book.

CLASSIFICATION OF ABILIITES RELATING TO MOVEMENT SKILLS

Skill and ability are two different terms although we sometimes use the term 'ability' when we really mean 'skill'.

Characteristics of ability	Explanation
innate/genetically determined	we are born with abilities, which are determined by the genes we inherit from our parents
stable and enduring	abilities tend to remain unchanged but can be affected by our experiences and are developed by maturation
support, underly or underpin	each skill usually needs several supporting, underlying or underpinning abilities if we are going to be able to learn the skill effectively

Table 3 Characteristics of abilities

There are currently about 50 identified abilities. Abilities are divided into gross motor abilities and perceptual motor abilities.

While it is accepted that abilities are stable and enduring, some psychologists argue that they can be modified by our experiences and by maturation. Abilities usually improve up to a certain age and then deteriorate as we get older.

EXAM TIP

Make sure that you know the differences between skill and ability.

Schmidt says that ability is:

'...an inherited, relatively enduring trait that underlies or supports various kinds of motor and cognitive activities or skills. Abilities are thought of as being largely genetically determined.'

TYPES OF ABILITY

There are two types of ability that you need to know and be able to give examples of. They are gross motor abilities and pyschomotor abilities.

Gross motor abilities

Gross motor abilities are also known as physical proficiency abilities. They usually involve movement and are related to physical fitness.

Gross motor ability	Example
dynamic strength	exerting muscular force over a period of time, e.g. press-ups
static strength	maximum strength that can be exerted against an external object
explosive strength	energy used effectively for a short burst of effort, e.g. jumping in a rugby lineout
stamina	capacity to sustain maximum effort involving the cardiovascular system, e.g. running a marathon
extent flexibility	flexing or stretching the trunk and back muscles, e.g. touching your toes
dynamic flexibility	making several flexing movements, e.g. high knee lift in sprinting
gross body co-ordination	organisation of several parts of the body while it is moving, e.g. performing on the gymnastics parallel bar
gross body equilibrium	being able to maintain balance by using the internal senses and without using vision, e.g. performing a handstand
trunk strength	the strength of the abdominal muscles, e.g. performing sit-ups

Table 4 Gross motor abilities

Psychomotor abilities

Psychomotor abilities usually involve the processing of information, making decisions and putting these decisions into action. These actions are usually movements.

Psychomotor ability	Example
multi-limb co-ordination	being able to organise the movement of several limbs at the same time, e.g. swimming front crawl
response orientation	choosing quickly the position to which an action should be made, e.g. forehand drive in tennis.
reaction time	being able to respond quickly to a stimulus, e.g. sprint start
speed of movement	being able to make gross rapid movements, e.g. sprinting
manual dexterity	being able to make rapid arm/hand movements involving objects at speed, e.g. catching the ball in cricket
rate control	being able to change the speed and direction of responses accurately, e.g. following a continuously moving target on a computer game
aiming	being able to aim accurately at a small object, e.g. putting in golf

Table 5 Psychomotor abilities

Explosive strength

Gross body co-ordination

EXAM TIP

Make sure that you can identify the supporting or underpinning abilities necessary for different activities. For example, gymnastics needs strength, co-ordination, balance and flexibility.

What do abilities do?

Abilities underpin or support skills. We need several abilities in order to learn a skill effectively; for example, a handstand – balance, strength, body co-ordination. If we have good levels of these abilities then we should be able to learn to do a handstand and other similar gymnastic activities quickly so we can perform them well.

Natural athletes

There is no such thing as a 'natural athlete' or 'games player'. Some people are lucky enough to have good levels of the abilities that are required to be successful in a group of activities, which, because the activities are similar, require the same combination of abilities to underpin or support them.

These people will still, even though they have these good levels of the necessary abilities, have to learn to apply and co-ordinate them through practice if they are to be successful.

When we learn a skill, we require different abilities at different stages of our learning.

How are abilities developed?

Abilities can be developed during early childhood if children:

- are given a wide range of experiences
- are given the opportunity to practise
- receive expert teaching and coaching
- have access to facilities and equipment
- have the support of their friends and families who may also be suitable role models.

EXAM TIP

Examiners sometimes ask how abilities are developed, so make sure that you can give examples of each of the points above.

CHECK

If you are satisfied with your knowledge and understanding, tick off the sections that you have revised so far. If you are not satisfied, then revisit those sections and refer to the pages in the 'Need to know more?' features.

- ☐ Classify movement skills by placing them on a variety of continua.
- ☐ Describe methods of manipulating skills practice to facilitate learning and improve performance.
- ☐ Evaluate critically these methods and their effectiveness in the learning of movement skills.
- ☐ Define and identify the characteristics of gross motor abilities and psychomotor abilities.

EXAM PRACTICE

Q.1 Developing movement skills is important if you want to follow a balanced, active and healthy lifestyle. Describe what is meant by discrete, serial, continuous, simple and complex skills. Use examples of motor skills to support your answer.
5 marks

Q.2 The progressive part method is one way of learning a movement skill.
Use a practical example to describe this method. What are the advantages of using this method?
5 marks

Q.3 Identify the characterisitics of abilities. Give examples of a gross motor ability and a psychomotor ability.
5 marks

Q.4 Compare the following methods of manipulating skills: part, whole, progressive part and whole–part–whole. Critically evaluate their effectiveness in the learning of movement skills.
10 marks

See page 167 for answers.

CHAPTER 5

The development of motor skills and the use of practice methods

CHAPTER OVERVIEW

By the end of this chapter you should be able to demonstrate knowledge and understanding of:

- Characteristics of Fitts and Posner's phases of learning
- Applying these phases of learning to practical activities
- Describing and critically evaluating different types of guidance used in different phases of learning to improve performance
- Describing practice methods and their impact on effective and efficient performance
- Describing and critically evaluating types of practice methods and their application to the performance of movement skills.

PHASES/STAGES OF LEARNING

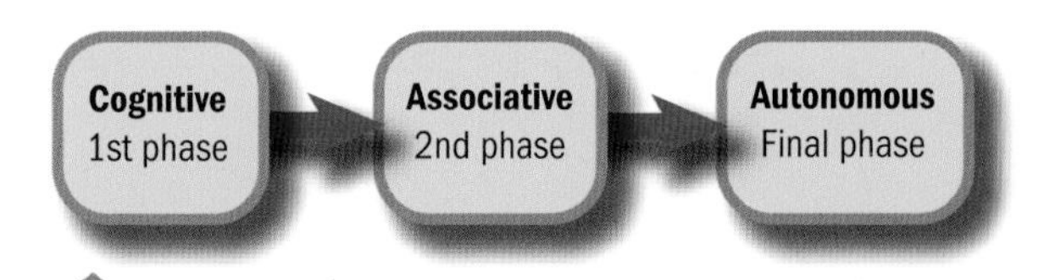

Fig 5.1 Fitts and Posner's three phases of learning

EXAM TIP

Do not confuse the cognitive phase of learning with cognitive learning theory. Although they sound similar they are unrelated and often confuse students.

Fitts and Posner suggested that learning is sequential and that we move through specific phases or stages as we learn. Learners do not suddenly move from one stage to the next but undergo a gradual change in learning characteristics from stage to stage.

Demonstrations are important in the cognitive phase of learning

Phase/stage	Characteristics	Example	Feedback
cognitive Earliest Stage of learning	initial/first phase: • demonstrations and verbal explanations are very important as the learner tries to form an accurate mental picture of the skill • learners should be given guidance as to the important cues to focus on (selective attention) • learners use trial and error and should receive positive feedback when successful	• teacher demonstrates overhead clear in badminton and explains the coaching points to the learner • this enables learner to form a mental picture of the skill	• external feedback important • positive feedback to reinforce successes • specific feedback to enable them to correct errors
associative Longest Stage of learning	the practice or second phase of learning; usually longer than cognitive phase, some learners never progress beyond this phase • learner begins to eliminate mistakes and errors are fewer and less gross; the basics of the skill are learned and become more consistent • motor programmes are developed and sub-routines become more co-ordinated leading to the skill becoming smoother • learner begins to use internal/ kinaesthetic feedback and detect some of their errors	1. learner has a good mental picture of the overhead clear and practises it 2. the clear goes high and over the net 3. teacher praises the learner for getting the shuttle high and over the net 4. the learner is told to focus on getting the shuttle to the back tramlines 5. learner starts to know what aspects of the clear they are getting right and those which are wrong without being told by the teacher 6. they try to correct these mistakes	the learner is able to utilise more detailed verbal feedback
autonomous Elite Staging.	final, third phase of learning: • after much practice the learner can execute the skill with minimum conscious thought and can focus on other factors; the motor programme has been established and stored in the long-term memory; the skill has been 'grooved' or overlearned • self-confidence increases and the learner is able to detect errors and correct them • practice needs to be maintained so that the learner does not go back to the associative stage	learner is now able to focus on where on the court to place the shuttle in relation to their opponent's position	• greater use of internal/intrinsic feedback • external feedback is used to highlight errors and to maintain improvement

Table 1 The three phases of learning

EXAM TIP

Visual guidance is best used in the cognitive stage of learning. Verbal guidance can be used effectively during the autonomous stage of learning.

Need to know more? For further information on phases/stages of learning see Chapter 5, pages 142–147 in your Student Book.

TYPES OF GUIDANCE AND THEIR IMPACT UPON EFFECTIVE PERFORMANCE AND PARTICIPATION

The four types of guidance that can be used by the teacher to help the learning process are: visual; verbal; manual; and mechanical (see Table 2).

EXAM TIP

You need to know the advantages and disadvantages of each method of guidance, and for which phases of learning they are most appropriate.

Type of guidance	Characteristics	Example	Advantages	Disadvantages
visual	• visual guidance helps the learner form their mental image of the skill • demonstrations provide an excellent means of transmitting information about the skill • vision is the dominant sense and we learn through imitation • demonstrations need to be accurate and focus on important aspects of the skill • visual guidance can also be: video, charts, diagrams, markings on floor etc.	• teacher demonstrates a chest pass drawing attention to hand position, extension of the elbows and transfer of body weight	• very effective in the cognitive/ early stages of learning • allows learner to form an accurate mental image of the skill by viewing demonstrations • allows skilled performers to analyse their performance	• demonstrations cannot be too complicated or long/contain too much information • demonstrations need to be very accurate • static visual aids do not give information about movement patterns

continued ▶

<table>
<tr><th>Type of guidance</th><th>Characteristics</th><th>Example</th><th>Advantages</th><th>Disadvantages</th></tr>
<tr><td>verbal</td><td>• most frequently used form of guidance
• often used in conjunction with visual guidance to direct learner to the important cues
• needs to be clear and concise
• teacher has to get the information across to the learners and they have to understand it and relate it to the skill being learned</td><td>• teacher/ coach giving information on tactics and strategies in a team talk
• teacher tells the learner the coaching points they need to focus on in the chest pass, e.g. hand and finger positions, flexed elbows, extend elbows, transfer body weight, extend fingers</td><td>• effective in the learning of open skills which require decision-making and perceptual judgements
• most effective in the autonomous phase when information can be detailed and technical</td><td>• amount of information has to be limited
• difficult to describe complex skills
• learners can become bored
• coach has to get information across and learners have to relate the information to the skill being learned</td></tr>
<tr><td>manual</td><td>• involves the teacher/coach holding and physically manipulating the body of the learner through the correct pattern of movement</td><td>• teacher supports the learner doing a handstand or guides the learner's arm through a forehand drive in tennis</td><td rowspan="2">• allows the learner to experience how the skill should feel
• useful in the early stages of learning to allow the learner to develop a kinaesthetic sense of the movement
• very useful in giving confidence and ensuring safety in dangerous skills
• allows the learner to experience the spatial and timing aspects of the movement</td><td rowspan="2">• the feel of the movement the learner experiences is different from the actual movement
• these forms of guidance have to be removed as soon as possible so the learner does not become dependent
• they are of limited use for the experienced performer
• as they are designed to eliminate errors they do not give the learner the opportunity to correct mistakes</td></tr>
<tr><td>mechanical</td><td>• involves the use of equipment to help support the learner and shape the skill</td><td>• trampolinist using a harness
• swimmer using floats, arm bands or rings</td></tr>
</table>

Table 2 Learning process – the four types of guidance

Need to know more? For further information on types of guidance see Chapter 5, pages 145–148 in your Student Book.

PRACTICE METHODS AND THEIR IMPACT UPON EFFECTIVE AND EFFICIENT PERFORMANCE OF MOVEMENT SKILLS

There are four methods of physical practice:

- massed
- distributive
- fixed
- variable.

Method	Characteristics	Example	Advantages	Disadvantages
massed	• learners practise a skill continuously without any breaks or rest intervals • practice sessions are usually long • can be used when coach wants to simulate performance conditions where there is an element of fatigue	basketball players practise their shooting skills by doing drills which involve many shots from different positions around the 'D'	• good for the grooving in of skills • good for experienced highly motivated performers who have good fitness levels • good for discrete skills of short duration • can save time as skills don't have to be re-introduced after breaks	• can lead to boredom or fatigue • beginners can be affected by lack of concentration • can cause fatigue and de-motivation which lead to poor performance and poor learning. • does not allow for extrinsic feedback
distributive	• practice sessions have rest intervals included • rest intervals allow time to recover both mentally and physically • research has shown this to be the most effective form of practice	the learner in the swimming pool swims a width of the pool and then rests while the teacher gives them some feedback	• good for beginners and learners with low levels of motivation and fitness • good for the learning of continuous skills • rest intervals allow learner to receive extrinsic feedback and to do mental practice • helps to maintain motivation and is good for dangerous or complex skills	more time-consuming than massed practice

continued ▶

Method	Characteristics	Example	Advantages	Disadvantages
fixed	• a specific movement pattern is practised repeatedly in the same, stable environment • allows movement patterns to be overlearned and become habitual • sometimes called a skill drill	• discus thrower practises in the discus circle and uses repetitive practices because the environment they perform in never changes • the diameter of the circle is always the same, the weight of the shot and the throwing area never change	most suitable practice method for closed skills that require specific movement patterns to be overlearned and become habitual	not suitable for open skills
variable	• a skill is practised in many environments • the practice conditions must be as realistic as possible • techniques are adapted to suit the environment	4 vs 5 passing practice in football/hockey – passing, support and positional play will be developed	• most suitable method for open skills • practising in a variety of environments develops schema • develops learner's perceptual and decision-making skills	the learner must have established the skill's motor programme in a fixed practice environment before being introduced to varied practice

Table 3 The four methods of physical practice

Need to know more? For further information on practice methods see Chapter 5, pages 148–151 in your Student Book.

Fixed practice is ideal for closed skills

MENTAL PRACTICE/MENTAL REHEARSAL

Mental rehearsal or practice is when the performer goes through the movement in their mind without any physical movement occurring. It has the following characteristics.

- Used in early/cognitive phase of learning to build up the mental picture of the skill to be learned; e.g. learner watches teacher demonstrate short badminton serve and goes over the skill in their mind.
- Advanced performers use it to rehearse complex skills or to go over strategies or tactics. The gymnast prior to performing will go through their routine visualising the performance of each movement in the routine.
- Can be used to reinforce successful movements, e.g. the golfer who has just hit a successful shot mentally practices the successful swing as they walk down the fairway.
- Experienced performers use mental rehearsal for emotional control and to establish optimum levels of arousal. It is also used to reduce anxiety, increase confidence and to focus on winning or being successful.
- When mental practice takes place the muscular neurones fire as if the muscle is active.
- Research has shown that mental rehearsal can improve performance both for experienced performers and learners.
- It should not be used as an alternative to physical practice as used on its own it is not as effective as physical practice.
- Used in conjunction with physical practice it can increase the speed of learning, e.g. learners' mental practice during the rest intervals of distributive practice sessions.
- It is most effective when used with skills that have a high cognitive element, e.g. team game strategies, gymnastic routines.

CHECK

If you are satisfied with your knowledge and understanding, tick off the sections that you have revised so far. If you are not satisfied, then revisit those sections and refer to the pages in the 'Need to know more?' features.

- ☐ Identify characteristics of Fitts and Posner's phases of learning.
- ☐ Apply these phases of learning to practical activities.
- ☐ Describe and evaluate critically different types of guidance used in different phases of learning to improve performance.
- ☐ Describe practice methods and their impact on effective and efficient performance.
- ☐ Describe and evaluate critically different types of practice methods and their application to the performance of movement skills.

EXAM PRACTICE

Q.1 What is distributive practice, when might it be used and what are the advantages of this type of practice?
5 marks

Q.2 Manual and mechanical guidance are similar methods widely used by Physical Education teachers and coaches.

What are mechanical and manual guidance? What are the advantages of using manual and mechanical guidance for teaching swimming to beginners?
5 marks

Q.3 It has been suggested that the learning of movement skills passes through the three phases. What is meant by the associative phase of learning?
4 marks

Q.4 Discuss the advantages and disadvantages of massed and distributed practice, explaining what type of skills they are most suited for use with. When might you consider using mental practice and what are its advantages when compared with physical practice?
10 marks

See page 171 for answers.

CHAPTER 6

Information processing during the performance of skills in physical activity

LEARNING OBJECTIVES

By the end of this chapter you should be able to demonstrate knowledge and understanding of:

- Models of information processing and their effectiveness in the learning and performance of movement skills
- The multi-store model of the memory process and apply it to the learning and performance of physical activities
- Reaction time and its role in developing effective performance in physical activities.

MODELS OF INFORMATION PROCESSING AND EFFECTIVENESS IN THE LEARNING AND PERFORMANCE OF MOVEMENT SKILLS

There are three stages to information processing:

1. **Stimulus identification**: Firstly detecting that there is a stimulus (information) and then interpreting the information, e.g. there is a ball coming and then determining its speed, flight and direction.
2. **Response selection**: Having interpreted the information (the speed, flight and direction of the ball), deciding what to do, e.g. move in the appropriate direction and put the appropriate limb in position.
3. **Response programming**: This is when the information is sent via the nervous system to the appropriate muscles to carry out the appropriate movement.

KEY TERMS

Stimulus – Information that stands out from the background and to which the performer pays attention.

Proprioception – The sense that allows us to know what position our body is in, what our muscles are doing and to feel things involved in our performance, e.g. the ball, the hockey stick. It consists of touch, kinaesthesis and equilibrium.

Perception – The process that involves the interpretation of information. This is the process by which we make sense of the stimuli we receive.

Motor programme – A series of movements stored in the long-term memory. They specify the movements the skill consists of and the order they occur. They can be retrieved by one decision.

Display
The surroundings/environment the performer is in. For the netball player this includes the ball, team mates, opponents, spectators, umpires, coach/teacher.

Sensory input
Senses detect information which stimulates their receptors. Senses involved are vision, hearing and proprioception. Proprioception is the sense that allows us to know what position our body is in, what our muscles are doing and to feel things involved in our performance, e.g. the ball or hockey stick. Proprioception consists of touch, kinaesthesis and equilibrium.

Perception
The process that interprets and makes sense of the information received. It consists of three elements: detection (a stimulus is present), comparison (comparing to stimuli in long-term memory) and recognition (matching it to one found in the long-term memory).

Memory
This plays an important role in both the perceptual and decision-making processes. It consists of short-term sensory stores (STSS), short-term memory (STM) and long-term memory (LTM)

Decision-making
(translatory mechanisms)
Once the information has been interpreted the correct response has to be put into action. This will be in the form of a motor programme.

Effector mechanism
The motor programme is put into action by sending impulses via the nervous system to the appropriate muscles to carry out the required actions.

Feedback
Once the motor programme has been put into action the display changes and new information is created. This new information is known as feedback. This is the information received by the performer during the movement and as a result of it. There are two major types of feedback: intrinsic and extrinsic feedback.

Fig 6.1 Basic processes of information processing

KEY TERM

Feedback – The information received by the performer during the course of the movement or as a result of it.

Intrinsic feedback	Extrinsic feedback
• feedback from internal proprioceptors about the feel of the movement • kinaesthesis is involved • important to experienced performers who are able to use it during a movement to control that movement • beginners need to be made aware of this type of feedback in order to experience the movement's feel • for example, feel of whether or not you have hit the ball in the middle of the bat in a cricket shot	• feedback from external sources such as the teacher/coach • received by the visual and auditory senses • used to augment intrinsic feedback • important for beginners as they are limited in their use of intrinsic feedback • for example, teacher telling you that you had got your short serve correct in badminton

Table 1 The two types of feedback

Feel from the bat is intrinsic feedback

Need to know more? For further information on feedback, see Chapter 6, pages 157–158 in your Student Book.

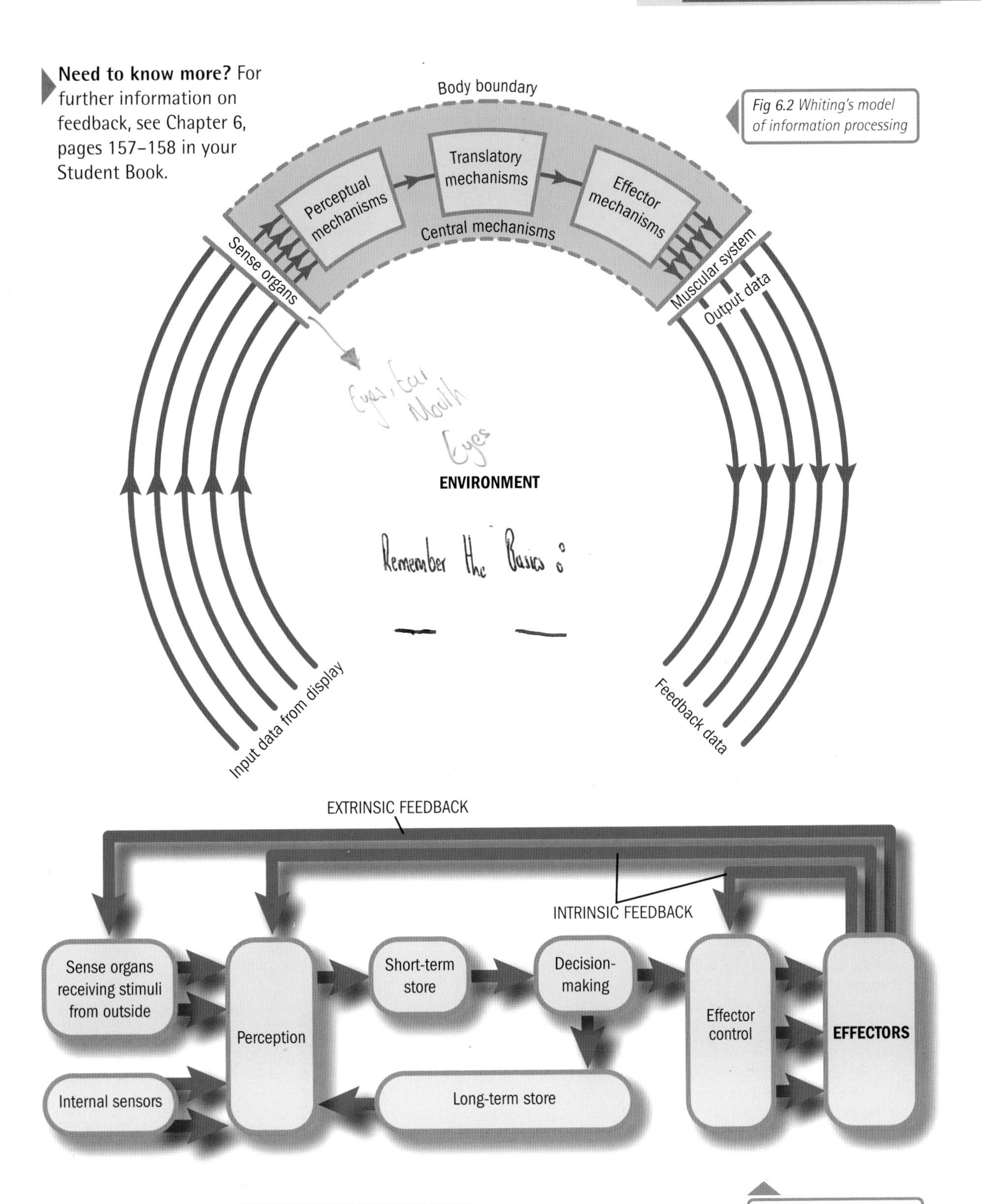

Fig 6.2 Whiting's model of information processing

Fig 6.3 Welford's model of information processing

EXAM TIP

Make sure that you know and understand both Whiting's and Welford's models and are able to draw them and explain their components by the use of practical examples.

Serial and parallel processing

Serial processing

Serial processing is when information is processed in stages (sequentially) – for example, a trampolining sequence consisting of:

- jump with 180° turn
- pike straddle jump
- swivel hips
- pike jump
- seat drop
- back drop.

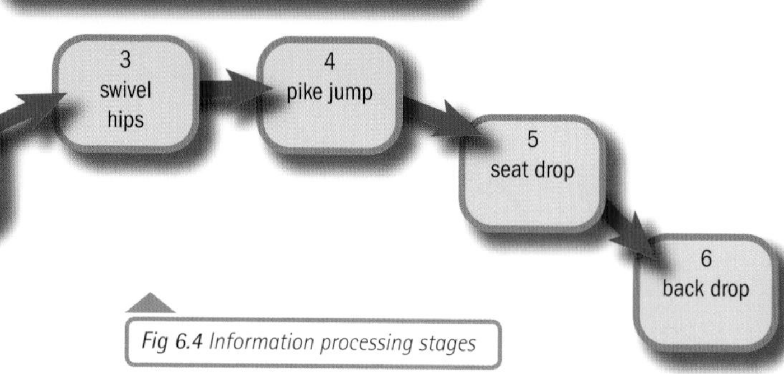

Fig 6.4 Information processing stages

The information would then be processed as shown in Fig 6.4.

Parallel processing

Parallel processing of information is where processes occur at the same time – for example, receiving a pass. The information relating to the following aspects of the pass is all processed at the same time:

- Speed of ball.
- Height of ball.
- Direction of ball.
- Position of team mates.
- Position of opposition.

Need to know more? For further information on serial and parallel processing, see Chapter 6, pages 158–159 in your Student Book.

MEMORY AND ITS ROLE IN DEVELOPING MOVEMENT SKILLS

Memory is important in:

- interpreting information when it compares information with that of our previous experiences
- determining the motor programme we are going to use to implement the action.

Selective attention

Rehearsal/repetition

Short-term sensory store
All information entering the information processing system is held here for a very short time (0.25–1 second). These stores have a very large capacity. There is a separate store for each sense. The perceptual mechanism determines which of the information is important to us and we direct our attention to it. This filtering process is called selective attention. This is the recognition aspect of perception. Irrelevant information is quickly lost from the sensory stores to be replaced by new information.

Short-term memory
This is known as the 'work place.' It is here that the incoming information is compared with that previously learned and stored in the long-term memory. This is the comparison aspect of perception. The short-term memory has a limited capacity in terms of how much information it can store and for how long. Generally these limits are between 5–9 pieces of information for up to 30 seconds. You can increase the amount of information by linking or 'chunking' bits of information together and remembering them as one piece of information. Think of how you remember phone numbers.
You can extend the period of time by rehearsing or repeating the information. Information considered important is rehearsed or practised and by this process passed into the long-term memory for future use. This process is called encoding.

Long-term memory
Long-term memory holds the information that is well rehearsed and practised. It has a limitless capacity and the information is held for a long time, perhaps permanently.
Motor programmes are stored in the long-term memory as a result of practising them many times. Think of how you never forget how to swim or ride a bike. The long-term memory is the recognition part of the perceptual process when the information stored in the long-term memory is retrieved and compared with the new information to see if it can be recognised.

Retrieval

Fig 6.5 The multi-store model of the memory process

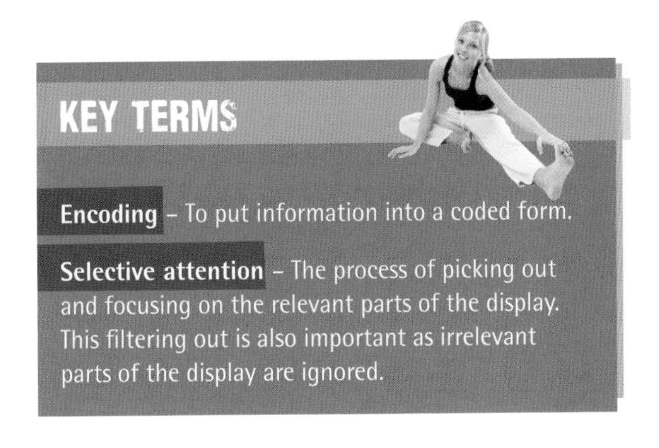

KEY TERMS

Encoding – To put information into a coded form.

Selective attention – The process of picking out and focusing on the relevant parts of the display. This filtering out is also important as irrelevant parts of the display are ignored.

The multi-store model of the memory process

Memory has three components, shown in Fig 6.5.

Selective attention

By focusing our attention on relevant information we filter this information through to the short-term memory. Selective attention enables the information important to our performance to be filtered and concentrated on. Information unimportant to the performance and therefore not attended to is filtered out.

The importance of this is indicated by theories which suggest that the amount of information we can process is limited. The process of focusing on the important and ignoring the irrelevant also helps us to react quickly.

The sprinter focuses their attention on the track and the gun and ignores the other athletes and the crowd. Knowing the important aspects of the display helps to avoid focusing on irrelevant cues.

When we do focus on irrelevant information this is known as attentional wastage and affects a beginner's learning and performance of skills.

Strategies to improve retention and retrieval

Now we realise how important the memory is to our performance it would help us if we were able to improve our ability to store information and to be able to remember it. Psychologists think that we can do this by the following methods.

Rehearsal/practice

When learning we need to practise or rehearse the skill as much as possible. Expert performers do a lot of skill practice until they have 'overlearned' the skill and it has become automatic. It is thought that practice carries the skills image 'to and fro' between the short- and long-term memories, establishing a memory trace. This helps both retention and retrieval.

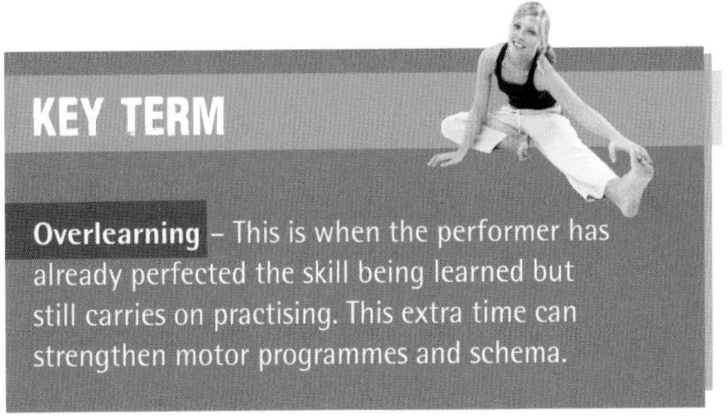

KEY TERM

Overlearning – This is when the performer has already perfected the skill being learned but still carries on practising. This extra time can strengthen motor programmes and schema.

Association/linking

Coaches and teachers should always try to link new information to that which the performer already knows. Specific sports skills can be linked to fundamental motor skills; for example, throwing the javelin can be linked to the overarm throw. This helps the learner mentally organise the skill. Linking parts of serial skills together both physically and mentally is also important. For example, parts of a basketball lay-up shot or parts of a gymnastics sequence.

Remember the limitation of the short-term memory. Teachers and coaches should give learners three coaching points to remember when they go to practise. When they have mastered these three, more can be given.

Simplicity

Learners should be given time to take in new information, which should be kept simple. More complex information can be added later. It is also important that similar information/skills should not be presented close together as they may interfere with each other. For example, beginners learning to swim should not be introduced to two different strokes in the same session.

Organisation

Information is more easily remembered if it is organised in a meaningful way. It is suggested that gymnastics and trampolining sequences will be remembered more easily if the individual movements are practised together in order that the performer links the end of one movement to the beginning of the next.

Imagery

Information can be remembered better by having a mental image. Demonstrations are really important in order that learners are able to create an image of the skill in their mind. Some coaches link images to words. For example 'chin, knee, toe' gives the learner the picture of the correct body position in the shot putt.

Meaningful

If the learner is made aware that the information being learned is relevant to them and their performance it becomes meaningful and is more likely to be remembered.

Chunking

Information can be grouped together allowing more to be dealt with at one time. Experienced performers use chunking to look at the whole field of play, recognise developing patterns and anticipate what will happen. This chunking together of information is particularly important in the short-term memory which has a limited capacity. In badminton if we have the grip, postion of the racket, position of feet and body weight stored as one item, i.e preparation, it frees up the capacity in the short-term memory to focus on other aspects.

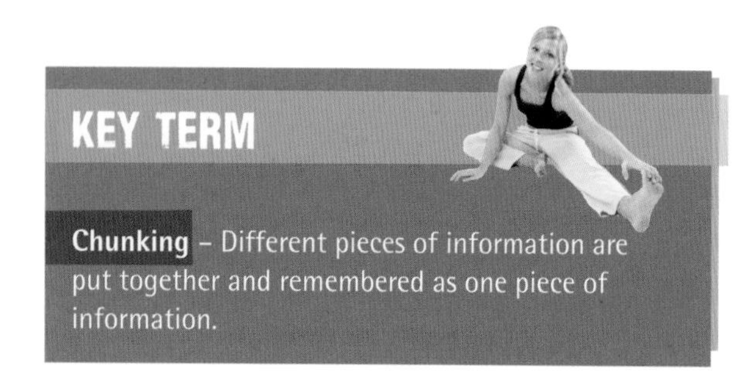

KEY TERM

Chunking – Different pieces of information are put together and remembered as one piece of information.

Uniqueness

If the teacher or coach presents information in an unusual or different way then it is more likely to be remembered.

Enjoyment

If the teacher can ensure that the learner enjoys the experience this will increase the possibility of it being remembered.

Positive reinforcement

Praise and encouragement when learning a skill will aid retention.

EXAM TIP

Make sure that you can describe strategies to improve storage and retrieval of information in both short- and long-term memory.

REACTION TIME AND DEVELOPING EFFECTIVE PERFORMANCE IN PHYSICAL ACTIVITY

- **Reaction time** – this is the time from the stimulus occurring to the performer starting to move in response to it.
- **Movement time** – this is the time taken from starting the movement to completing it.
- **Response time** – this is the time from the stimulus occurring to the completion of the movement.

For example, using the 100 metres sprint:

Starter's gun goes off	→	Sprinter pushes on blocks	=	Reaction time
Sprinter pushes on blocks	→	Sprinter crosses finish line	=	Movement time
Starter's gun goes off	→	Sprinter crosses finish line	=	Response time

Factors affecting reaction time

There are several factors that affect reaction time, which is an ability that varies between individuals, according to the criteria shown in Fig 6.6.

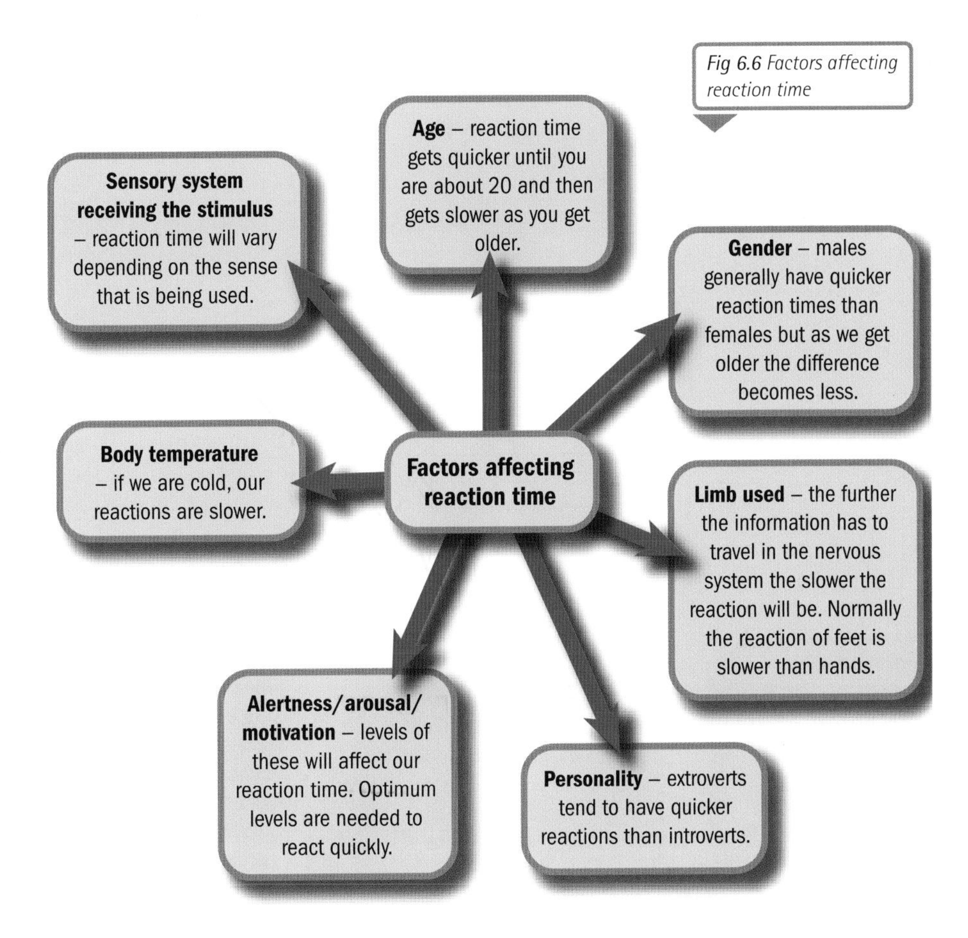

Fig 6.6 Factors affecting reaction time

Reaction time can also be affected by external factors.

- If a warning is given, for example, 'set' in sprint start.
- Intensity of stimulus, for example, orange ball for playing football in the snow.
- The likelihood of the stimulus occurring – if the stimulus has a good chance of happening, the reaction will be quicker.

Need to know more? For further information on reaction time, see Chapter 6, pages 162–165 in your Student Book.

EXAM TIP

Make sure that you know the definitions of reaction, movement and response times, as well as appreciating the differences between them. Be sure to be able to apply them to a practical activity.

Single channel hypothesis

This theory states that when we receive many stimuli from the environment the brain can only deal with one stimulus at a time. The way in which we process information is thought of as a single channel which can only deal with one piece of information at a time. This one piece of information has to be dealt with before the next piece of information can be dealt with. This is sometimes referred to as a bottleneck.

Choice reaction time

Choice reaction time occurs where there is more than one stimulus and/or more than one response. It occurs in many sporting situations.

Need to know more? For further information on choice reaction time, see Chapter 6, page 165 in your Student Book.

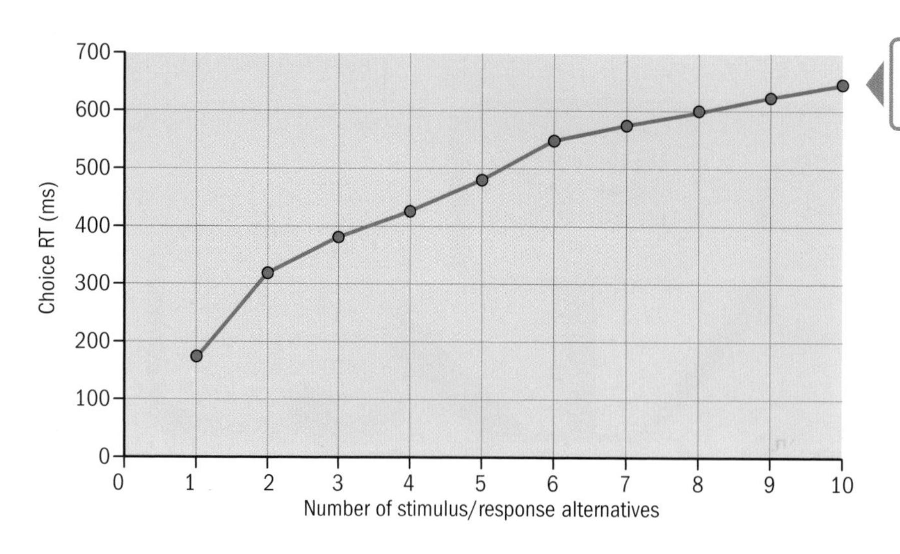

Fig 6.7 *Reaction time increases as the number of stimulus/response alternatives increases*

Response times can be improved by:

Level of arousal/motivation – The teacher/coach has to ensure that the performer is at the appropriate level of arousal/motivation for the activity.

Practice – The more often a stimulus is responded to the shorter the reaction time becomes. If enough practice is carried out the response becomes automatic and requires little attention.

Mental rehearsal – Practice can be in the form of mental rehearsal. This enables the performer to ensure that they attend to the correct cues and expect and respond to the correct stimuli. It also activates the neuromuscular system acting like physical training. It is also thought to have an effect on the control of arousal levels. Mental rehearsal works better with complex tasks which require a lot of information processing.

Concentration/selective attention – In simple reaction time situations you focus on the relevant stimulus and ignore everything else. This limits the information you process. For example, during a sprint start, focusing on the gun.

Experience – Playing the activity enhances the performer's awareness of the probability of particular stimuli occurring, e.g. practising passing in basketball/netball.

Warm-up – Ensuring that the cardio-respiratory, vascular and neuromuscular systems are adequately prepared.

Stimulus–response compatibility – If the response you are expected to make to the stimulus is the one you would normally make you will react quicker than with a different response, e.g. practising marking for set plays in a team game.

Cue detection – Analysing an opponent's play to anticipate what they are going to do. For example, analysing a badminton player's shots so that you are able to detect the difference between their overhead clear and drop shot.

Improve the performer's physical fitness – This will influence response time. The fitter you are, the quicker you will be.

Fig 6.8 *Possible ways to improve a performer's response time*

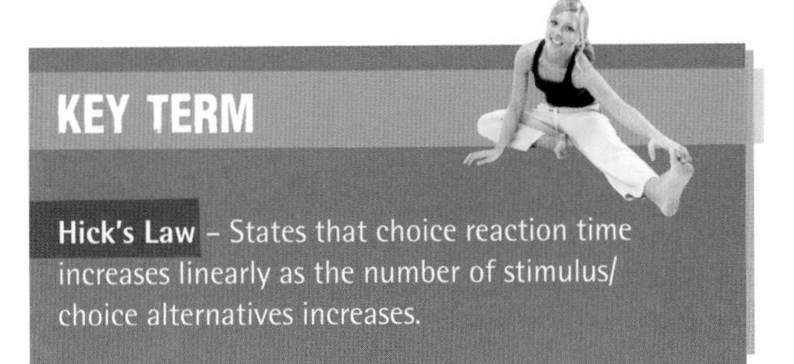

KEY TERM

Hick's Law – States that choice reaction time increases linearly as the number of stimulus/choice alternatives increases.

Hick's Law

Hick's Law has important implications in that we should always try to:

- disguise our intentions and therefore increase the number of possible alternatives that our opponents will have to select from; this will increase their reaction time
- pick up cues as to our opponents intended response as this reduces the number of alternatives and therefore reduces our reaction time.

How do teachers/coaches attempt to improve the performer's response time?

ANTICIPATION

We have left this to last because it is a very important strategy in reducing both types of reaction time. There are two main forms of anticipation.

- **Spatial** – predicting what will happen. The cricket batsman who has detected the difference in the fast bowler's action is able to pick out the disguised slower ball.
- **Temporal** – predicting when it will happen. The sprinter who has identified the period between the 'set' command and the gun will be able to move as the gun goes off.

Anticipation has very important implications for teachers and coaches. They should encourage their performers to look for relevant cues in their opponents' actions in order that they will then be able to predict what they will do and also to disguise their own actions to prevent opponents anticipating.

They should also ensure that their performers do not become too predictable in what they do.

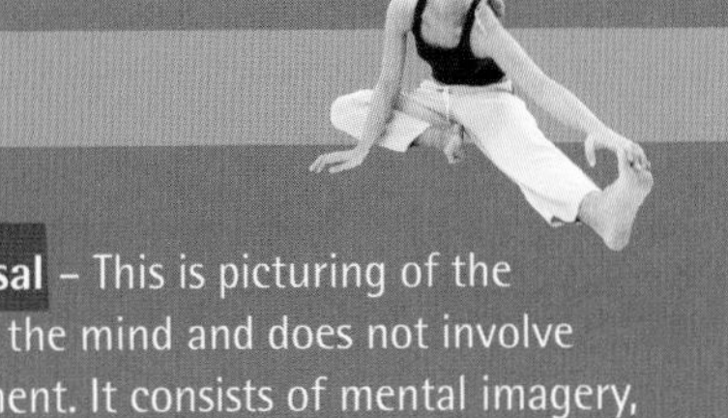

KEY TERM

Mental rehearsal – This is picturing of the performance in the mind and does not involve physical movement. It consists of mental imagery, viewing videos of the performance, reading or listening to instructions.

EXAM TIP

Ensure that you are able to explain the factors affecting response time and how they might be manipulated to improve response time in practical activities.

Psychological refractory period (PRP)

This is the negative side of anticipation. If we anticipate something and get it wrong, then our reactions are slower. If we detect a stimulus and are processing that information when a second stimulus arrives, we cannot attend to the second stimulus until we have finished processing the first. This delay makes our reaction time longer and the delay is known as the psychological refractory period (PRP).

Think of what happens when in badminton the shuttle hits the top of the net. How do you react?

What happens when the ball hits the top of the net in tennis?

Need to know more? For further information on the psychological refractory period, see Chapter 6, page 167 in your Student Book.

CHECK

If you are satisfied with your knowledge and understanding, tick off the sections that you have revised so far. If you are not satisfied, then revisit those sections and refer to the pages in the 'Need to know more?' features.

☐ Describe models of information processing and their effectiveness in the learning and performance of physical activities.

☐ Describe the multi-store model of memory process and apply it to the learning and performance of physical activities.

☐ Understand reaction time and its role in developing effective performance in physical activities.

EXAM PRACTICE

Q.1 Describe the components of the multi-store model of the memory process.

6 marks

Q.2 Performers use feedback in a variety of ways to improve their performance. Explain what is meant by the terms intrinsic and extrinsic feedback and use practical examples to describe how a performer could use these forms of feedback to improve their performance.

4 marks

Q.3 Why is it important to develop a quick reaction time when performing movement skills? What factors could affect response time in physical activities?

4 marks

Q.4 Anticipation can play an important role in sport. Identify two forms of anticipation. Explain the effect of anticipation on response time.

4 marks

See page 174 for answers.

CHAPTER 7

Motor control of skills and its impact upon developing effectiveness in physical activity

LEARNING OBJECTIVES

By the end of this chapter you should be able to demonstrate knowledge and understanding of:

- The nature and examples of motor and executive programmes stored in long-term memory
- How motor programmes link with open loop control and the autonomous phase of learning
- Open and closed loop control
- The role of open and closed loop control in the performance of motor skills
- How to evaluate critically different types of feedback to detect and correct errors
- Schema theory and its role in developing movement skills and strategies.

MOTOR AND EXECUTIVE PROGRAMMES

A motor programme (MP) or executive motor programme is the plan of a whole skill or pattern of movement. This plan is made up of generalised movements. Generalised movements are stored in long-term memory. Every skill performed in sport is the product of a motor programme.

Executive motor programmes are made up of sub-routines. Sub-routines are small components of executive motor programmes and are often called mini skills. Sub-routines underpin the executive motor programme hierarchy and are usually performed in sequence.

The example given in Fig 7.1 is of a tennis serve.

- Motor programmes are hierarchical and sequential.
- When a motor programme is stored in long-term memory it is said to have been grooved or overlearned.

When a motor programme has been overlearned the performer is said to be at the autonomous phase of learning. Once the motor programme has been overlearned it can be performed with little conscious control. The movement now appears to be automatic and this is the basis of open loop control.

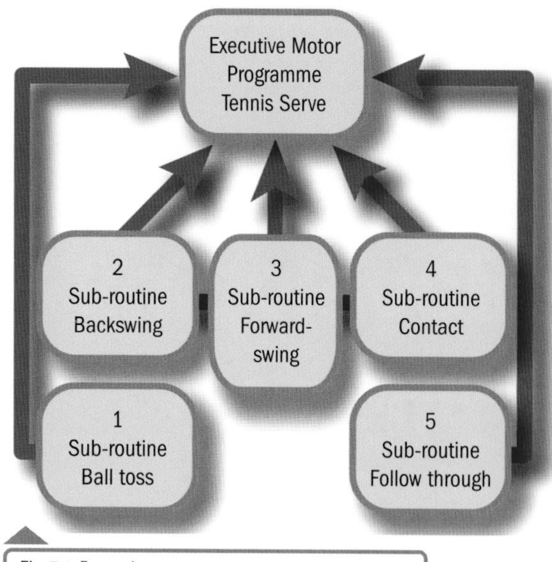

Fig 7.1 Executive motor programme – tennis serve

EXAM TIP

When defining or describing an executive motor programme remember to give a practical example, e.g. a smash shot in volleyball.

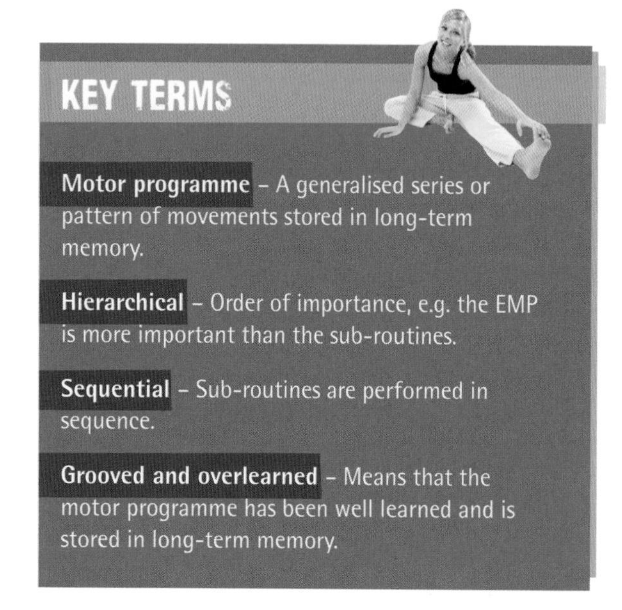

KEY TERMS

Motor programme – A generalised series or pattern of movements stored in long-term memory.

Hierarchical – Order of importance, e.g. the EMP is more important than the sub-routines.

Sequential – Sub-routines are performed in sequence.

Grooved and overlearned – Means that the motor programme has been well learned and is stored in long-term memory.

Need to know more? For further information on motor programmes, see Chapter 7, pages 171–172 in your Student Book.

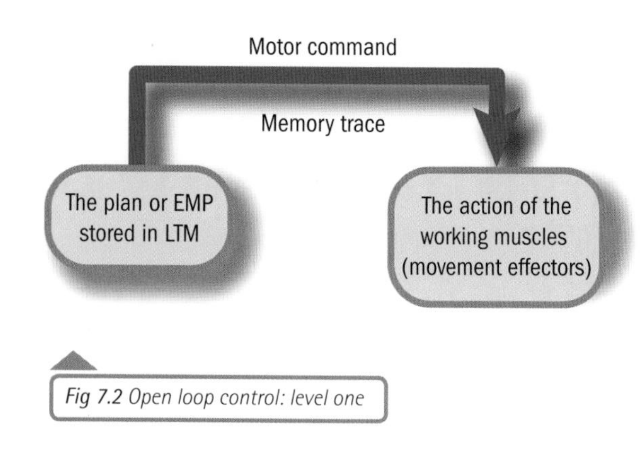

Fig 7.2 Open loop control: level one

OPEN LOOP CONTROL

Level one control

Open loop explains how rapid movements are performed in sport, e.g. a close catch in cricket. This rapid action occurs when the motor programme is triggered from long-term memory. The transfer of information from the long-term memory to the working muscle is done through the formation of a memory trace. There is no reference to feedback (see page 80).

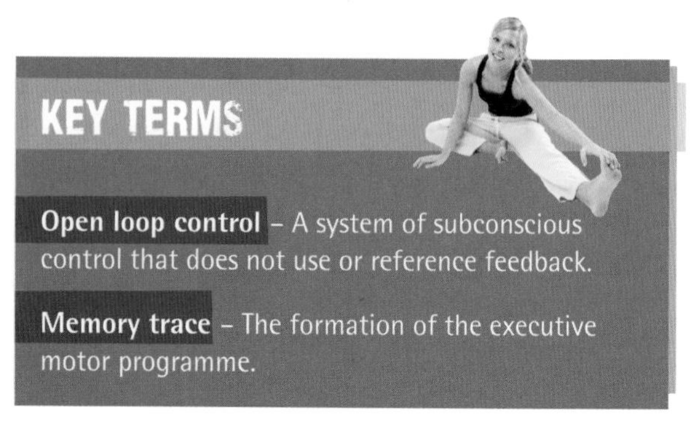

KEY TERMS

Open loop control – A system of subconscious control that does not use or reference feedback.

Memory trace – The formation of the executive motor programme.

Open loop is regarded as level one control and is thought to start (initiate) motor skills. Motor skills are adjusted and concluded by closed loop systems. Closed loop systems use feedback.

CLOSED LOOP CONTROL

Level two control

Closed loop involves feedback and this is termed the perceptual trace. At level two the feedback loop is short and involves internal feedback gathered through kinaesthesis and proprioception during the execution of the skill. This type of feedback allows quick subconscious corrections to take place, e.g. the slalom skier will make quick adjustments to retain balance.

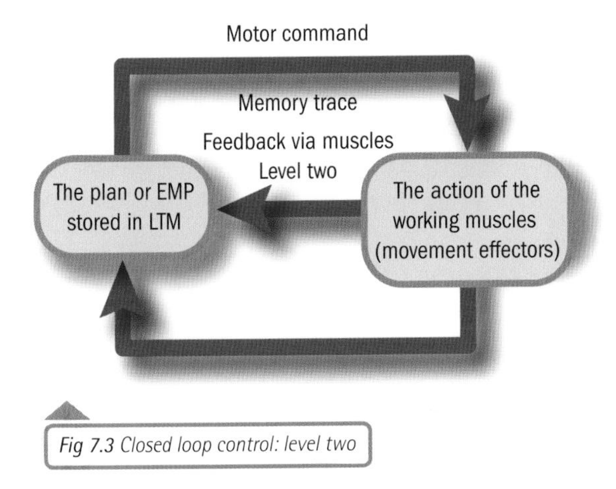

Fig 7.3 Closed loop control: level two

Although these changes are produced subconsciously, the adjustment is stored in long-term memory for future reference.

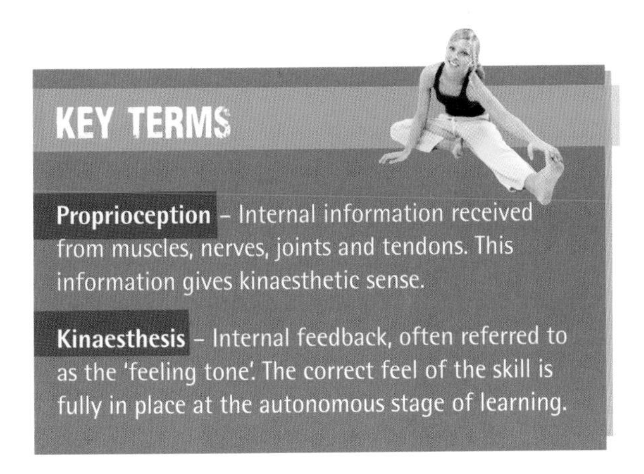

KEY TERMS

Proprioception – Internal information received from muscles, nerves, joints and tendons. This information gives kinaesthetic sense.

Kinaesthesis – Internal feedback, often referred to as the 'feeling tone'. The correct feel of the skill is fully in place at the autonomous stage of learning.

Level three control

- At level three, the feedback loop is longer because information on performance is relayed to the brain as a result of external feedback.
- The brain controls and modifies the movement by passing corrective messages back to the working muscles.
- External feedback is necessary when making decisions like running into position in invasion games.
- Furthermore, performers at the associative stage of learning rely and operate on external feedback as at this stage the correct feel of the skill (kinaesthesis) has yet to be acquired.
- The perceptual trace operates by comparing the performance as it is taking place with the plan formed by the memory trace.
- If performance matches the plan, the skill is reinforced and allowed to continue.

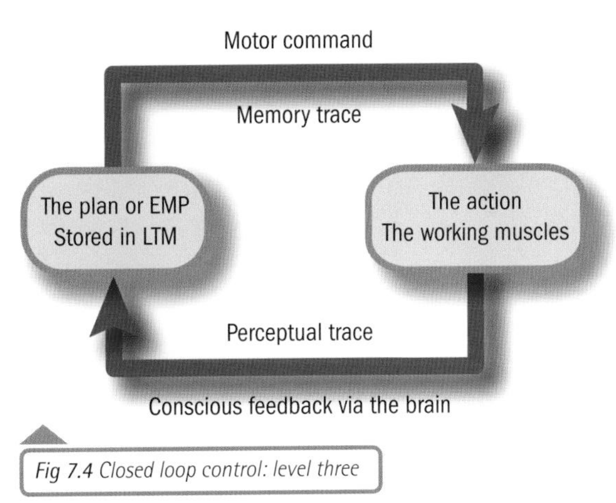

Fig 7.4 Closed loop control: level three

- Should performance not match the plan, the perceptual trace allows adjustment.
- This change or adjustment is stored as a new motor programme.

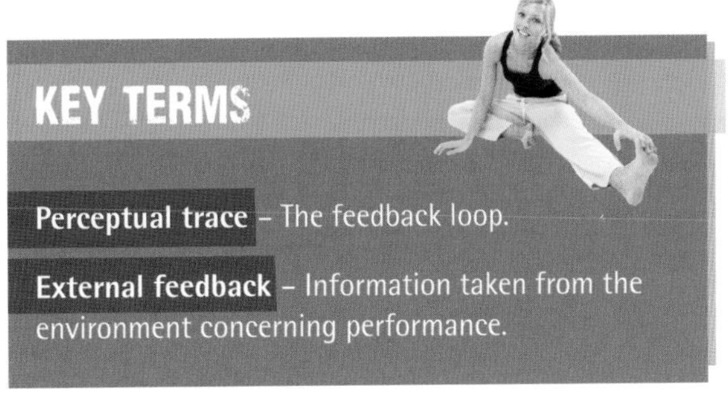

KEY TERMS

Perceptual trace – The feedback loop.

External feedback – Information taken from the environment concerning performance.

Need to know more? For more information on open and closed loop control, see Chapter 7, pages 173–175 in your Student Book.

Open and closed loop theory offers an explanation as to how motor skills are controlled and acquired but there are three drawbacks to the theory.

1. The theory implies that an infinite number of motor programmes would require storage.
2. If all motor programmes could be stored it would be difficult for the memory trace to recall the required plan in time to execute the skill.
3. The necessary motor programme might not exist to produce a 'novel' response.

A novel response is often spontaneous and creative but never instinctive. Novel responses usually emerge as open skills and are difficult to pre-programme. Such skills are difficult to explain through closed loop theory. Schema theory (see page 81) accounts for the execution of these skills.

Closed loop theory has drawbacks. How can this novel and creative response demonstrated by the footballer be executed if the motor programme does not exist in the memory?

EXAM TIP

Questions focusing on open and closed loop theory frequently refer directly to practical situations.

FEEDBACK

Before looking at schema theory it is necessary to define, explain and critically analyse feedback.

Feedback is the information received by the athlete both during and after the skill has been performed. You need to identify, explain and critically evaluate eight types of feedback.

Identification/explanation of feedback type	Critical evaluation of feedback
1. Positive feedback can be given externally by the teacher or coach when the player is praised following success	• positive feedback should clearly indicate the parts of the skill that were performed correctly • learners at the cognitive and associative stages of learning are motivated by positive feedback but discouraged by negative feedback
2. Negative feedback is received when the movement is incorrect; it can be intrinsic or extrinsic	• negative feedback must address how the skill can be improved • negative feedback is beneficial to expert performers as it helps to perfect their skills
3. Extrinsic feedback comes from external sources such as the teacher; this type of feedback is also called augmented feedback	• extrinsic feedback is received through visual and auditory systems • the learner can become dependent on external feedback and this does not help to develop kinaesthesis

continued ▶

Identification/explanation of feedback type	Critical evaluation of feedback
4. Intrinsic feedback is a form of sensory feedback about the physical feel of the movement as it is being performed; it is received via the internal proprioceptors	• intrinsic feedback can be accessed by performers at the autonomous stage of learning; performance will be fluent and well timed at this stage • performers at the associative stage are still learning what the skill should feel like; they require extrinsic (augmented) feedback
5. Terminal feedback is received after the movement has been completed and is extrinsic feedback	• terminal feedback given immediately is beneficial because the situation is fresh in the learner's mind • a delay in feedback can also be advantageous as it allows the athlete to think about the performance
6. Concurrent feedback is received during the performance of the skill	• concurrent feedback is good for continuous skills • it allows quick correction to take place
7. Knowledge of performance (KP) is feedback concerning the quality of the movement; KP can be internal as it arises from kinaesthetic awareness	• KP is used to good effect only by the expert performer • KP can also come from an external source, e.g. the teacher
8. Knowledge of results (KR) is feedback about the result or outcome of the movement and is extrinsic	• KR is essential in skill learning particularly during the early stages • KR helps to develop KP

Table 1 Feedback: identification and evaluation

Feedback is important to the sports performer because:

1. confidence will improve
2. motivation may increase
3. drive reduction could be prevented
4. it detects and corrects errors, therefore feedback is vital to learning and performance
5. good actions can be reinforced through feedback so that stimulus–response bonds are strengthened (see S/R bonding, page 91).

Furthermore, it is proven that feedback is more effective when given following the completion of a set goal.

EXAM TIP

You should be able to describe the function of feedback and to explain its value when learning and performing skills in sport. You need to be aware of the type of feedback that is required at each of the three phases of learning.

KEY TERM

Drive reduction – Loss of motivation.

Need to know more? For more information on feedback, see Chapter 7, pages 176–178 in your Student Book.

SCHEMA THEORY

Schema is a build up of experiences which can be adapted and transferred to meet the demands of new situations (see Transfer, pages 94–96).

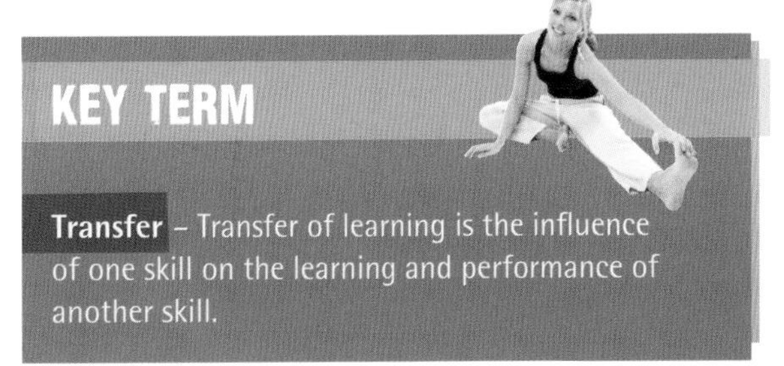

KEY TERM

Transfer – Transfer of learning is the influence of one skill on the learning and performance of another skill.

Schema theory is based on the idea that motor programmes are not stored as separate items as described by open loop theory. Instead they are retained in long-term memory as relationships with other motor programmes. These relationships are termed generalised movements and they allow the performer to adapt quickly in response to a situation.

Schema theory states that experience is gathered from four areas. These areas are termed memory items.

Four memory items are explained in the model in Fig 7.5, by using the example of two attackers approaching one defender in rugby. The example focuses on the attacker who is carrying the ball.

EXAM TIP

Schema is a topic that frequently appears on examination papers. Learn the memory items thoroughly. Be able to explain recall and recognition schema by using practical examples, preferably from your own experience, to support the explanation.

Fig 7.5 Schema theory

MEMORY ITEM 1
Knowledge of Initial Conditions:
Relates to whether the player in possession has previously experienced a similar situation in a similar environment, e.g. attacker approaching a defender.

+

MEMORY ITEM 2
Knowledge of Response Specifications:
Involves having knowledge of what to do in this situation, e.g. to pass, dummy, dodge or kick.

The collective term given to memory items 1 and 2 is Recall Schema

RECALL SCHEMA
has two functions:

- to store information about the production of the generalised movement
- to start or initiate the movement.

MEMORY ITEM 3
Knowledge of Sensory Consequences:
Applies to kinaesthesis (how the skill should feel), e.g. attacker would need to know how hard to pass the ball in order to reach the target.

+

MEMORY ITEM 4
Knowledge of Movement Outcome:
Involves knowing what the result of the skill is likely to be, e.g. a dummy would send the defender in the wrong direction.

The collective term given to memory items 3 and 4 is Recognition Schema

RECOGNITION SCHEMA
has two functions; it can:

- control the movement throughout its execution
- evaluate the effectiveness of performance.

Recognition schema enables the performer to store additional movement relationships which will help to adapt the motor programme in novel situations.

Need to know more? For more information on schema theory, see Chapter 7, pages 178–179 in your Student Book.

CHECK

If you are satisfied with your knowledge and understanding, tick off the sections that you have revised so far. If you are not satisfied, then revisit those sections and refer to the pages in the 'Need to know more?' features.

- ☐ Describe the nature and give examples of motor and executive programmes stored in long-term memory.
- ☐ Explain how motor programmes link with open loop control and the autonomous phase of learning.
- ☐ Describe open and closed loop control.
- ☐ Explain the role of open and closed loop control in the performance of motor skills.
- ☐ Evaluate critically different types of feedback to detect and correct errors.
- ☐ Understand schema theory and its role in developing movement skills and strategies.

EXAM PRACTICE

Q.1 The control of physical movement can be explained through closed loop theory. Use the example of a gymnast performing a handstand to explain closed loop control.
5 marks

Q.2 Describe three functions of feedback and explain the types of feedback that could be used by an advanced performer.
5 marks

See page 176 for answers.

CHAPTER 8

Learning skills in physical activity

PART I

Motivation and arousal

LEARNING OBJECTIVES

Chapter 8 is divided into three parts. By the end of this chapter you should be able to demonstrate knowledge and understanding of:

- Motivation and arousal and their impact upon young people's participation, performance and aspirations in physical activity
- Theories relating to the learning of movement skills and the development of positive behaviours associated with a balanced, active and healthy lifestyle
- Reinforcement of movement skill learning and behaviours associated with a balanced, active and healthy lifestyle
- Transfer of learning to develop effectiveness in physical activity.

At the end of Part I you should be able to:

- Demonstrate knowledge and understanding of arousal as a drive affecting levels of motivation
- Explain the major motivation and arousal theories, namely drive theory, inverted U theory and catastrophe theory
- Explain drive reduction theory and its impact on a lifelong, balanced, active and healthy lifestyle
- Demonstrate knowledge and understanding of motivational strategies and their application in order to encourage participation in a balanced, active and healthy lifestyle
- Evaluate critically motivation and arousal theories and the application of motivational strategies.

MOTIVATION

The term motivation implies the drive and energy an individual is prepared to expend to achieve a goal.

- Motivation is a factor that determines the amount of effort applied in sports performance.
- Feedback strongly influences motivation.

Although the terms motivation and arousal seem to be interchangeable there are differences between the two.

Motivation has two branches:

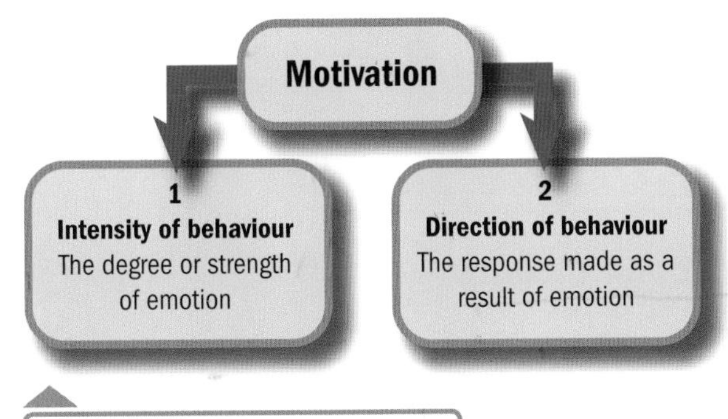

Fig 8.1.1 The two branches of motivation

The intensity of behaviour is the branch of motivation that relates to arousal. Arousal has two forms:

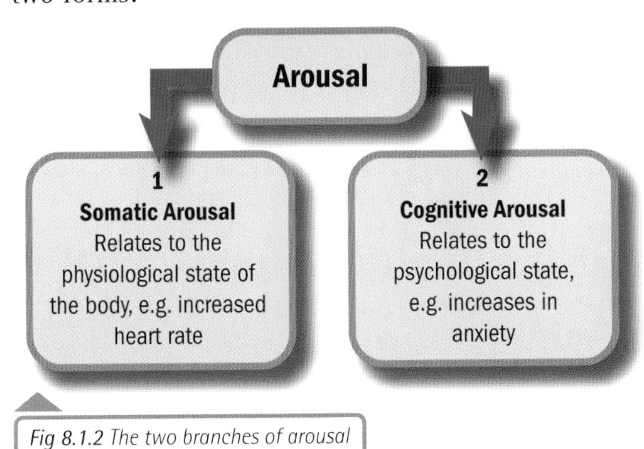

Fig 8.1.2 The two branches of arousal

EXAM TIP

The interaction of somatic and cognitive arousal is important in catastrophe theory of arousal.

Motivation has two sources:

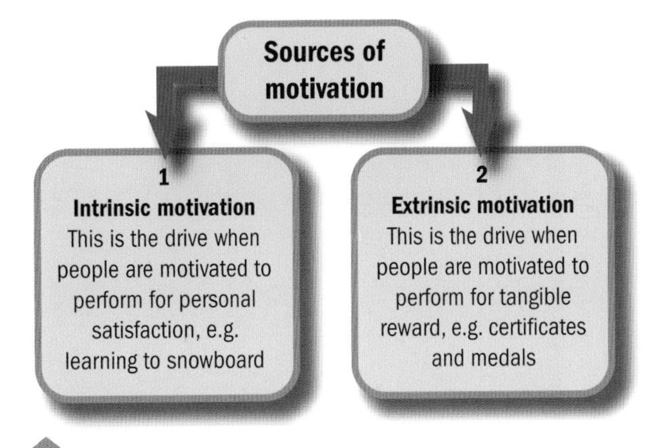

Fig 8.1.3 The two sources of motivation

EXAM TIP

You need to be aware that the application of extrinsic motivation and the development of intrinsic motivation impacts upon the inclination to participate in a balanced, active and healthy lifestyle.

- **Extrinsic reward** given to a novice performer can encourage initial involvement.
- Extrinsic reward, however, can eventually be a drawback to the learning process as effort may only be applied if reward is given.
- People who are **intrinsically motivated** are more likely to continue participation than those who seek reward.

KEY TERMS

Motivation – The drive to learn and perform well. It is described as the direction and intensity of behaviour.

Arousal – The degree of physiological and psychological readiness or activation. This varies on a continuum from deep sleep to intense excitement.

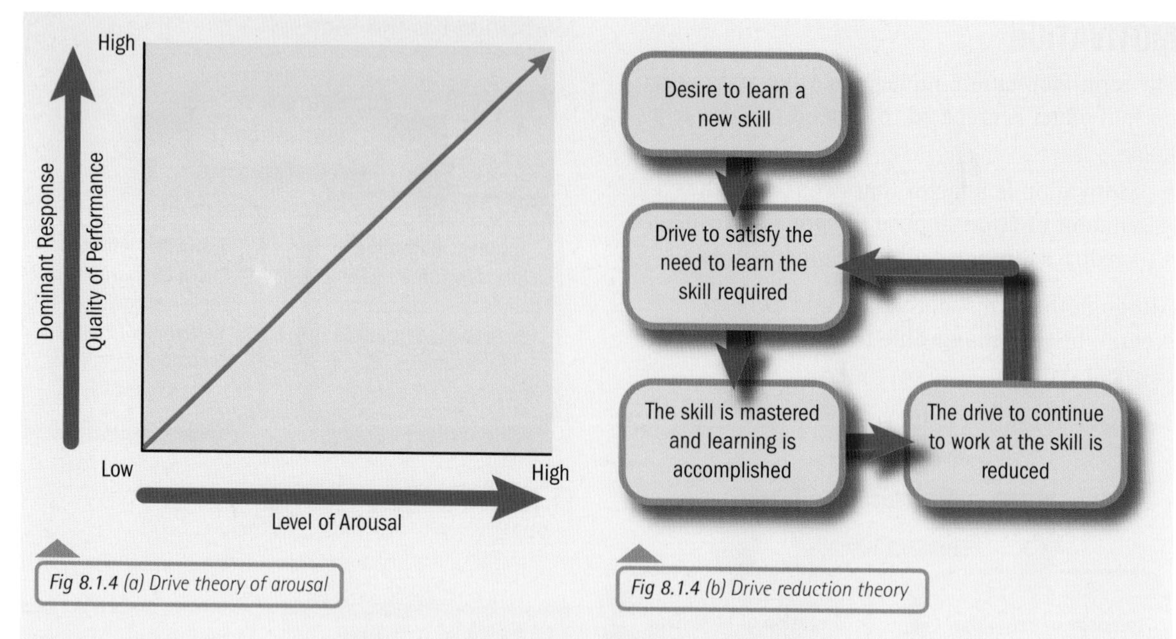

Fig 8.1.4 (a) Drive theory of arousal

Fig 8.1.4 (b) Drive reduction theory

Drive and drive reduction theories

Drive theory

Behaviour = Habit × Drive (B = H × D)

- Drive theory shows a relationship between arousal and performance.
- An increase in arousal is proportional to an increase in the quality of physical performance.
- The quality of performance depends on how well the skill has been learned.
- Motor programmes that have already been learned are said to be 'learned behaviours' and are therefore termed dominant responses.
- A dominant response is a response that is most likely to emerge when a performer experiences an increase in arousal.
- High arousal would be beneficial to the performer at the autonomous stage of learning.
- The dominant behaviour at this stage would tend to produce a response that is fluent and technically correct.
- Conversely the performance of a novice would be inhibited in conditions of high arousal.
- High arousal also helps the performance of gross and simple skills.

KEY TERM

Dominant response – the behaviour or response that is most likely to be given by the performer.

Drive reduction theory

- Drive reduction is the term given to a loss of motivation that may be experienced by the performer.
- Reduction of motivation could happen if a skill has been previously well learned or the task has become tedious.
- Decreased motivation occurs if too much practice has taken place and the skill has become overlearned.
- Overlearning may lead to inhibition, which reduces drive.
- At this point new goals or targets need to be put into place to re-motivate the athlete.
- Drive reduction must be avoided when encouraging a young person to develop a balanced, active and healthy lifestyle.

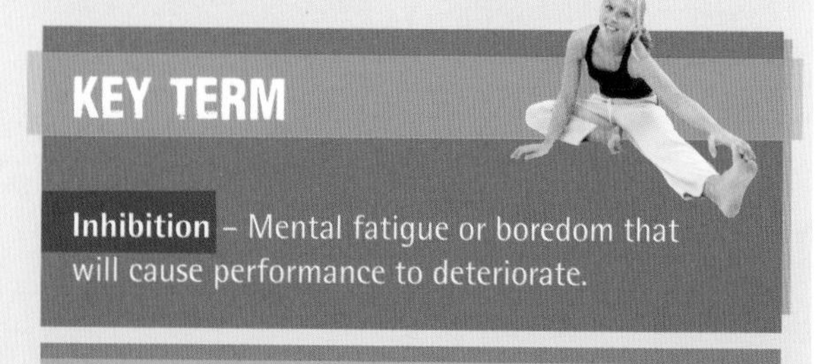

KEY TERM

Inhibition – Mental fatigue or boredom that will cause performance to deteriorate.

EXAM TIP

Students tend to confuse drive theory with drive reduction theory. They are different theories and should be considered carefully.

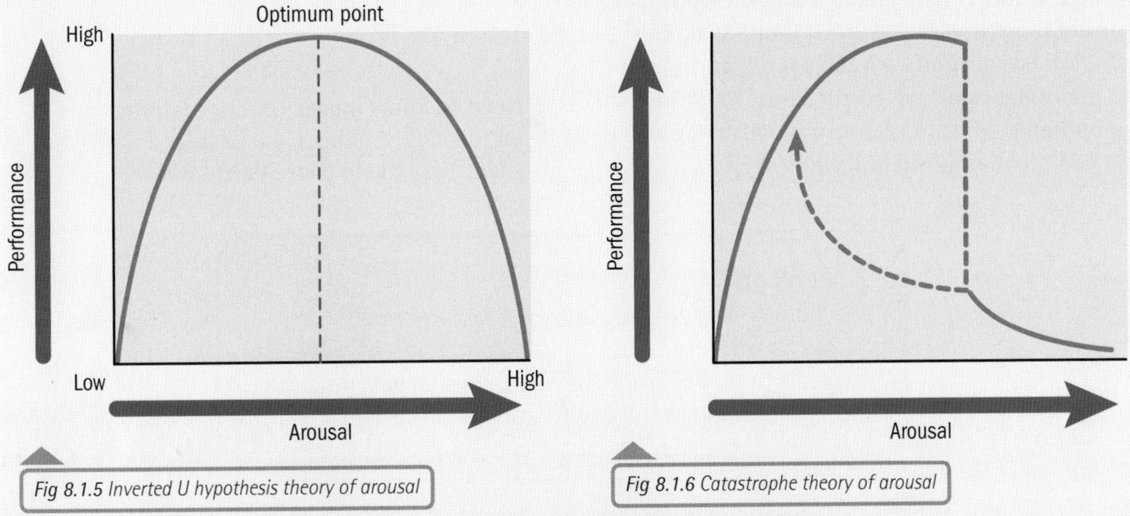

Fig 8.1.5 Inverted U hypothesis theory of arousal

Fig 8.1.6 Catastrophe theory of arousal

Inverted U and catastrophe theories

Inverted U theory of arousal

- The inverted U theory predicts that as arousal increases so does the quality of performance. Quality improves up to a point mid-way along the arousal axis.
- This point is called the optimum point or the threshold of arousal and predicts that best performance occurs at moderate levels of arousal.
- This is the perfect state in which the potential to learn and perform well is maximised.
- At the optimal point the attention field of the individual adjusts to the ideal width and as a result the learner or performer is able to concentrate fully.
- With increased focus the performer detects only the most important information.
- This process of selective attentiveness is called cue-utilisation.
- When under-aroused concentration is lost because the attention field of the performer widens excessively.
- This results in information overload.
- Over-arousal causes the field of attention to narrow excessively and as a result the relevant environmental cues are missed.
- This results in hypervigilence.

KEY TERMS

Attention field -The area of concentration.

Hypervigilence - A condition of nervousness and panic; often accompanied by extreme anxiety.

Information overload - An excess of sensory data.

Catastrophe theory

- Catastrophe theory, like the inverted U hypothesis, claims that as somatic arousal increases then the quality of performance improves.
- Catastrophe theory, however, adds a third dimension to this prediction by stating that performance will reach maximum potential at the optimum level only if cognitive arousal anxiety is kept low.
- If high cognitive arousal anxiety coincides with high somatic arousal the athlete will go beyond the optimum level of arousal and is thought to have 'gone over the edge'. Under these conditions performance drops.
- This drop is not on a smooth curve as predicted in inverted U theory but plummets vertically.
- This vertical descent depicts a performance 'disaster' or catastrophe.
- After a catastrophe the performer can rejoin the upward curve of arousal and once again attain the optimal threshold.
- This return requires the athlete to reduce cognitive anxiety.
- When somatic arousal is low skill learning and performance can be enhanced if cognitive arousal is increased.
- Serious debilitation in learning performance will arise when low levels of physiological and psychological arousal converge.

Inverted U theory also predicts that the optimum point of arousal varies for each individual. This variation has a significant impact on learning and the performance of movement skills. Variations in the optimum point of arousal are caused by one or any combination of the following factors.

Need to know more? For more information on theories of arousal, see Chapter 8, Part I, pages 185–188 in your Student Book.

1. Personality
The person who has an extroverted personality type performs and learns best under conditions of higher arousal. Conversely, introverted personalities function most effectively at a lower threshold of arousal.

2. Level of experience
An experienced athlete would reach their maximum performance level when arousal is high. The novice would perform best when the optimum point is lower.

3. Type of task
Gross and simple skills which are often ballistic and classified as closed are performed better when arousal is high. Fine and complex tasks requiring precision and decision-making, as with open skills, on the other hand are performed better when arousal is low.

4. Stage of learning
Learners at the cognitive and associative stages of learning operate more effectively in conditions of lower arousal whereas at the autonomous stage higher thresholds are beneficial.

A CRITICAL EVALUATION OF MOTIVATION STRATEGIES

1. External motivation
   - External motivation can come in the form of tangible or intangible rewards.
   - External motivation is thought to be of greatest importance in attracting young people into sport and during early learning.
   - Extrinsic rewards provide concrete proof of success.
   - The impact of external motivation must be considered a short-term strategy compared with internal motivation.

2. Internal motivation
   - Internal motivation is the key to lifelong participation.
   - It involves giving learners positive feelings about their performance.
   - Once interest has been stimulated, the teacher can endorse the value of participation by indicating that sport promotes confidence, personal satisfaction and self-realisation.

Other motivational strategies which will help to promote a balanced, active and healthy lifestyle include those shown in Fig 8.1.7.

Fig 8.1.7 Motivational strategies that help to promote a balanced, active and healthy lifestyle

Motivational strategies that help to promote a balanced, active and healthy lifestyle

Progression
Learners are inspired if sports participation is leading somewhere

Positive reinforcement
Praise from teachers, parents and peers encourages participation

Fun activities
Practices and activities should be enjoyable and provide fun

Transfer of skills
If new skills can be built on previously learned skills, they do not seem so difficult

Social experience
If young people perceive that sport is a social experience they are more likely to participate

Role models
Young people like to copy successful sports players

Skills and fitness
If young people feel that fitness and skill levels are improving, they are more likely to continue

Attainable targets
If targets and goals are met during learning, motivation is enhanced

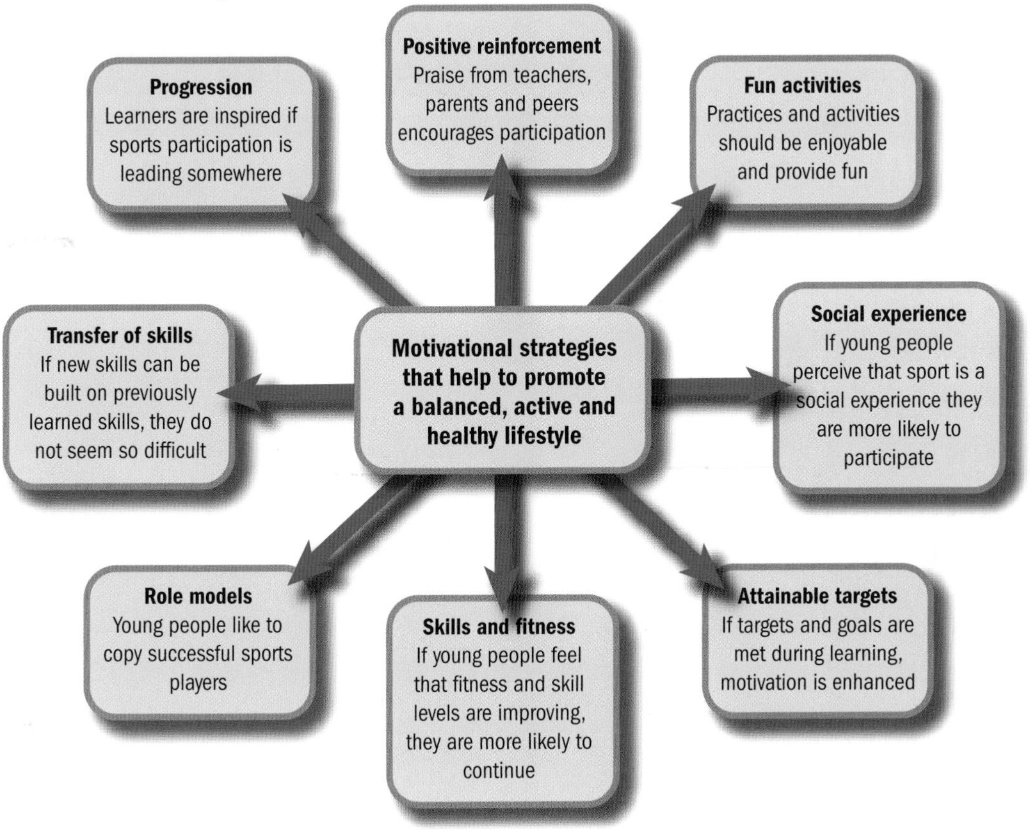

Need to know more? For more information on motivational strategies, see Chapter 8, Part I, pages 190–191 in your Student Book.

CHECK

If you are satisfied with your knowledge and understanding, tick off the sections that you have revised so far. If you are not satisfied, then revisit those sections and refer to the pages in the 'Need to know more?' features.

- ☐ Demonstrate knowledge and understanding of arousal as a drive affecting levels of motivation.
- ☐ Explain the major motivation and arousal theories, namely drive theory, inverted U theory and catastrophe theory.
- ☐ Explain drive reduction theory and its impact on a lifelong, balanced, active and healthy lifestyle.
- ☐ Demonstrate knowledge and understanding of motivational strategies and their application in order to encourage participation in a balanced, active and healthy lifestyle.
- ☐ Evaluate critically motivation and arousal theories and the application of motivational strategies.

EXAM PRACTICE

Q.1 Drive theory, inverted U theory and catastrophe theory are the major motivation and arousal theories.

By using your knowledge of these theories explain how arousal can influence the performance of motor skills.
10 marks

Q.2 Explain how the application of drive reduction and other motivational strategies could be used to develop an active, healthy and balanced lifestyle.
10 marks

See page 177 for answers.

CHAPTER 8: PART II

Theories relating to the learning of movement skills and the reinforcement of movement skill learning and behaviours associated with a balanced, active and healthy lifestyle

LEARNING OBJECTIVES

By the end of this part you should be able to demonstrate knowledge and understanding of:

- The associationist/connectionist theory of operant conditioning (Skinner)
- The cognitive theory related to the work of Gestaltist principles
- Social/observational learning theory; the importance of significant others (role models) in the adoption of a balanced, active and healthy lifestyle
- Bandura's model and the factors that affect modelling
- Reinforcement of movement skill learning and behaviours associated with a balanced, active and healthy lifestyle
- Positive reinforcement, negative reinforcement and punishment
- Thorndike's Laws as they apply to the formation and strengthening of the Stimulus–Response learning bond
- Appropriate use of reinforcement in skill learning and in promoting positive, healthy lifestyle behaviour.

OPERANT CONDITIONING

Operant conditioning involves the learner forming and strengthening a stimulus–response (S–R) bond. The link between the stimulus and the response is often called a connection or association. Hence operant conditioning is referred to as a connectionist or associationist theory.

By directing behaviour towards a stimulus, operant conditioning modifies the performer's response.

Explanation and practical application of operant conditioning

1. The teacher would first structure or manipulate the environment to bring about the desired response. For example, when learning to play a cross-court forehand in tennis a target may be drawn at the back of the opponent's court during practice.

2. A period of trial-and-error learning will occur as the learner attempts to perform the desired action, e.g. to land the ball in the target.
3. During this period the learner's response or behaviour is being shaped or modified.
4. A good response is positively reinforced by the teacher in order to strengthen the S–R learning bond.
5. Similarly, negative reinforcement can serve to strengthen a correct learning bond.
6. Any response receiving no reinforcement will disappear.
7. Complete reinforcement after every attempt increases the speed of learning but the drawback with this method is that behaviour tends to be forgotten more easily than if partial reinforcement is applied.
8. When the desired behaviour has been overlearned the target is taken away.
9. A positive learning outcome facilitated by the process of reinforcement will promote behaviours associated with a balanced, active and healthy lifestyle.

EXAM TIP

When giving an example make it skill specific, e.g. a pass in football. No marks will be given to the candidate who just states football as the example.

Need to know more? For more information on operant conditioning, see Chapter 8, Part II, pages 194–195 in your Student Book.

REINFORCEMENT

Reinforcement is the process that causes a response to reoccur by forming and strengthening the S–R learning bond.

There are two types of reinforcement.

- **Positive reinforcement.**
  - After a successful response or after the desired behaviour has been demonstrated by the learner the teacher would present a satisfier or make a show of approval.
  - Approval may be in the form of praise and is an intangible reward, e.g. well done.
  - Positive reinforcement could be presented by some other form of 'satisfier', e.g. a certificate is a tangible reward.
- **Negative reinforcement.**
  - Negative reinforcement involves withdrawing a negative or aversive stimulus.
  - An aversive stimulus is often called an 'annoyer'. For example:
    - the teacher may show disapproval when a poor response is given by the learner
    - when the learner eventually responds correctly the aversive stimulus of disapproval is withdrawn and replaced by a 'satisfier'.
  - Negative reinforcement is an operation that weakens the incorrect learning bond but it also strengthens the correct learning bond.

Punishment

In the above context, remember that we also have to consider 'punishment'.

- Punishment involves giving an unpleasant stimulus to a performer to prevent a response from occurring.
- The unpleasant stimulus is called a noxious stimulus.
- A noxious stimulus is designed to break an undesired learning bond.

KEY TERMS

Complete reinforcement – Refers to the process that rewards every successful response.

Partial reinforcement – Is administered when a number of correct responses occur. This process takes longer but the result is more permanent than complete reinforcement.

Need to know more? For more information on reinforcement, see Chapter 8, Part II, pages 198–199 in your Student Book.

THORNDIKE'S LAWS

A psychologist named Thorndike strongly believed that connecting S–R bonds was the most effective way to learn. Thorndike applied three rules to the connectionist theory.

1. The Law of Effect states that reinforcement affects the S–R bond.
2. The Law of Exercise states that the S–R bond will be strengthened by practice and repeated reinforcement.
3. The Law of Readiness states that if reinforcement is to strengthen the learning bond the performer must be both physically and mentally capable of performing the skill.

In the early stages of learning, positive reinforcement is an important motivational aid. It provides the learner with confidence and therefore encourages a positive, healthy lifestyle behaviour.

COGNITIVE THEORY OF LEARNING

The cognitive learning theory supports the view that learning is best achieved by presenting the whole skill to the learner in the context of a realistic situation.

In order to arrive at a solution, the learner must understand and think about the problem as a whole. This cognitive thought process is dependent on perception, which is the driving force in cognitive learning. Many factors influence the process of perception but most importantly the learner will use intelligence, current knowledge and previous experience to plan or predict a solution.

To help understanding, the learner would focus on the problem by using mental rehearsal. Mental processes that occur to bring about a solution are called 'intervening variables'. The process of solving the whole problem by using the process of thought is called insight or intuitive learning.

The cognitive view on learning is often termed Gestalt theory. Gestalt means whole patterning or wholeness of form and states that 'the whole is greater than the sum of the parts'.

If the skill is too complex for a beginner to learn as a whole, problem solving can be facilitated by creating, adapting or conditioning games, e.g. Kwik cricket.

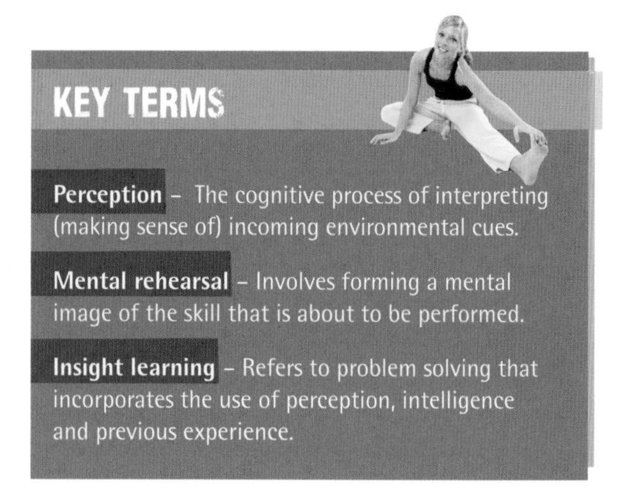

KEY TERMS

Perception – The cognitive process of interpreting (making sense of) incoming environmental cues.

Mental rehearsal – Involves forming a mental image of the skill that is about to be performed.

Insight learning – Refers to problem solving that incorporates the use of perception, intelligence and previous experience.

EXAM TIP

Candidates frequently confuse cognitive learning theory with the cognitive stage of learning. They are two separate theories.

Need to know more? For more information on the cognitive theory of learning, see Chapter 8, Part II, pages 195–196 in your Student Book.

OBSERVATIONAL LEARNING

Observational learning involves copying a demonstration of a motor skill and is a form of visual guidance.

Bandura's model of observational learning

Learning by demonstration is not a fail-safe method. A psychologist named Bandura indicates that observational learning takes place only if the learner can put into place the four following parts or sub-processes.

1. Attention.
The learner must focus directly onto the model that is being demonstrated. The teacher can give verbal guidance to the learner to draw their attention to an important part of the demonstration.

↓

2. Retention.
An image of the demonstration must be stored or retained by the learner if it is to be copied successfully. Mental rehearsal helps this process.

↓

3. Motor reproduction.
The learner must have the physical ability and schematic development to copy or replicate the skill that is being demonstrated.

↓

4. Motivation.
In order to reproduce the demonstration, the observer must have the drive to match the performance of the skill being modelled. External reinforcement of the demonstration will increase the motivation to replicate it.

And so:

- demonstrations are important at all stages of learning
- during the cognitive phase it is easier for the novice to understand a visual model rather than follow verbal instructions
- at the autonomous stage, a demonstration is useful in highlighting detailed and specific points in the performance
- behaviour is most likely to be copied if demonstrated and reinforced by a role model who is significant and of high status.

Need to know more? Go back to Chapter 8, Part II, page 197 in your Student Book.

CHECK

If you are satisfied with your knowledge and understanding, tick off the sections that you have revised so far. If you are not satisfied, then revisit those sections and refer to the pages in the 'Need to know more?' features.

- ☐ The associationist/connectionist theory of operant conditioning (Skinner).
- ☐ The cognitive theory related to the work of Gestaltist principles.
- ☐ Social/observational learning theory; the importance of significant others in the adoption of a balanced, active and healthy lifestyle.
- ☐ Bandura's model and the factors that affect modelling.
- ☐ Reinforcement of movement skill learning and behaviours associated with a balanced, active and healthy lifestyle.
- ☐ Positive reinforcement, negative reinforcement and punishment.
- ☐ Thorndike's Laws as they apply to the formation and strengthening of the stimulus–response learning bond.
- ☐ Appropriate use of reinforcement in skill learning and in promoting positive, healthy lifestyle behaviour.

EXAM PRACTICE

Q.1 The formation of an S–R bond through reinforcement is the basis of the connectionist theory known as operant conditioning.
Use an example from Physical Education or sport to explain how a performer learns by operant conditioning.
6 marks

Q.2 Cognitive theories of learning related to the work of the Gestaltists explain how we learn movement skills.

Describe four of the **key terms** of the cognitive learning theory and give a practical example of how cognitive theories of learning can be applied to the teaching of a skill in Physical Education or sport.
5 marks

See page 180 for answers.

CHAPTER 8: PART III

Transfer of learning to develop effectiveness in physical activity

LEARNING OBJECTIVES

By the end of this part you should be able to demonstrate knowledge and understanding of:

- The types of transfer that occur in practical performance
- Ways of optimising the effect of positive transfer
- Ways of limiting the effect of negative transfer
- How to critically evaluate different types of transfer and their impact on the development of movement skills
- The effects of transfer of learning on schema development and the importance of variable practice.

EXAM TIP

Understanding the link between variable practice, transfer and schema theory is a key issue.

THE DIFFERENT TYPES OF TRANSFER

KEY TERM

Transfer of learning – 'Transfer' means the influence that one skill has on the learning and performance of another. The process is extremely important to the acquisition of movement skills because practically all learning is based on some form of transfer.

You need to learn five types of transfer.

1. **Positive transfer** – occurs when one skill helps or enhances the learning and performance of another skill. For example, the skill of throwing transfers positively to the racquet arm action of a tennis serve.
2. **Negative transfer** – arises when one skill hinders or impedes the learning and performance of another skill. For example, a loose wrist required to play a badminton shot transfers negatively to the firm wrist needed to perform a tennis stroke.
3. **Proactive transfer** – occurs when a previously learned skill influences a skill that is currently being learned. Similarly, a skill being learned at present will eventually influence a skill to be learned in the future. For example, a throwing motor programme learned as a child will later transfer positively and proactively to an overarm volleyball serve.

4. **Retroactive transfer** – occurs when a newly learned skill influences a previous learned skill. For example, the acquisition of a successful tennis serve may influence the previously learned overarm throw used in cricket.
5. **Bi-lateral transfer** – refers to the capacity of the performer who may be dominantly right sided to perform a skill with the left side of the body. For example a footballer who can shoot with the right and left foot with matching power and accuracy is a considerable asset to the team.

Need to know more? For more information, on the transfer of learning, see Chapter 8, Part III, pages 203–205 in your Student Book.

The teacher must ensure both that:

- **positive transfer** is taking place and that its effects are optimised, while taking care to ...
- ... limit the possibility of **negative transfer.**

Each of these issues is addressed in the text that follows. (See Table 1 for more information on how transfer takes place.)

KEY TERM

Optimising transfer – the effects of transfer are maximised and have a full influence on the learning and performance of movement skills.

OPTIMISING THE EFFECTS OF POSITIVE TRANSFER

Transfer – key points	Explanation and/or example
1. Learning situations need to allow for positive transfer	variability of practice, such as two-touch football, would recreate the conditions experienced in a real game and help to improve passing skills
2. The learner must be made aware of the transferable elements of a previously learned skill	the elbow position when the point at which the ball is released in a football throw-in transfers positively to the elbow position during the throwing phase in javelin
3. Clear and concise demonstrations must be used	the learner will be able to transfer elements of the demonstration to aid performance, e.g. the demonstration of bowling in cricket
4. The environmental conditions need to be similar to the real situation	passing skills in hockey should for the most part be practised in a changing environment, e.g. a varied practice
5. The elements of information processing may be similar	'cutting' in basketball has the same perceptual requirements as getting free in netball
6. The closer the practice is to the replication of the game situation, the greater is the chance of positive transfer	this condition is stated in the identical elements theory (Thorndike)
7. Transfer will only operate successfully if previous skills have been well learned	development of a good throwing schema will enhance the learning and performance of a clear in badminton
8. Diverse experiences enhance the probability of transfer	a child must therefore learn a wide range of fundamental motor skills; it is from this 'pool of experience' that sophisticated executive programmes are learned at secondary school
9. Reinforcement ensures that positive transfer can take place	the teacher will know that strong S–R learning bonds from related skills are good foundations on which new skills can be established
10. Simplify the task during initial learning and transfer it later into the real situation	feeding the ball underarm to the learner practising a drive shot in cricket

Table 1 Transfers: explanations and examples

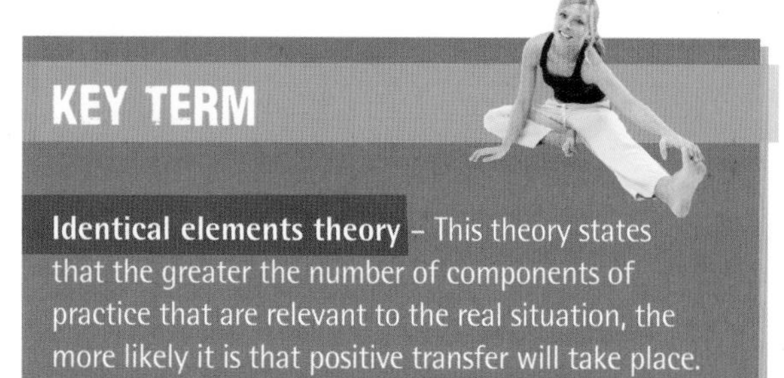

KEY TERM

Identical elements theory – This theory states that the greater the number of components of practice that are relevant to the real situation, the more likely it is that positive transfer will take place.

LIMITING THE EFFECT OF NEGATIVE TRANSFER

- The performer must be helped to understand the requirements of the task before beginning practice.
- The environment in which the skill is learned and practised must match that experienced in the applied situation.
- The learner's attention must be drawn towards motor programmes that transfer positively to the skill being currently performed and drawn away from movements causing negative transfer.
- Negative transfer can be avoided if conflicting skills, e.g. badminton and tennis strokes, are not taught close together in time.
- Should a part presentation method of delivery be used by the teacher the first sub-routine must be thoroughly learned before progressing to the second sub-routine.

EXAM TIP

You need to be aware of the strong relationship between the topics of transfer of learning, schema development and variability of practice.

Varied practice

Open skills are best practised in a varying environment in which the situation is constantly changing, e.g. a three on two attack and defence drill in basketball. The changing environmental conditions will facilitate improvements in positional play and passing technique in a situation directly reflecting the game.

Variability of practice will develop decision-making and perceptual skills. The player will also learn to adapt motor programmes in order to respond effectively to the situational demands.

Adaptations are stored in long-term memory and this is how the experience, or the schema, of the performer is expanded. When a new situation is encountered the appropriate schema is transferred to produce a modified pattern of movement.

EXAM TIP

Avoid the word 'thing' (on its own, or as part of a word) in your answers. This includes the terms 'everything' and 'something'. Use of these words will tell an examiner that the candidate has not learned the appropriate technical language!

Need to know more? For more information on varied practice see Chapter 8, Part III, page 206 in your Student Book.

CHECK

If you are satisfied with your knowledge and understanding, tick off the sections that you have revised so far. If you are not satisfied, then revisit those sections and refer to the pages in the 'Need to know more?' features.

- ☐ Describe types of transfer that occur in practical performance.
- ☐ Demonstrate knowledge and understanding of ways of optimising the effect of positive transfer.
- ☐ Demonstrate knowledge and understanding of ways of limiting the effect of negative transfer.
- ☐ Critically evaluate different types of transfer and their impact on the development of movement skills.
- ☐ Explain the effects of transfer of learning on schema development and the importance of variable practice.

EXAM PRACTICE

Q.1 Transfer of training is a major process in motor skill learning. What is transfer of training? Explain proactive and retroactive transfer and give practical examples of each.
5 marks

Q.2 Explain how the teacher or coach can optimise the effect of transfer when teaching a motor skill in sport.
6 marks

See page 181 for answers.

CHAPTER 9

Physical activity

LEARNING OBJECTIVES

By the end of this chapter you should be able to demonstrate knowledge and understanding of:

- Physical activity as an umbrella term
- The meaning of the terms: exercise, healthy balanced lifestyles, lifetime sport/lifelong physical activity, lifelong participation, physical prowess, physical endeavour, sportsmanship, gamesmanship, deviance
- The benefits of regular participation in physical activity
- Factors contributing to increasingly sedentary lifestyles
- Recommendations in terms of frequency, intensity and type of physical activity
- Possible barriers to regular participation in physical activity by young people
- Definitions, characteristics and benefits of: physical recreation, outdoor recreation, Physical Education, Outdoor Education and sport.

EXAM TIP

You need to be able to explain the meaning of all key words from the specification with an example from sport.

WHAT ARE THE BENEFITS OF REGULAR PARTICIPATION IN PHYSICAL ACTIVITY?

Adults who are physically active have a 20–30 per cent reduced risk of premature death and a 50 per cent reduced risk of developing a major chronic disease. The estimated cost of physical inactivity in England is £8.2 billion annually. In addition the obesity cost is £2.5 billion annually.

These are National Health Service (NHS) costs and absence from work costs. Fifty per cent of boys, and between 33 and 50 per cent of girls have activity levels that may put their health at risk.

The benefits of physical activity can usefully be revised under the following headings.

- **Physical**, e.g. improved cardiovascular fitness or maintenance of a healthy body weight.
- **Mental**, e.g. stress relief, mood enhancement, or a feel good factor.
- **Personal**, e.g. knowing own strengths and weaknesses or increasing self-esteem.
- **Social**, e.g. a feeling of belonging or having healthy relationships.

EXAM TIP

You need to be able to give examples of physical, mental, personal and social benefits of regular participation in physical activity.

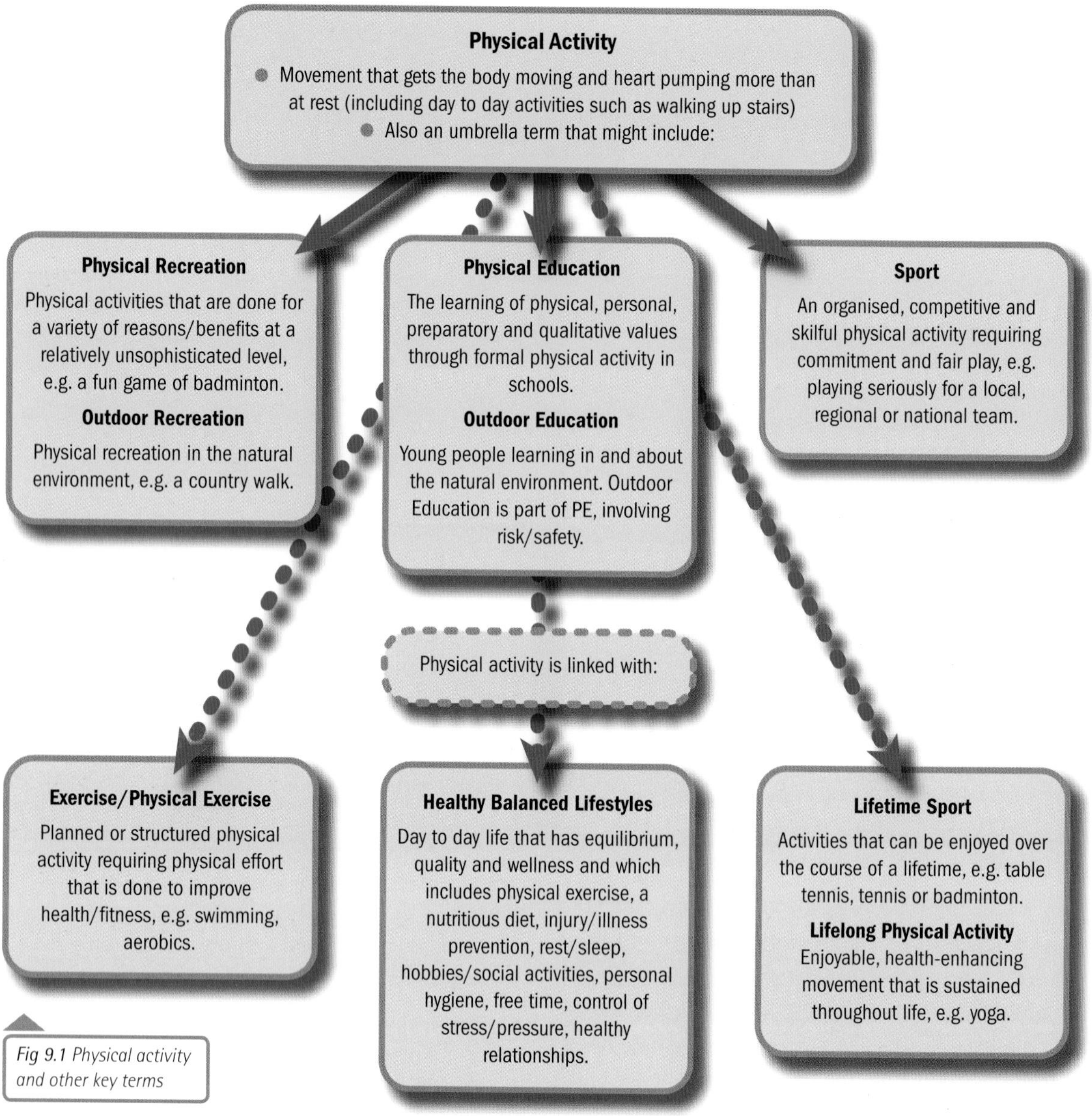

Physical Activity

- Movement that gets the body moving and heart pumping more than at rest (including day to day activities such as walking up stairs)
- Also an umbrella term that might include:

Physical Recreation

Physical activities that are done for a variety of reasons/benefits at a relatively unsophisticated level, e.g. a fun game of badminton.

Outdoor Recreation

Physical recreation in the natural environment, e.g. a country walk.

Physical Education

The learning of physical, personal, preparatory and qualitative values through formal physical activity in schools.

Outdoor Education

Young people learning in and about the natural environment. Outdoor Education is part of PE, involving risk/safety.

Sport

An organised, competitive and skilful physical activity requiring commitment and fair play, e.g. playing seriously for a local, regional or national team.

Physical activity is linked with:

Exercise/Physical Exercise

Planned or structured physical activity requiring physical effort that is done to improve health/fitness, e.g. swimming, aerobics.

Healthy Balanced Lifestyles

Day to day life that has equilibrium, quality and wellness and which includes physical exercise, a nutritious diet, injury/illness prevention, rest/sleep, hobbies/social activities, personal hygiene, free time, control of stress/pressure, healthy relationships.

Lifetime Sport

Activities that can be enjoyed over the course of a lifetime, e.g. table tennis, tennis or badminton.

Lifelong Physical Activity

Enjoyable, health-enhancing movement that is sustained throughout life, e.g. yoga.

Fig 9.1 Physical activity and other key terms

WHAT ARE THE FACTORS CONTRIBUTING TO INCREASINGLY SEDENTARY LIFESTYLES?

In the last 150 years Britain has changed from a rural to an urban society; from manual labourers to those who are deskbound. Walking and cycling as modes of transport have also declined 20 per cent over the last 25 years. Today, for most people in the UK, exercise is now a lifestyle choice rather than a daily necessity.

Modern technology has reduced the need to move around. Cars, lifts, escalators, washing machines, sit-on mowers, TV channel zappers and other labour-saving gadgets and machines have all contributed to inactivity.

Add to this more hours in front of the TV and computer (including shopping online) as well as many parents fearful of their young children walking to school and we see why we are leading increasingly sedentary lifestyles.

WHAT ARE THE RECOMMENDED AMOUNTS OF PHYSICAL ACTIVITY FOR A BALANCED ACTIVE AND HEALTHY LIFESTYLE?

Adults should do a minimum of 30 minutes of moderate intensity physical activity five times per week (5 a week).

Children and young people should do 60 minutes of moderately intensive physical activity each day. At least two sessions should include higher impact activities to improve bone health, muscle strength and flexibility.

Moderate intensity is when you are able to hold a conversation during exercise, feel a bit breathless but are back to normal within 10 minutes of stopping. The time can be made up of 10-minute chunks over the day.

Any type of activity that is safe, enjoyable and that gets the heart and lungs working is suitable. (Recommendations from the Department of Health.)

WHAT ARE THE POSSIBLE BARRIERS TO REGULAR PARTICIPATION IN PHYSICAL ACTIVITY BY YOUNG PEOPLE?

Lack of:

- energy
- perceived ability/skills
- friends who participate
- suitable facilities nearby
- money, e.g. to join a gym
- suitable/correct kit.

Also:

- anxiety about being out after dark
- preference to stay inside when it is cold or wet outside
- dislike of exercise and/or sweating
- embarrassed to show body.

In brief:

- lack of opportunity
- lack of provision
- lack of esteem.

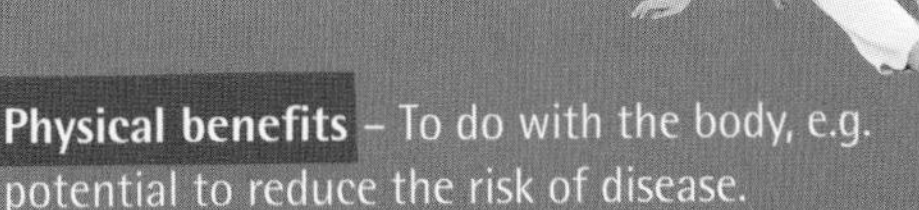

KEY TERMS

Physical benefits – To do with the body, e.g. potential to reduce the risk of disease.

Mental benefits – To do with the mind, e.g. stress relief.

Personal benefits – To do with self, e.g. improved self-esteem.

Social benefits – To do with others, e.g. having positive relationships.

Opportunity – The chance to take part based on factors such as time, money etc.

Provision – The availability of facilities which allow for participation.

Esteem – Confidence.

EXAM TIP

Key words = marks! Add detail/development to your key words to score well particularly on your ten-mark question at the end of each section.

Need to know more? For more information on physical activity see Chapter 9, pages 210–217 in your Student Book.

Physical recreation

Physical recreation is more than just an activity – it is also a potentially valuable experience. It involves activities that are pursued at a relatively unsophisticated level, e.g. a fun game of badminton. When carried out as physical recreation, activities are done with a playful attitude in a leisurely environment.

EXAM TIP

When asked to identify the characteristics of physical recreation in an exam it is important to be specific and clear in your answers. If simple, bland terms such as 'anyone, anywhere, any time' are given as characteristics they will not gain marks. Always be specific rather than vague in your answers.

Physical recreation – enjoyment is a key characteristic

In physical recreation the emphasis is on:

- participation, not standard of performance
- taking part, not winning
- enjoyment and satisfaction, not record breaking.

Need to know more? For more information on physical recreation see Chapter 9, pages 217–219 in your Student Book.

KEY TERMS

Physical recreation – Physical activities that are pursued for a variety of reasons and benefits at a relatively unsophisticated level.

Outdoor recreation – Physical activities which take place in the natural environment and which are pursued for a variety of reasons and benefits.

EXAM TIP

You need to be able to compare characteristics of physical recreation with characteristics of sport.

BENEFITS OF OUTDOOR RECREATION

- **Appreciation of the natural environment** – a chance to get back to nature/live more simply/escape from modern hectic lifestyles/a time to tune in to one's inner self, thoughts and feelings.

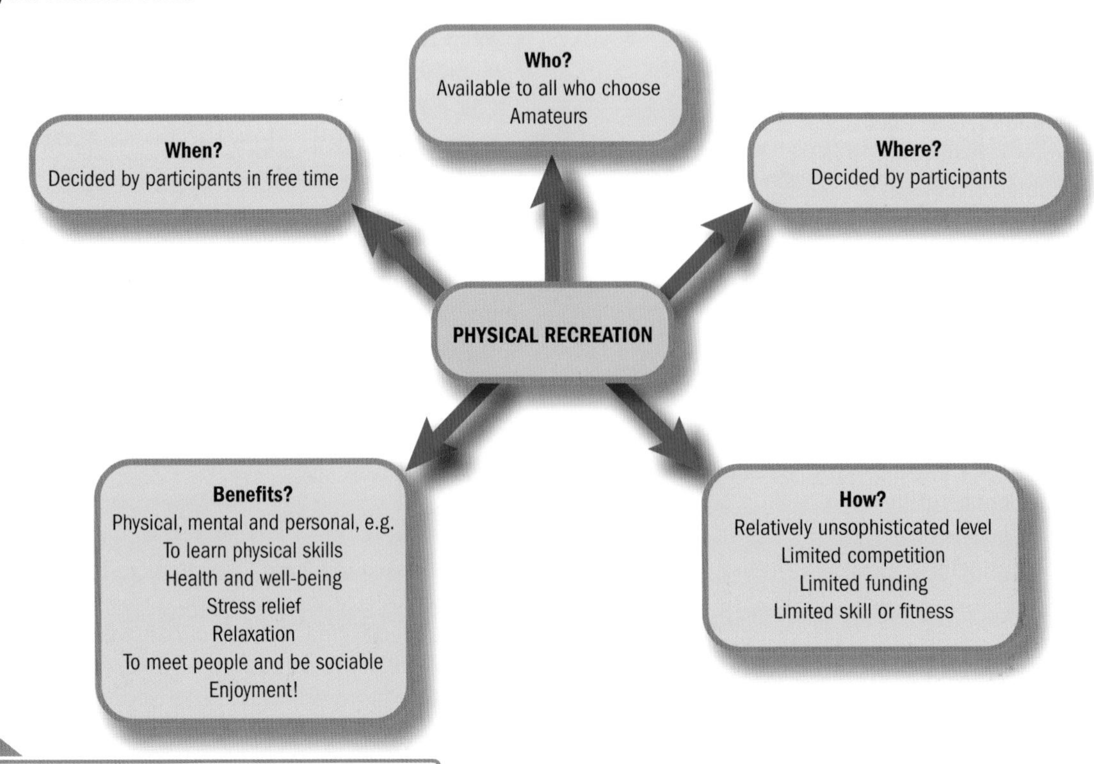

Fig 9.2 Physical recreation: characteristics and benefits

- **Respect for the natural environment** – being in the natural environment can intensify appreciation of need to preserve, conserve, value and protect the natural environment.
- **Gaining a sense of adventure** – due to the unpredictable, risky and sometimes potentially dangerous nature of the natural environment. Once all real risk has been eliminated and safety measures followed, a sense of excitement, exhilaration and adventure can be experienced.

Remember that outdoor recreation **is** physical recreation – in the natural environment, e.g. a walking holiday.

EXAM TIP

Remember that outdoor recreation means using the natural environment, (e.g. hills, lakes or rivers) to gain physical, mental, personal and social benefits.

Outdoor recreation is not just playing a game of hockey or golf which happens to be outside.

PHYSICAL EDUCATION

PE can be described/defined as:

- learning about and through physical activity, or
- the learning of physical, personal, preparatory and qualitative values through formal physical activity in schools.

Benefits

Among other things, a high-quality school PE experience enables young people to do the following things.

- Enjoy, succeed and become confident in a variety of physical activities.
- Have a healthy balanced lifestyle.
- Develop a love of exercise leading to lifelong involvement in physical activity.
- Learn a range of skills, tactics and strategies.
- Develop creativity and decision-making skills.
- Develop observational and communication skills.
- Develop personally and socially from working alone, in groups and in teams.
- Develop qualities such as fair play and responsibility.
- Lead, coach and officiate as part of their PE programme.
- Be effective in competitive, creative and challenging situations.

These benefits can usefully be considered under the headings in the diagram in Fig 9.4.

Need to know more? For more information on Physical Education see Chapter 9, pages 220–222 in your Student Book.

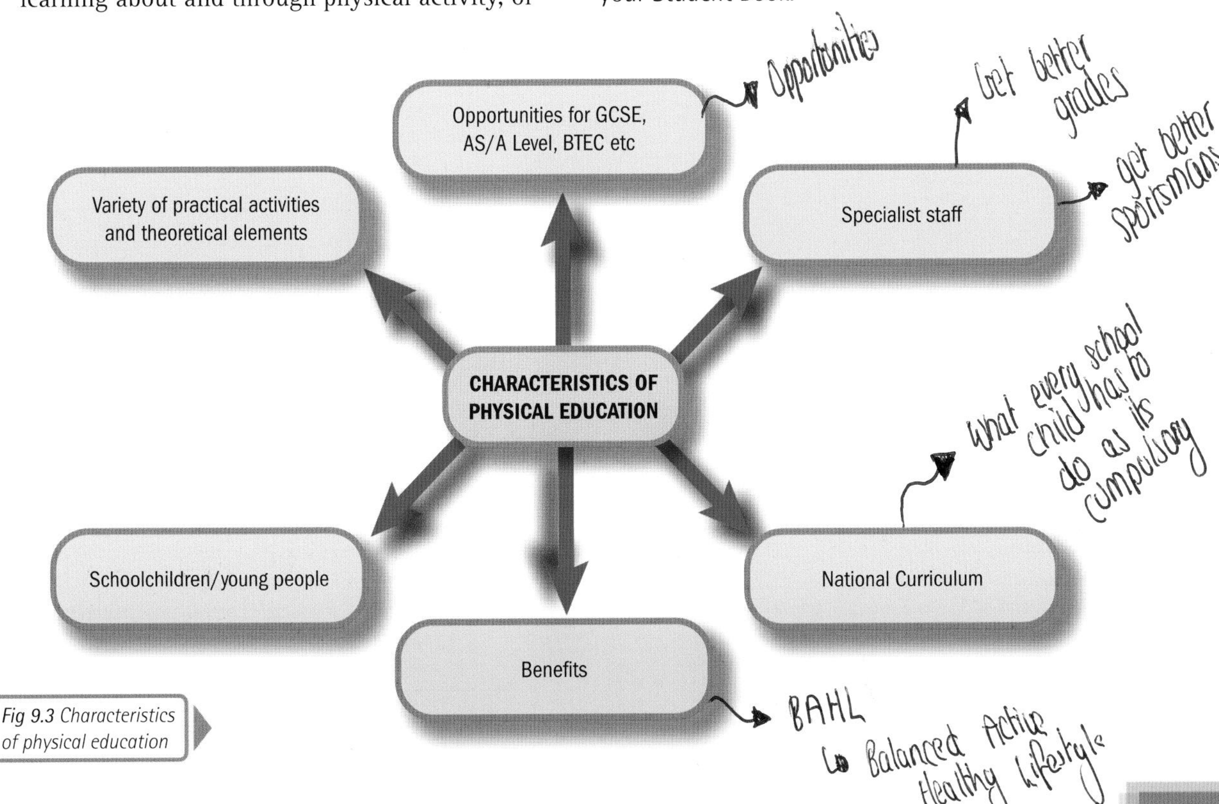

Fig 9.3 Characteristics of physical education

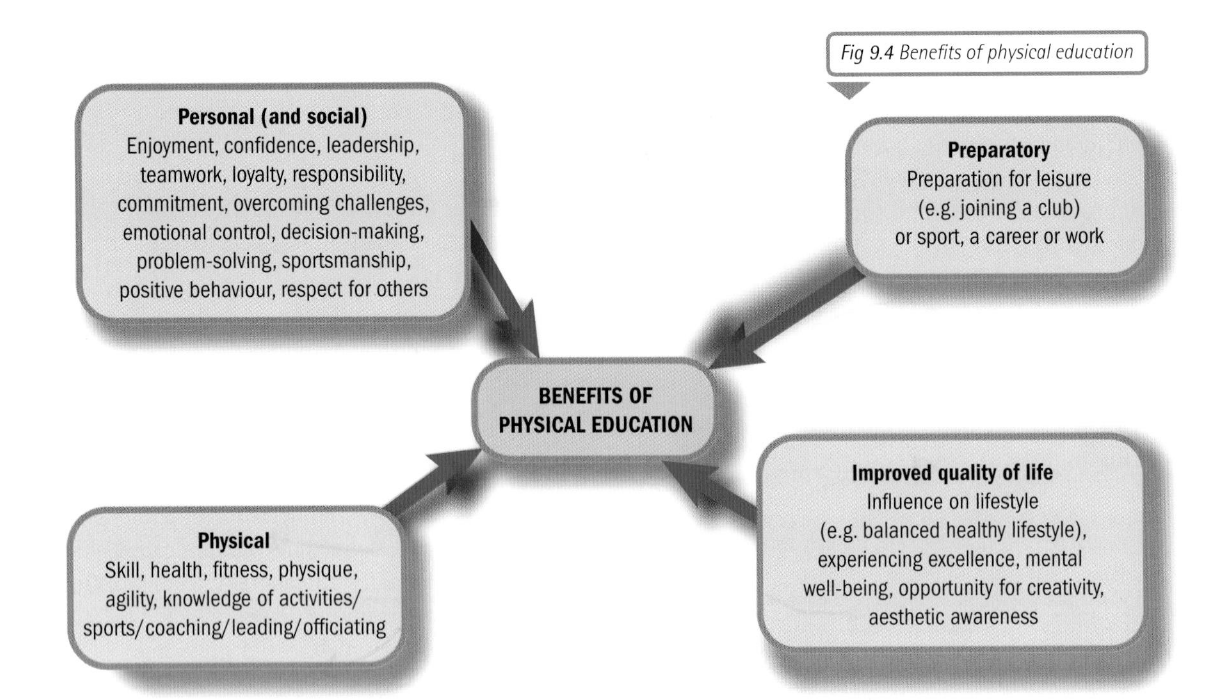

Fig 9.4 Benefits of physical education

Outdoor Education

Outdoor Education is part of PE and involves young people learning in and about the natural environment. What distinguishes Outdoor Education from the rest of PE is the element of risk and unpredictability.

Risk might be the possibility of a natural disaster or freak accident that must be avoided at all costs while unpredictability could be weather conditions that change suddenly and which result from the natural or semi-natural environment.

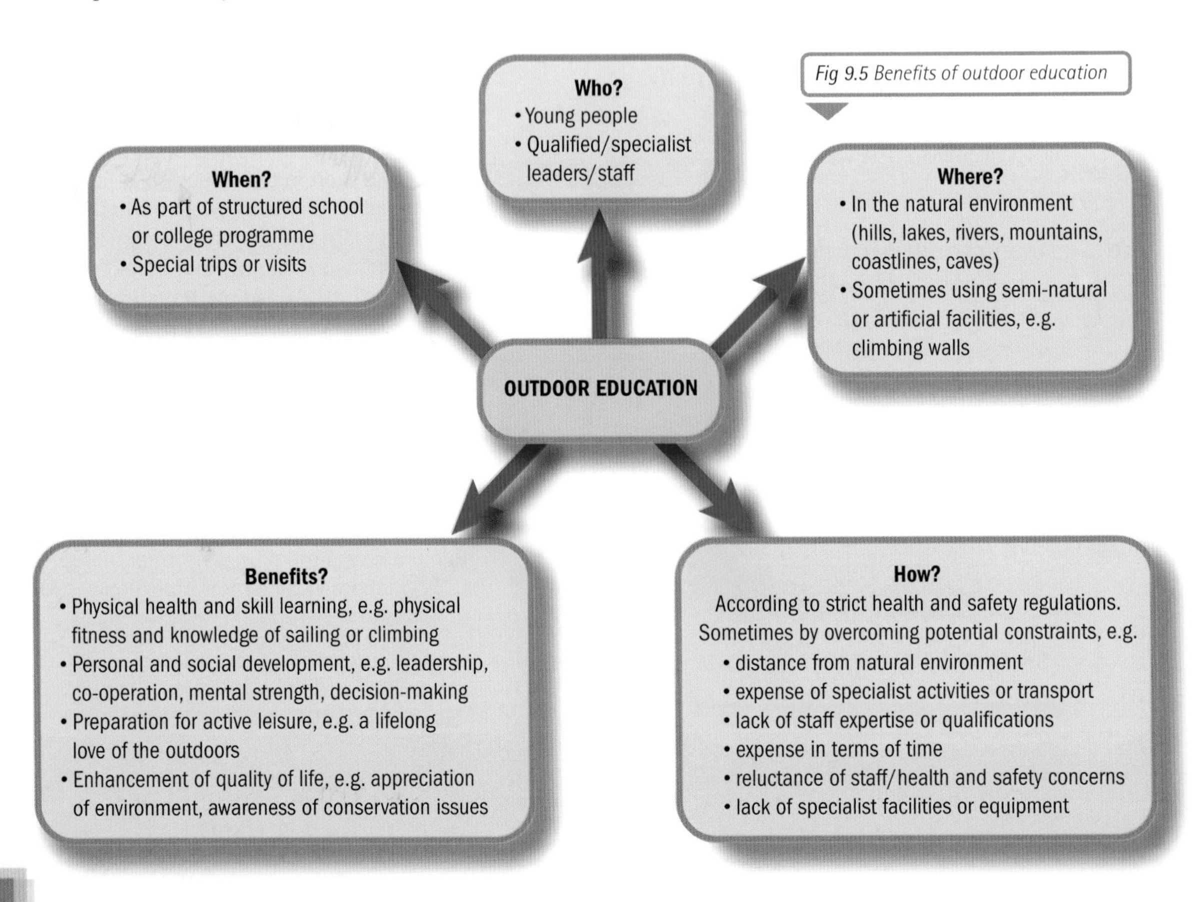

Fig 9.5 Benefits of outdoor education

Abseiling as an Outdoor Education activity

Fig 9.6 Real and perceived risk

You need to be aware of the differences between real and perceived risk and the need for safety in Outdoor Education.

Constraints on widespread participation in Outdoor Education by young people

Several factors restrict or stop school PE departments from offering a regular varied Outdoor Education programme to young people.

- Lack of adequate funding either for transport to the natural environment or for the specialist, time-consuming and expensive training of specialist staff.
- Possibility of insufficient voluntary contributions from pupils.
- Natural facilities are often distant from many urban and suburban schools which make them inaccessible on a regular basis.

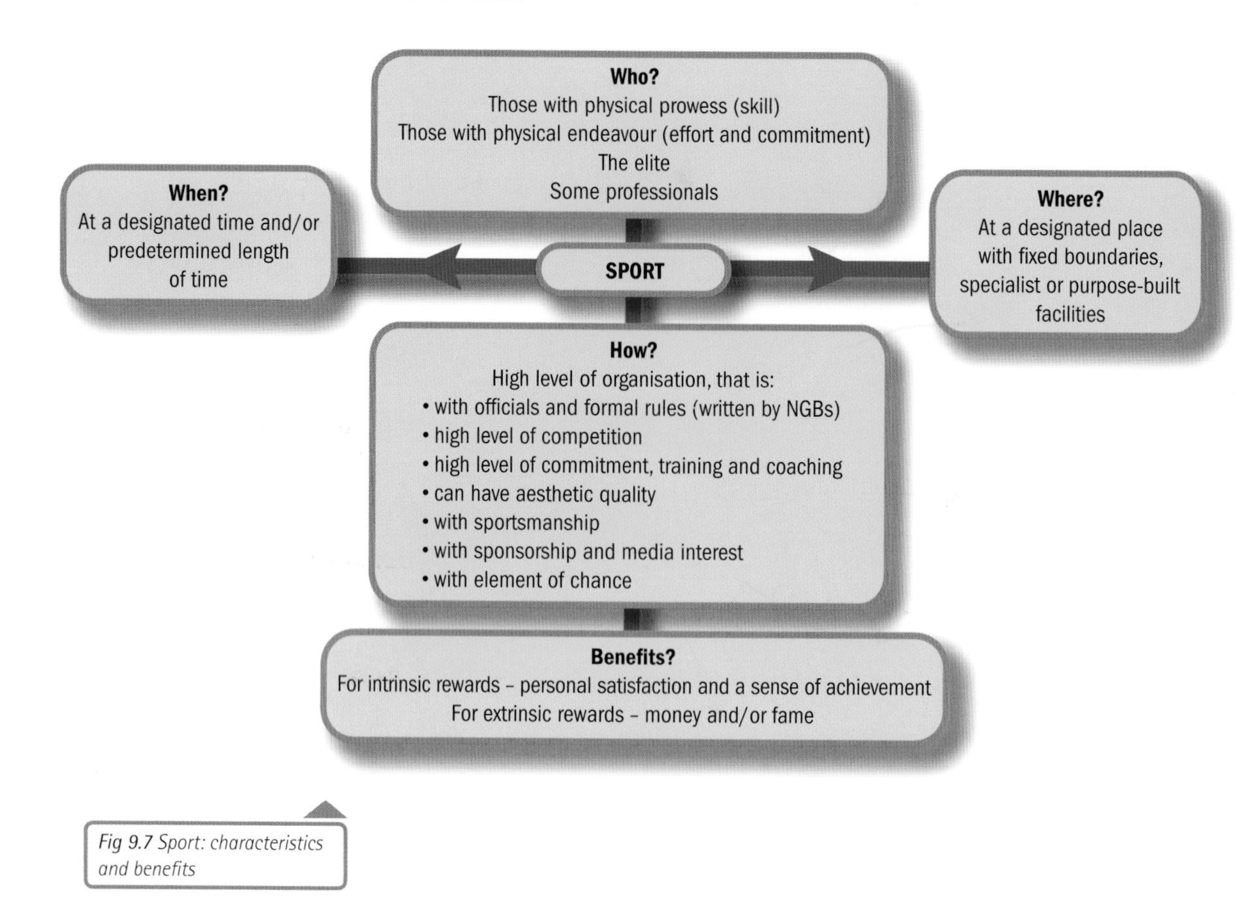

Fig 9.7 Sport: characteristics and benefits

- Outdoor Education can take up a lot of curriculum time so is one of the first subjects to be squeezed out.
- Some parents have health and safety concerns and staff may be reluctant to take on the responsibility.

Need to know more? For more information on Outdoor Education, see Chapter 9, pages 223–224 in your Student Book.

Sport

Sport can be defined as organised, competitive and skilful physical activity requiring commitment and fair play.

What makes a sport a sport?

The more of the following features that fit a particular activity, the more likely it is that it can be classified as sport.

- **Tradition** – do we traditionally call the activity a sport in this country?
- **Vigorous physical exertion** – does the activity involve strenuous movement?
- **Competition** – does the activity involve competition against oneself or others?
- **Administration** – does the activity follow National Governing Body rules?
- **Behaviour** – does the performer show commitment, skill and fair play?

So what about aerobics, skipping, body building, fishing or ballroom dancing – could/should they be classified as sports?

KEY TERMS

Aesthetic – Movement that is pleasing to the eye or beautiful to watch.

Physical prowess – Skill.

Physical endeavour – Effort.

Sportsmanship – Fair play.

Gamesmanship – Stretching the rules to gain an unfair advantage.

Deviance (in sport) – Seriously breaking the rules and norms (of sport).

Sledging – Attempting to undermine opponent (often in cricket) by verbally abusing, taunting, intimidating or antagonising.

CHECK

If you are satisfied with your knowledge and understanding, tick off the sections that you have revised so far. If you are not satisfied, then revisit those sections and refer to the pages in the 'Need to know more?' features.

- ☐ Physical activity as an umbrella term.
- ☐ The meaning of the terms: exercise, healthy balanced lifestyles, lifetime sport/lifelong physical activity, lifelong participation, physical prowess, physical endeavour, sportsmanship, gamesmanship, deviance.
- ☐ The benefits of regular participation in physical activity.
- ☐ Factors contributing to increasingly sedentary lifestyles.
- ☐ Recommendations in terms of frequency, intensity and type of physical activity.
- ☐ Possible barriers to regular participation in physical activity by young people.
- ☐ Definitions, characteristics and benefits of: physical recreation, outdoor recreation, Physical Education, Outdoor Education and sport.

EXAM PRACTICE

Q.1

a) What is being described in i) ii) and iii) below?

i) Planned or structured physical activity requiring physical effort that is performed to improve health and fitness.

ii) Activities that can be enjoyed over the course of a lifetime e.g. table tennis, tennis or badminton.

iii) Day to day life that has equilibrium, quality and wellness.

b) Identify factors contributing to increasingly sedentary lifestyles.

6 marks

Q.2 Outline some of the barriers to regular participation in physical activity by young people.

5 marks

See page 182 for answers.

CHAPTER 10

Sport and culture

LEARNING OBJECTIVES

By the end of this chapter you should be able to demonstrate knowledge and understanding of:

- Surviving ethnic sports and games in the UK
- The role of nineteenth-century public schools in promoting and organising sports and games
- The relatively recent move from the traditional amateur approach to a more professional approach in sport in the UK
- Characteristics of the USA and Australia and the nature of sport in each of those countries
- American football and Australian Rules football.

SPORT AND CULTURE

Sports and games reflect the culture in which they exist – in other words people play games that suit them and their environment. In this chapter we will look at how sport and physical activity reflect a community's true nature and personality.

THE UNITED KINGDOM

Here are some examples of surviving ethnic sports and games in the UK.

- The Highland Games – Scotland.
- Royal Shrovetide Football – Ashbourne, Derbyshire.
- Cheese rolling – Gloucestershire.
- Tar Barrel Burning – Devon.

Ethnic Sports → Surviving Sports

EXAM TIP

You need to remember an example of a surviving ethnic sport in the UK – be specific, i.e. don't just say 'mob football' but name a specific mob football game.

Each of the sports, games or festivals listed above has at least some of the characteristics shown in the spider diagram, Fig 10.1.

EXAM TIP

You need to be able to describe the characteristics of surviving ethnic sports and give reasons for their continued existence and popularity – Fig 10.1 gives you the details!

Need to know more? For more information on surviving ethnic sports and games see Chapter 10, pages 233–236 in your Student Book.

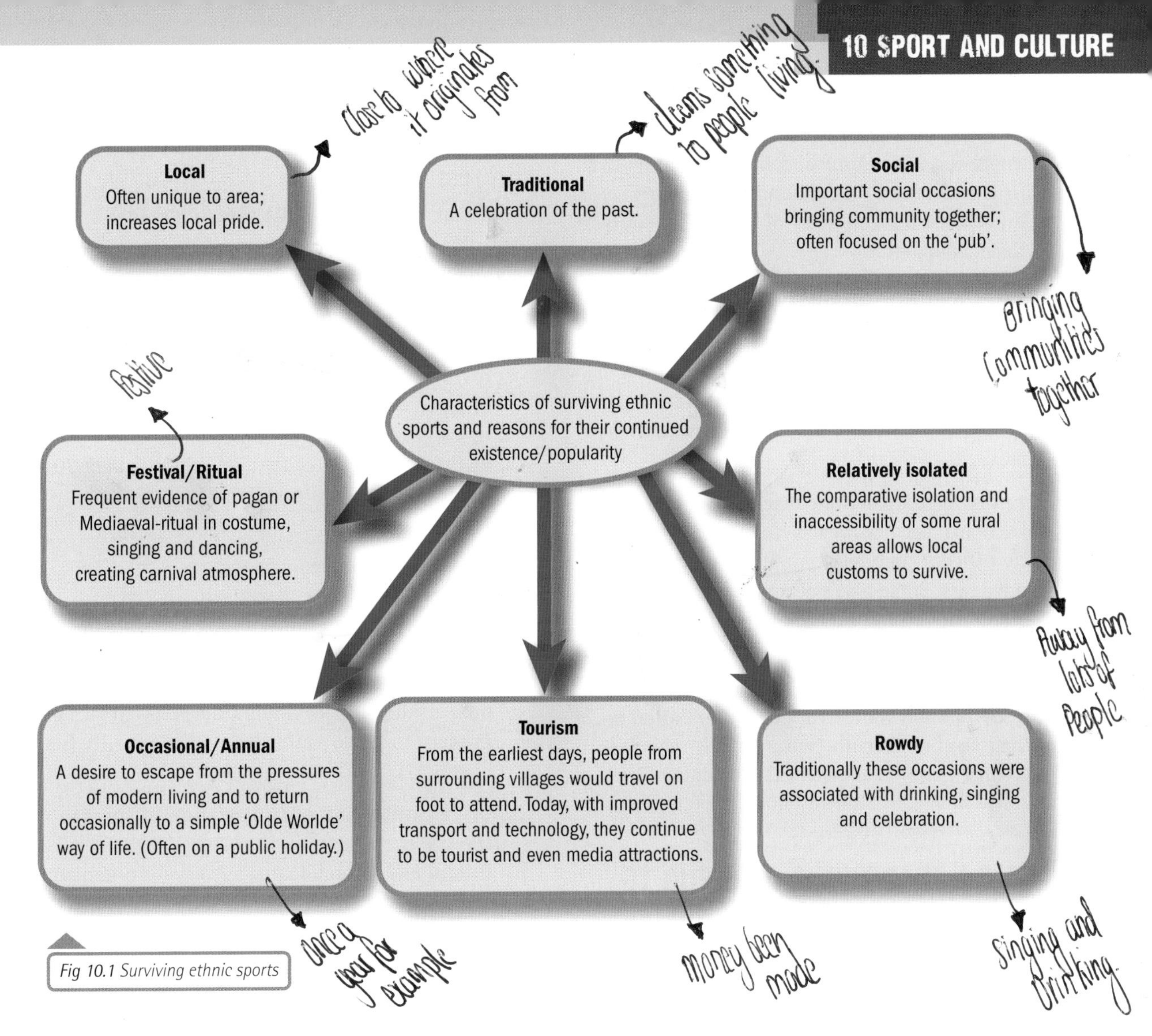

Fig 10.1 Surviving ethnic sports

THE ROLE OF NINETEENTH-CENTURY PUBLIC SCHOOLS IN PROMOTING AND ORGANISING SPORTS AND GAMES

What was going on in the nineteenth century (1800–1900)?

- The RSPCA was formed in 1824 and started to reduce cruel blood sports and baiting sports, e.g. dog fighting.
- Queen Victoria reigned for 65 years from 1837–1902.
- The growth of the railways in the 1850s had a huge impact on the development and spread of sport.
- Public baths were built in towns to try to reduce disease.
- Working class children either didn't attend school or went to local state/village schools. Upper and middle class boys (and later girls) attended elite, fee paying, public boarding schools.
- Towards the end of the century the working and living conditions of the working class improved.

In what ways did the public schools help to promote and organise sports and games?

- They had plenty of **funding** to:
  - build specialist facilities
  - employ specialist coaches.
- Being boarding schools, there was plenty of **time** to practice.
- There was usually plenty of **space** e.g. for cricket and rugby pitches and for building new specialist facilities, e.g. squash courts or swimming baths.
- Games were usually compulsory every day.
- The boys were fully involved in the organisation of games.
- Over time, both boys and masters became obsessed with team games.

- Fixtures between different schools became more regular as transport improved after 1850.
- It was believed that playing team games developed the **character** of a boy, e.g. courage, leadership, etc.

How did team games spread around Britain and the rest of the world?

The ex-pupils from these schools took on major leadership roles in society. In these leadership roles they spread their belief in, and passion for, team games.

For example they became teachers back in their old schools, became wealthy industrialists, vicars, army officers, parents, community members and leaders. Some also became key founders of National Governing Bodies (NGBs) and so were largely responsible for the spread of team games.

Need to know more? For more information on the role of nineteenth-century public schools in promoting sports and games see Chapter 10, pages 236–238 in your Student Book.

FROM A TRADITIONAL AMATEUR TO A MORE PROFESSIONAL APPROACH TO SPORT

The word amateur stems from the Latin word *amare* which means 'to love.' In the nineteenth century amateurs took part in sport for love not money. Wealthy upper and upper-middle class men who excelled at games were knows as 'gentleman amateurs.' They could afford to spend time away from work playing sports and games for enjoyment. In the late 1800s and well into the twentieth century being an amateur meant abiding by a set of unwritten rules about behaviour in life as well as behaviour in sports and games.

Unlike gentlemen amateurs, working class men could not afford to miss work to play. If a working class man had great talent they might get a chance to play full time for payment. They then became a 'working class professional'. Today, the word 'professional' is used to describe an expert, skilful performer as well as someone who is paid to play.

A professional approach in modern sport involves full-time commitment, planning, policy and high levels of funding.

The move from amateurism to professionalism

Let's look at four key areas, which it could be argued have become more professional in approach.

1. Mass participation
   Mass participation means getting more people involved in sport. Initiatives/action plans are in place both locally and nationally to try to improve participation rates. The Government wants 70 per cent of the population taking 30 minutes of moderate exercise five times per week by 2020.
2. Sporting excellence
   Sporting excellence means winning medals. UK Sport is the organisation responsible for all Olympic and Paralympic sport in the UK. UK sport is aiming for 4th place in the medals table at the 2012 Olympic Games. Strategies are in place to try to make this dream a reality (see page 141).
3. Organisation and administration of sport in the UK
   Britain has a complicated system for organising sport as most NGBs were formed over 100 years ago. NGBs are working towards more smooth running, proficient and professional systems to match the needs of modern day sport (see page 119).
4. Government support for sport
   The Department for Culture, Media and Sport appoints the Minister for Sport and gives an annual grant to key organising bodies, e.g. to UK Sport. The Government of the UK does not have an outstanding reputation for supporting sport with high levels of funding!

   However, The National Lottery has greatly improved funding for both mass participation and sporting excellence in the UK since 1994 (see page 118).

THE UNITED STATES OF AMERICA

Characteristics of the USA

- The USA is a powerful, relatively young nation.
- Native Indians are the indigenous or original population.
- George Washington was the first president in 1787.

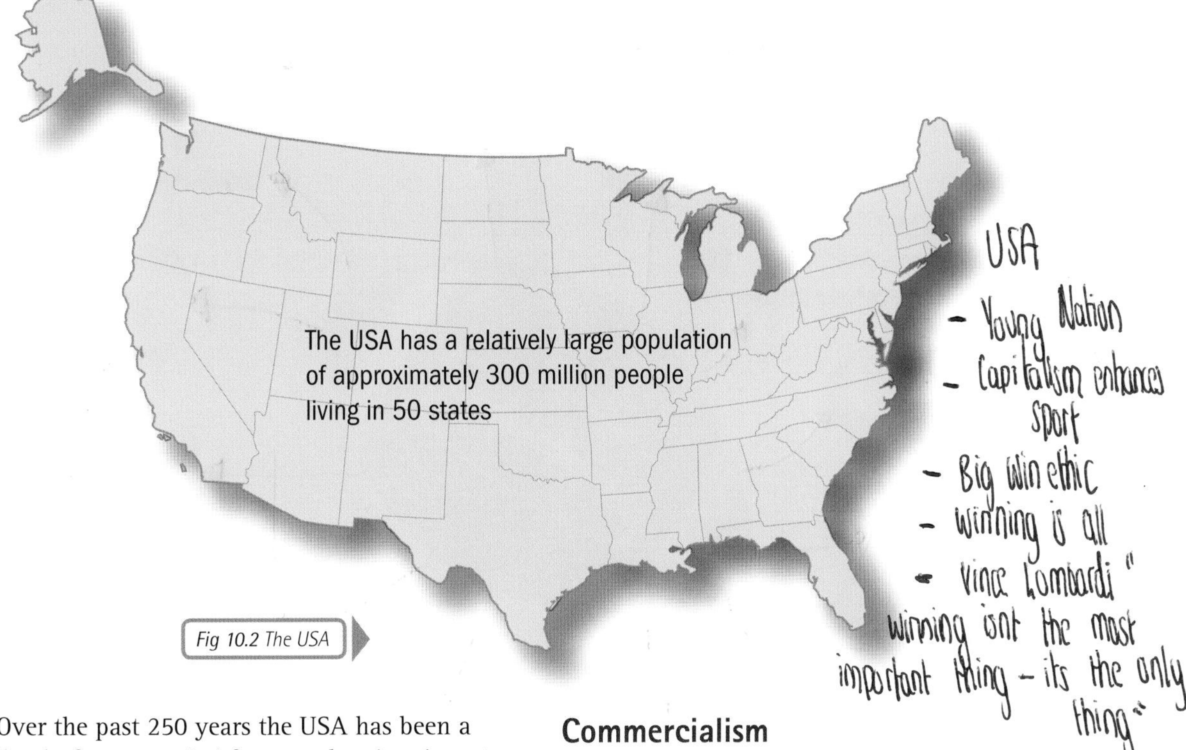

Fig 10.2 The USA

- Over the past 250 years the USA has been a 'land of opportunity' for countless immigrants.
- The country has a belief in individualism where each person is responsible for their own destiny and success.
- The individualism leads to capitalism which is a system based on private or corporate ownership and the investment of money for profit.
- Capitalism influences the nature of sport in the USA.

The nature of sport in the USA

Win Ethic

- The 'win ethic' dominates sport at all levels in the USA.
- Winning is more important than taking part.
- The result is what matters.
- Second place is not an option.
- According to legendary American football coach Vince Lombardi, 'winning isn't the most important thing – it is the only thing'.

Vehicle for achieving the American Dream

- The American Dream is the dream of success, freedom, equality and security.
- The Dream gets you from 'Rags to Riches' or from 'Zero to Hero'.
- Prosperity and success depend on ability and hard work – not class.
- Anyone can achieve the 'Dream' – age, gender or ethnic background should not stop you.

Commercialism

In America sport means big business! Sport is a commodity and companies use it to promote their products and to achieve goodwill. The high-scoring and action-packed games of the USA are well suited to commercialism.

TV and advertising fund top level professional sport with sport, sponsorship and the media enjoying a strong and mutually beneficial relationship. This three-way relationship is sometimes referred to as the 'golden triangle'. In the USA money determines the location, timings and nature of sport.

Though comparatively few performers become super-rich the very best are on multi-million dollar playing contracts. They can also earn millions from advertising and sponsorship deals.

American football

Origins and nature of the game

Also called 'gridiron' (from the original pitch markings that went both width and lengthways forming a grid of squares) the game developed in the influential 'Ivy League' universities such as Yale, Harvard, Princeton and Rutgers. In the early 1800s there were no generally accepted rules – some universities allowed running with the ball while others did not.

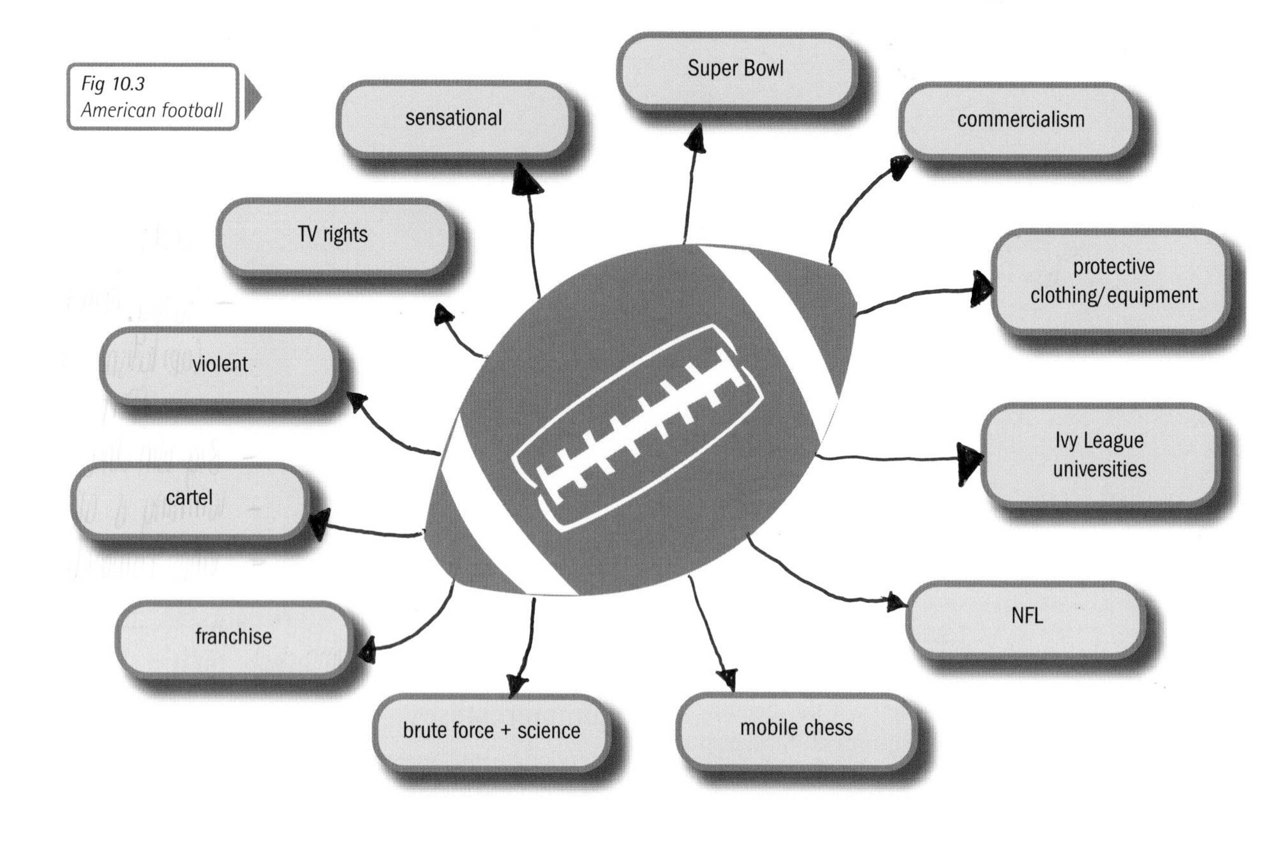

Fig 10.3 American football

Characteristics

In the early days, serious injury and even death were not uncommon as players wore very little protective clothing. Play was so rough that some universities banned it for a time. In 1869 Rutgers and Princeton universities competed in the first intercollegiate match. Handling or carrying of the (then) round ball was not allowed and there were 25 players a side. Characteristics of toughness, endeavour and courage which were needed to be successful in the game reflected the spirit of the early settlers to the USA. After adaptations, revisions and modifications, American football developed its own rules, tactics and style of play.

Physicality

By 1900 the game had developed into a violent, sensational, hazardous conflict with survival and success dependent almost entirely on physical force. It is a tough collision sport which today involves intricate planning and complicated, carefully concealed tactical and strategic moves. Each player has a specialist role in each play or move.

Physical contact is allowed between players who are not in possession of the ball and obstruction of opponents' moves by deliberate body-checking is allowed. The game has been described as both 'mobile chess' and 'a mixture of brute force and science'.

Players must wear special protective equipment, such as padded plastic helmets, shoulder pads, hip pads and knee pads and various rule changes have been brought in which emphasise safety.

Injury

Even so, injuries remain very common. Twenty-eight players (mostly school age) died from direct football injuries between 2000–2005 (*National Center for Catastrophic Sport Injury Research*). The dangers and expensive equipment make it impractical for casual/recreational play. In fact it could be argued that the safety equipment has increased levels of violence as players can hurl themselves at one another at high speeds with less chance of injury.

Commercialism

American football is a multi-billion dollar business. The National Football League (NFL) is a group (or cartel) of companies with teams either privately owned (e.g. Chicago Bears) or run as public companies (e.g. the Green Bay Packers Foundation). Teams are bought or inherited and run as 'franchises'.

Competition between TV networks for coverage rights inflates the cost of NFL franchises which sometimes relocate hundreds of miles from their traditional fan base just for profit. The Super Bowl is the championship game of the NFL and is much more than a football game. It takes place on 'Super Bowl Sunday' which has become the second-largest food consumption day in the US after Thanksgiving!

The Super Bowl

In recent years the Super Bowl has become the showcase for extravagantly expensive adverts with the estimated cost of a 30-second commercial break being $2.6 million. Half time at the Super Bowl is an hour long and many TV networks take advantage of the huge TV audience by scheduling independently produced half-time entertainment. In recent years, the Rolling Stones, Joss Stone, Justin Timberlake, Janet Jackson (who suffered a wardrobe malfunction!) and Paul McCartney have performed during the half-time show.

Television

In the early days of commercialism (1960s) some universities went dangerously into debt to provide themselves with expensive stadiums. The professionals then agreed not to play on Saturdays so that colleges could have their share of TV coverage. The game was redesigned back in the 1960s to suit television and is thus characterised by many and regular commercial breaks.

Need to know more? For more information on the nature of sport in the USA see Chapter 10, pages 242–245 in your Student Book.

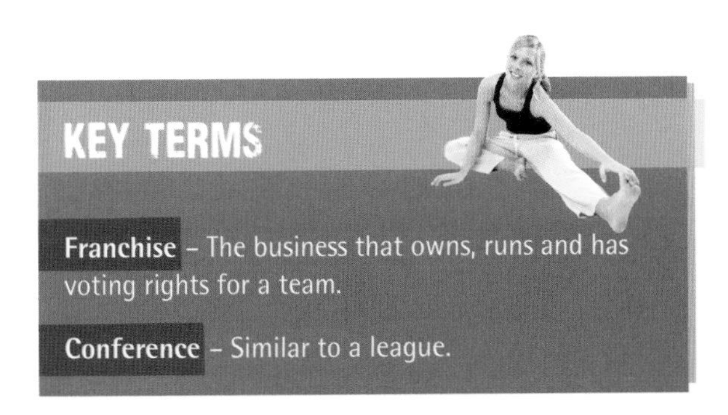

KEY TERMS

Franchise – The business that owns, runs and has voting rights for a team.

Conference – Similar to a league.

AUSTRALIA

KEY TERMS

Colonialism – When a more dominant country takes over and rules a less dominant country and imposes its ways of life including sports and games.

White Australia policy – The laws and policies that restricted non-white immigration to Australia from 1901 to 1973.

Bush culture – The individuality, pioneering spirit, ruggedness and stamina of early settlers which suits sport today.

Characteristics of Australia

Australia is a comparatively **young nation**; until a few hundred years ago it was inhabited solely by Aboriginal people. In 1770 James Cook sailed into Botany Bay and claimed Australia as a colony for Britain. Australia is massive – it takes six hours to fly from one side of the country to the other.

Australia is **sparsely/thinly populated** with just 21 million people compared with 300 million in the USA and 60 million in Britain. The country consists of six states and two territories. With most of the country uninhabitable, the majority of the population live in one of the eight main cities. Eighty-five per cent of the population live in only just over 3 per cent of the land.

Colonial influence

- The British Union flag is still in the corner of the Australian flag as a symbol of British **colonialism.**
- When colonialists arrived over 200 years ago they brought the British way of life, government, education and judicial systems plus sports and games with them.
- Most schools have sports afternoons and many schools have school colours in the English tradition.
- Australia adopted many English games and a great sporting rivalry between the two countries developed which continues today.
- Perhaps the passionate desire for victory has been reversed in more recent years with England now fighting for victory against its former outpost.

- In 1901 Australia became an independent commonwealth country of the British Empire.
- Although historically Australia is steeped in colonial values, we should not underestimate the assimilation of new culture and identity that has taken place.

Immigration

- Captain Cook's arrival in 1770 was followed in 1788 by an influx of British convicts.
- Throughout the nineteenth century (1800–1900), the population of Australia continued to grow.
- More convicts were transported, then Chinese and European immigrants arrived seeking their fortunes in the gold rush of the 1850s.
- After the Second World War (post-1945) the Australian government launched a massive immigration campaign due to the perceived need to 'populate or perish'.
- Britons who emigrated for a better life 'Down Under' via a £10 one-way passage were collectively known as *Ten Pound Poms.*
- Since the abolition of the 'White Australian' policy in the early 1970s multiculturalism has been promoted and Australia has been committed to a policy of multiculturalism.
- More recently Australia has embarked on a policy of reconciliation aimed at ending the discrimination against the Aboriginal people, which started in the colonial period.

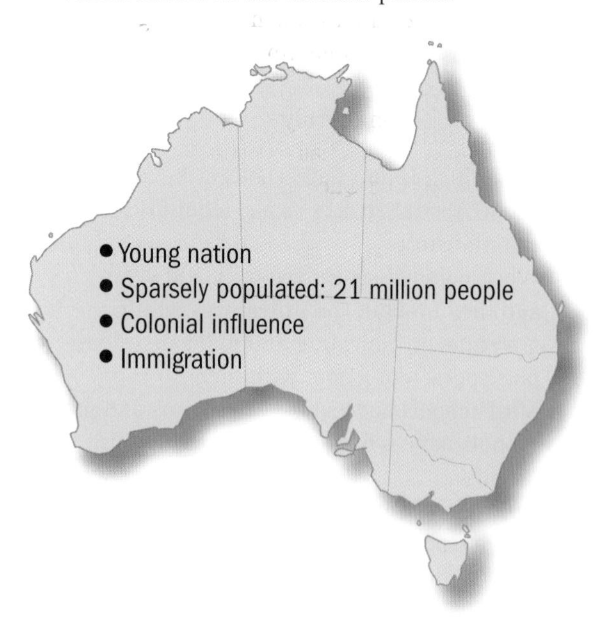

Fig 10.4 Some basic facts about Australia

The nature of sport in Australia

Sport is a national preoccupation in Australia. Up to 90 per cent of Australians participate in sport and sport accounts for 15 per cent of TV time. Sporting articles appear regularly on the front page of national newspapers and nearly everyone is either directly involved in or at least interested in sport.

Australian Rules football

Origins

The game of Australian Rules football strongly reflects Australian society and culture. It is also known as 'Aussie Rules' or 'footy' (pronounced 'fudy'). It is played on gigantic cricket 'ovals' with nine officials and 22 players per side, many of whom often run up to 15 miles during a game.

It was the idea of English-born Tom Wills as winter training for cricketers. Wills probably combined an Aboriginal leaping game with what he had seen as a schoolboy at Rugby in the mid-nineteenth century. Some argue that the game is just a mixture of Rugby and Gaelic football. Either way the rules of 'footy' were established before most other forms of modern football.

It is the fourth most played team sport in Australia after netball, soccer and cricket and there has been a 42 per cent increase in participation from 2001 to 2005. Aboriginal players make up 16 per cent of the AFL elite competitors though only 3 per cent of the population as a whole.

Fig 10.5 The Australian flag

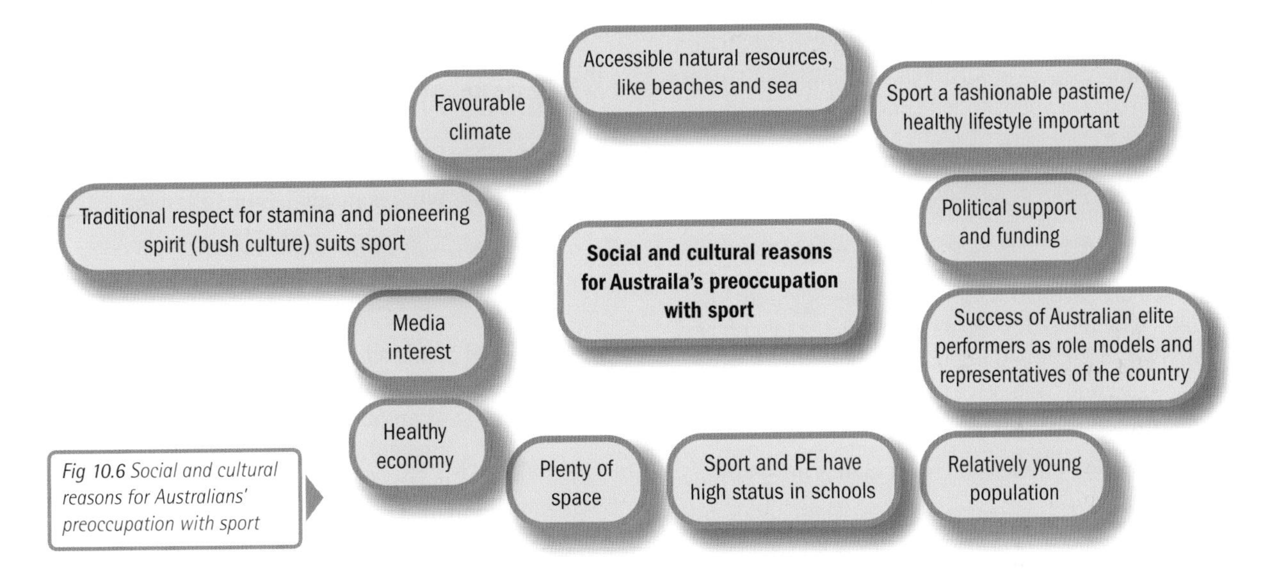

Fig 10.6 Social and cultural reasons for Australians' preoccupation with sport

Factors that have shaped the development of the game

- Australians living and travelling abroad have taken the game with them.
- Exhibition matches have increased interest.
- Players have converted from rugby union, league and soccer to the game.
- It is widely taught in Australian schools and there are extensive pathway programmes.
- The game appeals to all.
- It can be played by men and women.
- It can be played successfully by all body types from 6'10" (2.1 m) 'ruckmen' weighing 16 stone (102 kg) to 5'6" (1.7 m) 'rovers' weighing 9 stone (57 kg).
- The introduction of truly national competitions at elite level has spread the game into New South Wales and Queensland (traditional rugby states).

Commercialism and impact of the media

Australian Rules football is a multi-million (Australian) dollar business that has blossomed as a result of commercialism. Interest in the game is at an all-time high, making it the most highly attended spectator sport in Australia. The game is a great media product with regular commercial breaks.

Modern-day players are attracted by the financial rewards from advertising, sponsorship, endorsement and linked commercial ventures. Some also welcome the celebrity status. Since the development of national competitions the game has received greater exposure in both the electronic and print media.

Need to know more? For more information on the nature of sport in Australia see Chapter 10, pages 248–250 in your Student Book.

CHECK

If you are satisfied with your knowledge and understanding, tick off the sections that you have revised so far. If you are not satisfied, then revisit those sections and refer to the pages in the 'Need to know more?' features.

☐ Surviving ethnic sports and games in the UK.

☐ The role of nineteenth-century public schools in promoting and organising sports and games.

☐ The relatively recent move from the traditional amateur approach to a more professional approach in sport in the UK.

☐ Characteristics of the USA and Australia and the nature of sport in each of those countries.

☐ American football and Australian Rules football.

EXAM PRACTICE

Q.1

a) What is meant by the following terms:
– amateurism
– professionalism.

b) With reference to sport in the UK, give reasons for the relatively recent move from a traditional amateur approach to a more professional approach.

5 marks

Q.2 Discuss the game of American Football with reference to its origins and its link with commercialism.

10 marks

See page 183 for answers.

CHAPTER 11

Contemporary sporting issues

PART I

Impact on young people's aspirations and participation

LEARNING OBJECTIVES

Chapter 11 is divided into three parts. By the end of this part you should be able to demonstrate knowledge and understanding of:

- Public, private and voluntary funding (including the national lottery)
- UK Sport; and home country organisations such as Sport England
- Current government and national governing body initiatives that influence and promote participation in physical activity
- The sports development pyramid and the continuum from mass participation to sporting excellence
- Opportunity, provision and esteem – in the context of mass participation and sporting excellence.

This large chapter has been split into three parts. In Part I we will look at how physical activity is funded in the UK; then, in Part II, at some organisations that influence **mass participation** (taking part) and **sporting excellence** (getting to the top as an elite performer); and, finally, at the factors affecting mass participation and sporting excellence. This will include identifying the opportunity, provision and esteem of certain societal groups such as people with a disability.

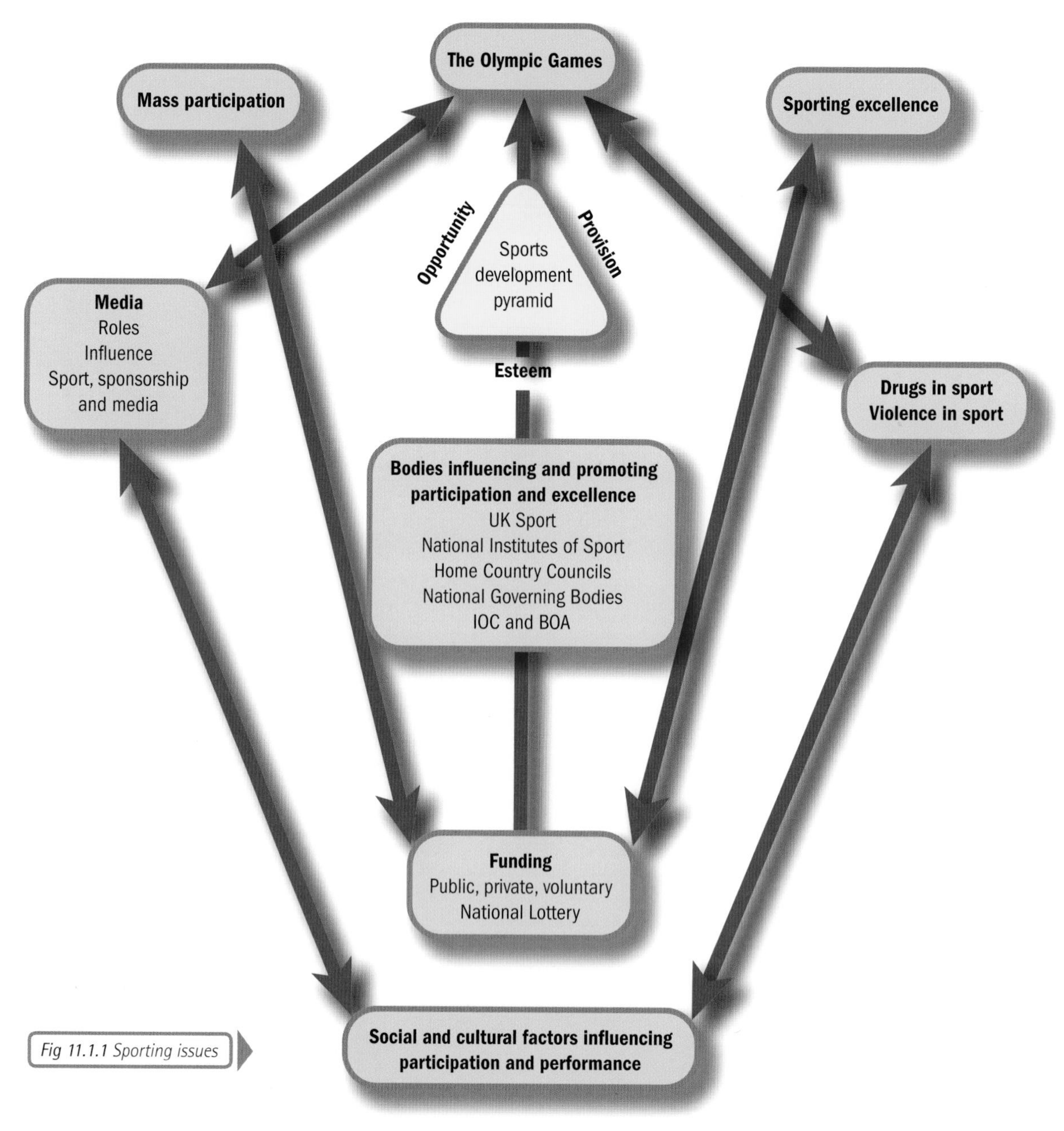

Fig 11.1.1 Sporting issues

FUNDING OF PHYSICAL ACTIVITY

You need to be aware of the following three types of funding:

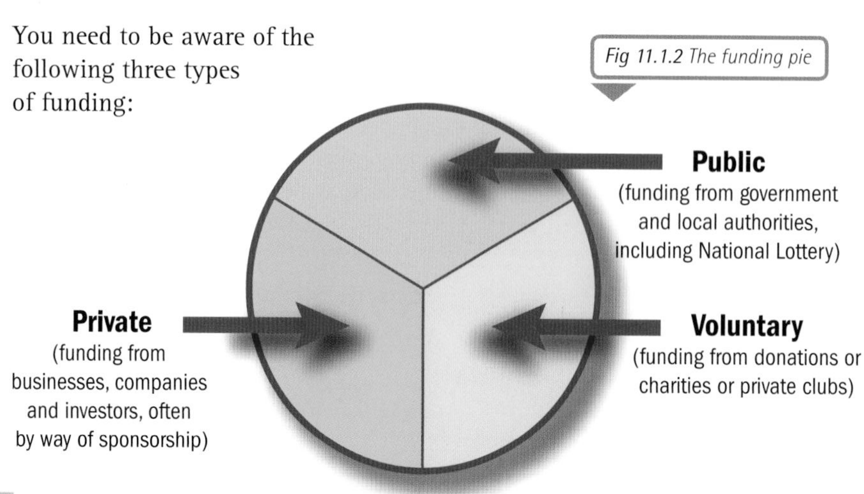

Fig 11.1.2 The funding pie

Note that: public funding includes the National Lottery and that, as the national lottery sports fund (among other things) funds the World Class Pathway Programme (see page 118), UK Sport, (page 119), and the home country organisations such as Sport England (see page 121), these are all important too.

Public sector			
Central government		**Local authorities**	
In	**Out**	**In**	**Out**
from: • taxes • gaming duties • National Lottery ticket sales	cost of: • local authorities • awards and grants e.g. to UK Sport • Sportsmatch sponsorship • Sport for Armed Forces	from: • Government • council taxes • grants from central government and lottery • business/ commercial sources • charges for facility use	cost of: • schools – staff and facilities • community sport facilities • grants to local clubs

Private sector	
In	**Out**
from: • business profit • ticket sales • sale of TV rights	cost of: • sponsoring of individuals and/or teams • running and maintaining private sports clubs and facilities • buying TV rights • Sport Aid grants • National Sports Foundation

Voluntary sector	
In	**Out**
from: • National Lottery grants and awards • Awards for All (lottery grant scheme) • Sportsmatch grants • local authority grants • National Governing Bodies • fundraising • Foundation for Sport and the Arts • National Sports Foundation • commercial sponsorship • members' subscriptions	cost of: • facility building, maintenance and development • developing performers (e.g. coaching fees) • running the club

Table 1 Funding that comes in and goes out of the public, private and voluntary sectors

The National Lottery

- Since 1994, The National Lottery has had a huge impact on British sport and is now the primary source of sports funding in the UK.
- Fewer people buy lottery tickets now than when the scheme was first established so the amount of lottery money generated through sales has declined.
- The Lottery Sports Fund provides grants of around £200 million annually.
- These grants go to and are distributed by UK Sport and the four home country sports councils (see pages 119 and 121) to support and encourage both:
  - mass participation, and
  - sporting excellence.
- It is widely accepted that Britain would never have achieved the number of medals at either the Athens (2004) or Sydney (2000) Olympic Games without the National Lottery.
- The World Class Pathway Programme and the World Class Events Programme are funded by the Lottery Sports Fund.

World Class Pathway Programme

The programme gives three different levels of support to elite Olympic performers as shown in Fig 11.1.3.

World Class Events Programme

This supports the bidding for and staging of major sporting events in the UK. Currently, UK **Sport** distributes approximately £3.3 million of lottery funding each year to the World Class Events Programme. The idea is to give sporting, social, cultural and economic benefits to the host nation via hosting major sporting events (e.g. London 2012).

The National Lottery and mass participation

Over £1 billion of grant aid has been awarded to thousands of sporting projects throughout the UK since the lottery was established. Home country councils (such as Sport England and the Sports Council for Wales) invest in a range of projects. Priorities are:

- increasing participation by young people
- improving sports provision in schools
- supporting deprived areas, ethnic minorities, people with disabilities and women via Sport Action Zones.

Fig 11.1.3 The World Class Pathway Programme

1. World Class podium funding
- For likely medalists at next Olympic Games.
- Sports receive this funding based on Olympic results, competitive record and record of producing elite athletes through pathway programmes.
- Distributed through NGBs.

2. World Class development
- For performers who are about six years away from a medal.

3. World Class talent
- Highly gifted performers with world class talent are selected by NGBs.
- For performers who are a maximum of eight years from a likely medal.

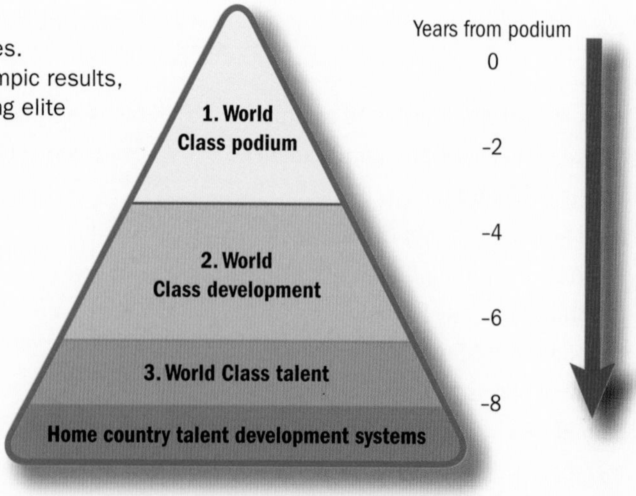

1. World Class podium
2. World Class development
3. World Class talent
Home country talent development systems

Years from podium
0
-2
-4
-6
-8

BODIES INFLUENCING AND PROMOTING PARTICIPATION IN PHYSICAL ACTIVITY AND THE ACHIEVEMENT OF SPORTING EXCELLENCE

Sport in the UK involves many different sporting organisations/bodies. They include those for grass roots recreational performers in the community up to elite performers who represent the UK on the world stage. Grass-roots clubs and local associations are self-governing or autonomous. Central government provides relatively little in terms of overall sporting policy.

Fig 11.1.4 shows the UK's complicated and inter-connected system. This pattern of organisation has evolved over many years. It is a decentralised system – meaning that power is spread out rather than centrally held.

In recent years and particularly since the awarding of the 2012 Olympic Games to Britain, there has been some organisational change and attempts at improvement. UK Sport is particularly keen to reduce organisational inefficiency in the system as a whole. NGBs are also working hard to improve their management and systems.

Note that while small private clubs continue to depend on volunteers, larger and more determined clubs and associations have an increasingly businesslike and professional approach.

KEY TERMS

Organisational bodies – Organisations or agencies that run sport.

Decentralised – When parts of a system are self governing or when power is not centrally held.

Grass roots clubs – Community clubs that exist for people at the base of the sports development pyramid.

UK Sport – The organisation that is responsible for developing elite sport in the UK. It provides strategic support.

You will only be asked direct questions on the following.

- UK Sport.
- Home country organisations (i.e. Sport England, Sports Council for Northern Ireland, sportscotland, Sports Council for Wales).
- Current government initiatives.
- Current National Governing Body (NGB) initiatives.

Let's look at each of these in turn.

Name	UK Sport
Overall aim	to develop elite sport in UK
What does UK Sport do?	• manages and distributes National Lottery funding through the World Class Programme • promotes ethical behaviour – has anti-doping programme (100% ME – see p133) • co-ordinates work to attract major sporting events • encourages administrative efficiency in the UK system as a whole • works with home country councils • manages the UK's international sporting relationships • helps elite performers' development of 'sporting lifestyle' • supports world class coaches • supports development of NGBs through Mission 2012 • manages the Talented Athlete Scholarship System (TASS), a government funded programme/ partnership between sport and higher and further education that aims to bridge the gap between non-funded grass roots sport and world-class sport

Table 2 UK Sport

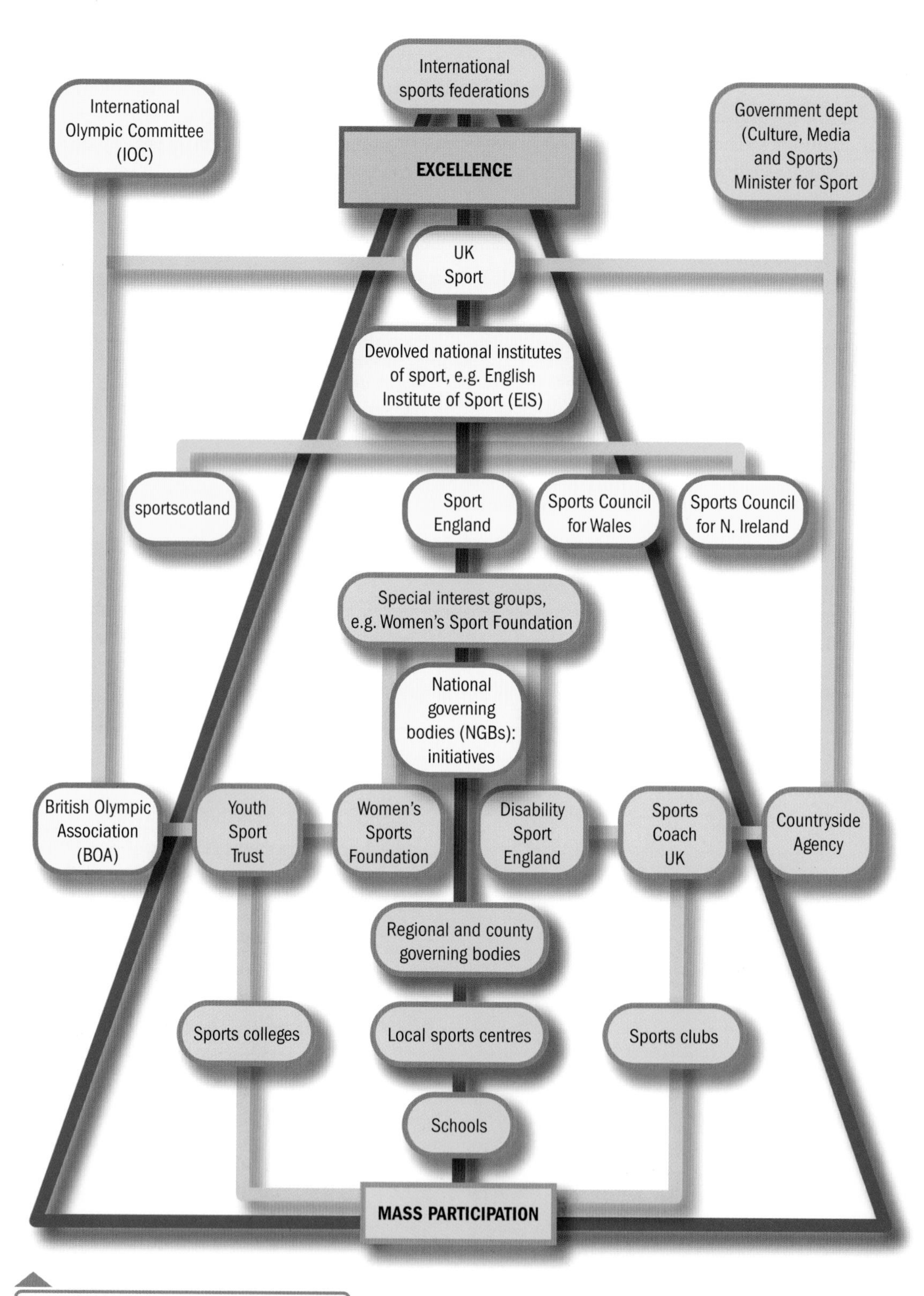

Fig 11.1.4 Bodies influencing and promoting participation and excellence in physical activity

Name	Devolved national institutes of sport – a network of centres in England, Scotland, Northern Ireland and Wales
Overall aim	to provide Britain's best performers with the practical support needed to compete and win at the highest level
What do they provide?	• sport science and sports medicine • medical consultation and medical screening • physiology • biomechanics • nutritional advice • podiatry (care of feet and ankles) • performance analysis and planning • psychology • physiotherapy • strength and conditioning • career, education and lifestyle advice • sports massage • sports vision • performance lifestyle advice

Table 3 Devolved national institutes of sport

Home country organisations

Name	Sport England
Overall aim	to get people more active and involved!
What does Sport England do?	• invests in, advises on and promotes community sport • promotes volunteering, coaching, leadership and officiating • focuses on priority groups such as people with disabilities • supported the government's initial target for school sport '*that by 2008 at least 85% of school children aged 5–16 spend at least two hours each week on high-quality PE and school sport*' and the government's updated aim (July 2007) for '*the equivalent of an hour of "sport" every school day*' • works closely with local, regional and national partners and brings together NGBs, regional sporting bodies, coaches, clubs and volunteers – all in order to increase participation • creates and funds initiatives such as **Sporting Champions** – which organises visits by world-class athletes to schools and communities to raise awareness and to motivate • develops school/club links • works with partners to ensure that the London 2012 Olympic and Paralympic Games leave a lasting sporting legacy • is responsible for funding elite performers in sports such as squash and netball that are non-Olympic

Table 4 Sport England

Name	Sports Council for Northern Ireland
Overall aims	• to increase participation especially among young people • to improve performance in sport • to improve the management of sport and the image of Northern Ireland using sport
What else?	Sport Northern Ireland has a community sport programme to: • increase participation in disadvantaged areas and by people with disabilities • improve knowledge and skills enabling more people to make a contribution in their local communities and to stay involved in sport long term

Table 5 Sports Council for Northern Ireland

Name	sportscotland
Overall aims	to increase participation and improve performances in Scottish sport
What else?	• to develop sporting people, organisations and facilities • to create pathways of opportunity for people to take part in sport at any level and at any stage in life • to tackle discrimination and promote equality of opportunity ensuring safe and fair participation and performance

Table 6 sportscotland

Name	Sports Council for Wales
Overall aims	to get more people more active more often
What else?	• particularly active young people • active communities (they encourage adults to be active for 30 minutes a day, and children for 60 minutes a day) • high-level performance and excellence which focuses on the talented performer and surrounds them with support

Table 7 Sports Council for Wales

In short, each of the home country councils want people to **start getting active** and **stay being active**.

EXAM TIP

Key sporting bodies and organisations such as **UK Sport** are not told what to do by the Government. UK Sport is, however, answerable to the Government because of the government funding it receives.

Need to know more? For more information on bodies promoting participation and excellence see Chapter 11, Part I, pages 262–269 in your Student Book.

GOVERNMENT INITIATIVES

We need to look at government initiatives (schemes, proposals, plans or ideas) that impact upon participation and sporting achievement by young

EXAM TIP

It can be difficult to stay up to date with some aspects of your socio-cultural studies, e.g. initiatives that were current when this book was published may have been replaced by the time you read it! Don't worry; examiners will be reasonable regarding what is current. Keep your eye on relevant websites to check what is happening and changing, e.g. at www.teachernet.gov

people in state schools. Government departments involved in sport include the Department for Culture, Media and Sport (DCMS) and the Department for Children, Schools and Families (DCSF).

The National Curriculum

This has been compulsory in schools since 1988 and has four key stages as follows:

- KS 1 (5–7 yrs)
- KS 2 (7–11 yrs)
- KS 3 (11–14 yrs)
- KS 4 (14–16 yrs).

Though the specific requirements of each key stage are different the themes throughout are as follows.

1. Competence (body and mind skilfulness).
2. Performance (applying competence).
3. Creativity (problem-solving techniques and tactics).
4. Healthy active lifestyles (physical activity for health).

The PE, School Sport and Club Links Strategy (PESSCLS)

- The PESSCL strategy has different strands – as shown in Fig 11.1.5.
- It aims to increase participation by 5–16-year-olds.
- It aims for the equivalent of an hour of sport every school day for every school child (including two hours within the curriculum and three hours extra curricular/community participation).

It also wants:

- more **coaches** in schools and coaches and volunteers in the community
- more **competition** – within (intra-) and between (inter-) schools
- more sports days and inter-school tournaments.

Some aspects of the PESSCL strategy

Specialist sports colleges

Specialist sports colleges aim to:

- raise standards in PE and sport
- be regional focal points for promoting excellence in PE and community sport
- develop links between families of schools, sports bodies and communities
- share resources and good practice
- provide a structure through which young people can progress, perhaps to careers in sport and PE.

School sport partnerships (SSPs)

These clusters or 'families' of schools work together to develop PE and sport for young

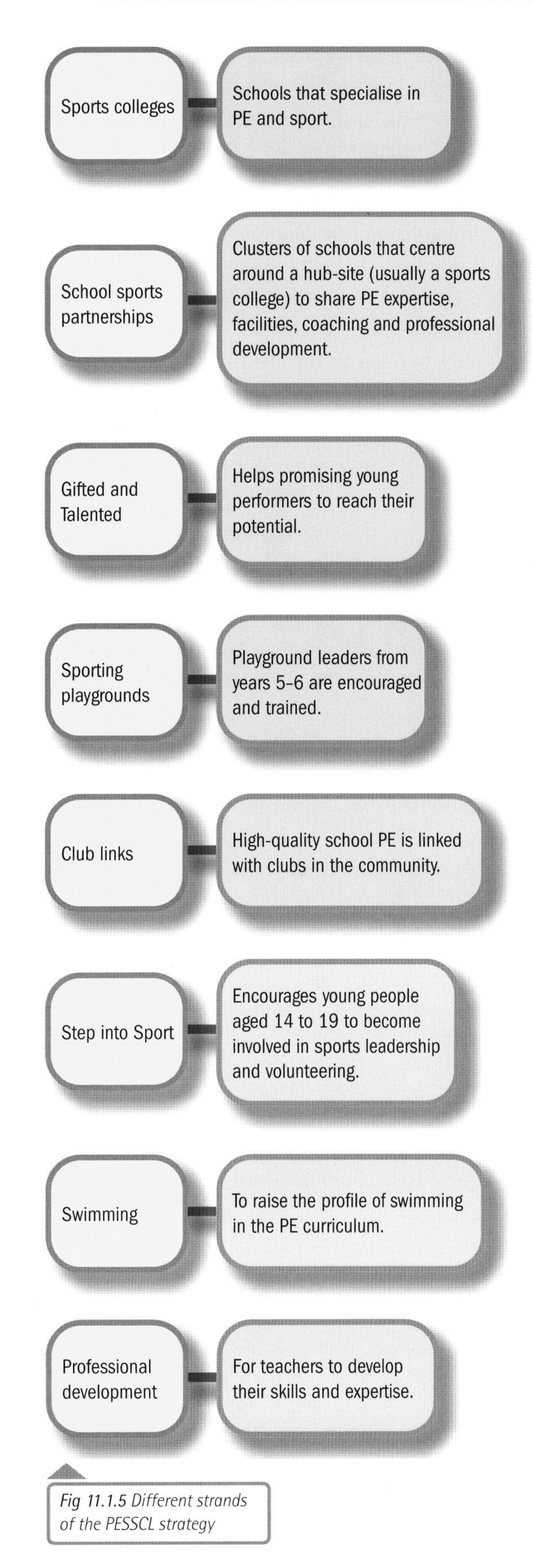

Fig 11.1.5 Different strands of the PESSCL strategy

people within their cluster. A typical school sport partnership (SSP) model may consist of:

- a full-time partnership development manager (PDM) – based in sports colleges
- up to eight school sport co-coordinators (SSCos) who do this work for up to two days per week
- primary (and special school) link teachers (PLTs) who are based in their primary or special school and get support from the SSCo and PLT.

Gifted and Talented

- Aims to improve the identification of and support and provision for gifted and talented pupils in schools.
- Provides professional development for teachers.
- Facilitates teachers to identify talent in their own schools.
- Provides a network of Multi-skill Academies to develop core skills.
- Supports talented athletes via the Junior Athlete Education (JAE) programme, which gives lifestyle management and performance planning to young people and their teachers.

Kite marking

Special kite marks are awarded to maintained schools within a partnership and reward delivery of the national PESSCL strategy. The kite marks are:

- Activemark (primary and special schools)
- Sportsmark (secondary and special schools)
- Sports Partnership Mark.

Other relevant Government initiatives

- *'Sport: Raising the Game'* – 1995
- *'A Sporting Future for All'* – 2001
- *'Game Plan'* – 2002; the action plan based on *'A Sporting future for All'*.
- The National Sports Foundation – a government-led initiative to encourage partnerships between private investors and community sports projects in England.

EXAM TIP

You can only be asked questions on material that is clearly in the specification. So, you will **not** get a specific question on the PESSCL strategy (now renamed PESSYP). 'Current government initiatives' are in the specification and this is just one example. When in doubt, and with the help of your teacher/s, check the specification!

NATIONAL GOVERNING BODIES (NGBs)

Each sport is controlled by its National Governing Body (NGB), for example BADMINTON England.

You need to know and understand current NGB initiatives that impact upon mass participation and sporting excellence, for example whole sport plans.

Whole sport plans (WSPs)

These are produced by English NGBs. One stop plans (OSPs) are produced for sports development in Wales, Scotland and Northern Ireland. Plans must include strategies:

- from grass roots to elite level
- to increase participation, clubs, coaching and volunteering
- to increase international success
- for the effective running of their organisation.

In other words NGBs must map out their vision and get people to start, stay and succeed in their sport.

NGBs receive funding from their home country councils as a result of their WSPs. The councils are then able to check NGB 'results' against clearly identified plans and predictions and either continue with or cut funding. The aim is for individual sports and sport in general to benefit and be ready for the Olympics in 2012 and to fit the needs of 21st century sport.

It might include the appointment of performance directors and the building of new national centres. NGBs for professional, media-friendly sports such as The Football Association (FA) and the Rugby Football Union (RFU) have a comparatively high level of independence due to their capacity to attract media funding for TV rights.

EXAM TIP

There will be five parts to your AS Socio-cultural Studies question. The final part will have ten marks and may ask you to 'evaluate critically' an issue or item. For the highest marks you will need to show evidence of your ability to think and make judgements. Add relevant material/data from your extra research and reading especially in the final-part question worth ten marks.

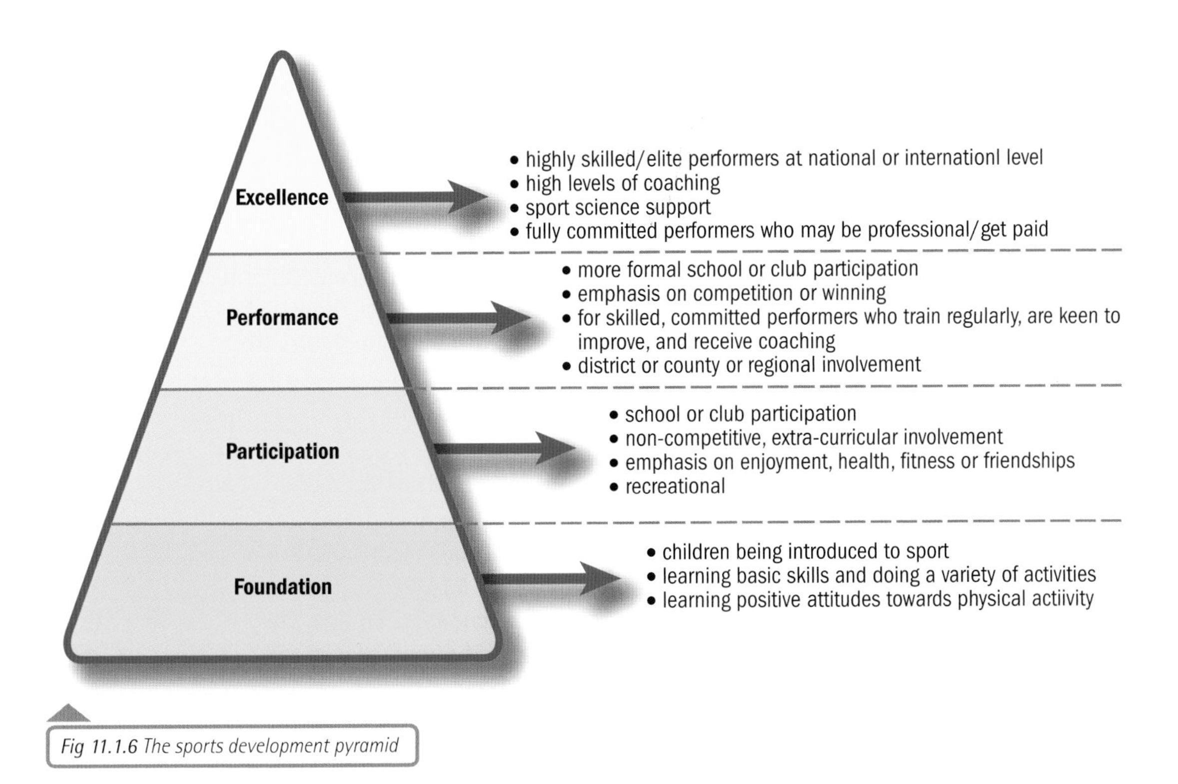

Fig 11.1.6 *The sports development pyramid*

EXCELLENCE AND PARTICIPATION IN THE UK

You need to understand and be able to explain sports development in terms of the sports development pyramid and the continuum from mass participation to sporting excellence.

EXAM TIP

You could be asked to name and explain each layer of the sports development pyramid in the examination. Ensure that you are clear about the two layers beginning with the letter 'P.' Candidates often get those two muddled up!

Need to know more? For more information on excellence and participation in the UK see Chapter 11, Part I, pages 279–280 in your Student Book.

The continuum from mass participation to sporting excellence

At one end of the continuum is mass participation – an inclusive concept where taking part is more important than winning. Here physical activity is pursued, among other reasons, for health or fitness or enjoyment. At the other end of the continuum is sporting excellence.

Mass participation is associated with lifelong physical activity and lifetime sport that can result in lifelong participation. A benefit of mass participation is that it (theoretically at least) enlarges the pool from which talent can be trawled and supported to the top; it supports the idea that everyone should have the chance to take part in sport, as regularly as they wish and at whatever level they choose, irrespective of where they live, the school they attend, their ability, age, wealth, gender, race or religion.

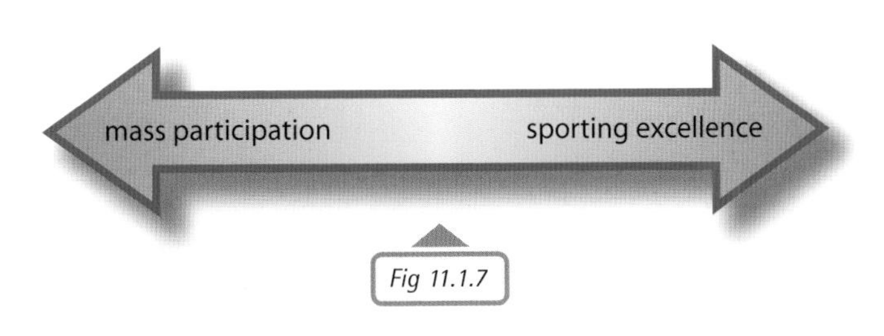

Fig 11.1.7

Sporting excellence involves elite or professional, highly skilled and highly committed performers taking part at national or international level to win. Here, sporting excellence is a selective or exclusive idea and very few make it to this level.

OPPORTUNITY, PROVISION AND ESTEEM

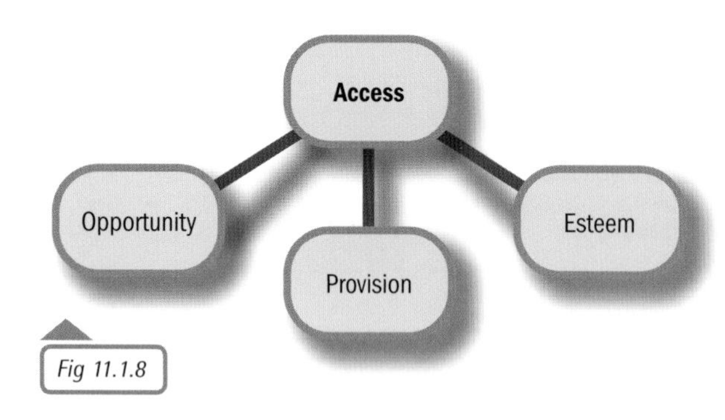

Fig 11.1.8

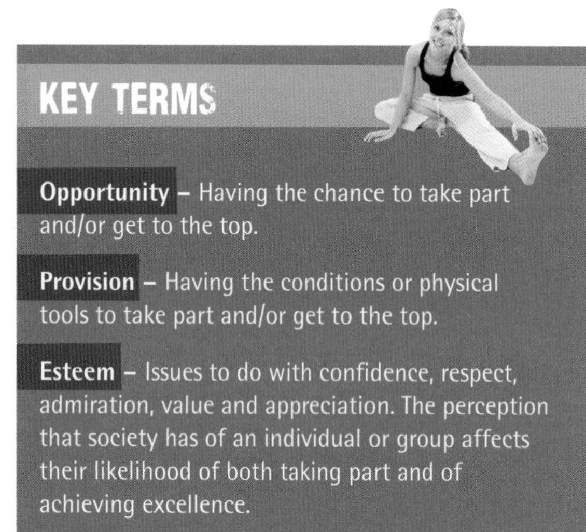

KEY TERMS

Opportunity – Having the chance to take part and/or get to the top.

Provision – Having the conditions or physical tools to take part and/or get to the top.

Esteem – Issues to do with confidence, respect, admiration, value and appreciation. The perception that society has of an individual or group affects their likelihood of both taking part and of achieving excellence.

Social and cultural factors

- Social and cultural factors (things to do with society and culture) impact upon both mass participation and sporting excellence.
- By society we mean the people in the communities we live in.
- By culture we mean the traditions, customs and way of life within those communities.

Society

- Society is stratified, which means that it has imaginary layers into which groups fit.
- This unfair layering or 'stacking' of society is most evident in places with high immigration.
- The dominant group in society (in the UK this is the white, middle-class male group) is at the top of the stack.
- The dominant group has the greatest freedom and opportunity while other groups, such as Asian women, often have less opportunity.
- Not everyone within a group has the same needs and wants.
- Combinations of factors can lead to double deprivation, more under-representation and more under-achievement. For instance, the constraints or restrictions for a black female with a disability are multiplied.

Discrimination

Discrimination is unfair treatment. It occurs when a group is constrained or held back by factors that are not applied to the dominant group. In a stratified or layered society where stacking occurs, minority groups often experience discrimination. This discrimination is then likely to exist in physical activity and sport.

Minority groups

You need to know, understand and be able to assess the impact of (critically evaluate) various factors that affect the following.

- Young people.
- The elderly.
- People with a disability.
- Women.
- Ethnic minority groups.

These societal groups are most likely to experience discrimination and social exclusion in the UK. They are also most likely to be targeted by organisations such as Sport England who are keen to increase their participation and achievement of sporting excellence.

See Fig 11.1.9, which shows the factors that are likely to affect participation.

EXAM TIP

When you are thinking of measures to increase participation and excellence (i.e. thinking of solutions to a problem), start by thinking of the problem and then solve it! For example, think of the problem that there are not enough specialist coaches for people with a disability. Then solve the problem by saying 'train more specialist coaches'. Easy!

Factors relating to opportunity, provision and esteem that can influence mass participation and sporting excellence	
Mass participation	**Sporting excellence**
OPPORTUNITY – having the chance to take part and/or get to the top	
disposable income	funding and financial support, e.g. National Lottery or sponsorship money
ability, skill, health or fitness or playing standard	skill level and performance lifestyle
the amount of time available after work and other commitments	chance to train full time
Do you actually want to take part? Are suitable and appealing activities available?	whether individuals choose to make the sacrifices and give the all-round commitment needed to get to the top
PROVISION – having the conditions or physical tools to take part and/or get to the top	
the presence or absence of suitable equipment and/or facilities	the availability of world class facilities and equipment
access – for example for wheelchairs if necessary	the availability of sport science and other 'high-tech' support (see Student Book, Chapter II, pages 265–267 and 299–300); modern technological products
availability of suitable transport – privately owned or public transport	distance from or access to high performance or National Institute centres, e.g. the National Tennis Centre in Roehampton, SW London; warm weather training in Cyprus or high altitude training venues for athletes
suitable and available clubs, activities, leagues, competitions or courses nearby	suitable and regular competitions with and against other high-level performers
the right coaching at the right level by suitably qualified staff	the right highly qualified and experienced coaches
well-maintained and equipped, private and clean changing and social areas	performance lifestyle advice and a holistic approach to excellence
ESTEEM – issues to do with respect, admiration, value and appreciation; the perception that society has of an individual or group affects the chances of their both taking part and of achieving excellence	
self-confidence and self-belief – which influences self-perception	self-confidence and self-belief, which impact on performance
respect from others and social acceptance of everyone's 'right' to take part in any chosen activity	respect from others – including team mates, opponents and the media
positive or negative perceptions of certain physical activities	recent results (good and/or bad) and national and international ranking
status in society, i.e. if from a disadvantaged group	status in the sporting world

Table 8 Influences on mass participation and sporting excellence

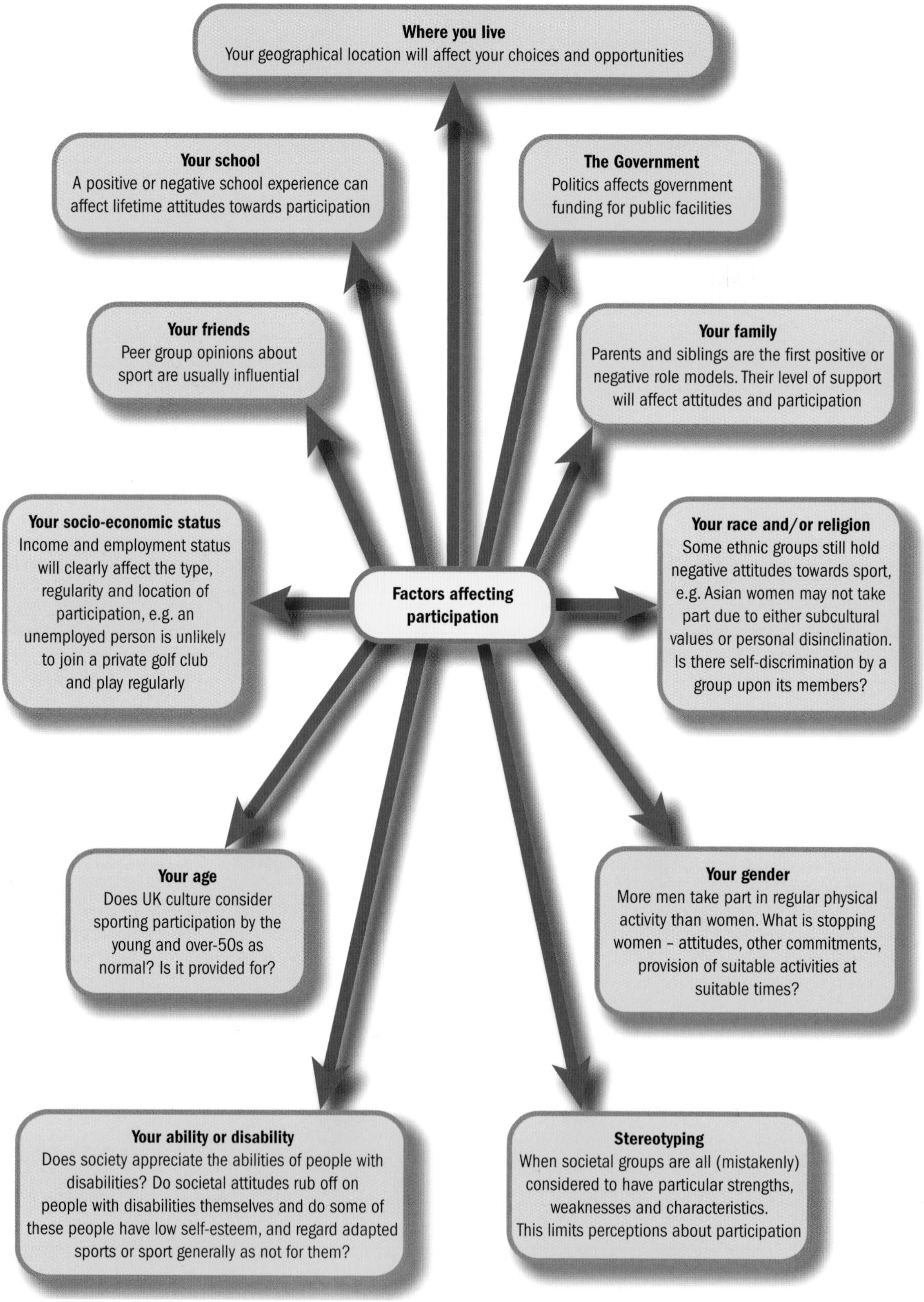

Factors affecting participation

Where you live
Your geographical location will affect your choices and opportunities

Your school
A positive or negative school experience can affect lifetime attitudes towards participation

The Government
Politics affects government funding for public facilities

Your friends
Peer group opinions about sport are usually influential

Your family
Parents and siblings are the first positive or negative role models. Their level of support will affect attitudes and participation

Your socio-economic status
Income and employment status will clearly affect the type, regularity and location of participation, e.g. an unemployed person is unlikely to join a private golf club and play regularly

Your race and/or religion
Some ethnic groups still hold negative attitudes towards sport, e.g. Asian women may not take part due to either subcultural values or personal disinclination. Is there self-discrimination by a group upon its members?

Your age
Does UK culture consider sporting participation by the young and over-50s as normal? Is it provided for?

Your gender
More men take part in regular physical activity than women. What is stopping women – attitudes, other commitments, provision of suitable activities at suitable times?

Your ability or disability
Does society appreciate the abilities of people with disabilities? Do societal attitudes rub off on people with disabilities themselves and do some of these people have low self-esteem, and regard adapted sports or sport generally as not for them?

Stereotyping
When societal groups are all (mistakenly) considered to have particular strengths, weaknesses and characteristics. This limits perceptions about participation

Fig 11.1.9 Factors impacting on physical activity and participation in sport

Factors to consider	Possible measures to increase participation and excellence
Young people	
• there is a post-school gap of non-participation into which many school leavers fall • school-age children need to have a positive experience of PE to ensure they continue with physical activity after they leave school • young people need a varied and interesting programme at all levels of the performance pyramid	Government initiatives including: • the National Curriculum • the different PESSCL strands (see page 123) The work of organisation such as: • UK Sport (for excellence) • Home country councils (for mass participation) • NGBs
The elderly	
• factors such as poor self-image; lack of transport or disposable income; physical challenges; negative previous experience of physical activity; relatively few role models etc. can all limit participation • see diagram, Fig 11.1.10 for fuller explanation of limiting factors	• increased opportunity, e.g. reduced entrance fees, more choice of activities • increased provision, e.g. more exclusive clubs and more specialist leaders for the elderly, and improved local transport • increased esteem, e.g. respect and encouragement from others; highlighting efforts and achievment of others
People with a disability	
• six million people in Britain have a sensory, physical or mental impairment • society continues to discriminate against and impose barriers on people with disabilities; three-quarters of disabled adults rely on state benefits as their main source of income so they are financially disadvantaged, which adds to the problem/their constraints • it is increasingly recognised that attitudes, assumptions, myths and stereotyping, along with inadequately designed environments all limit people with disabilities in terms of physical activity • since 1988 many disabled young people have been integrated into mainstream schools, which can have both negative and positive consequences	• promote positive images of disabled performers at both recreational and elite level • smash myths and ignorance by educating via school, media etc. • increase awareness of sports facilities and organisations which cater for people with disabilities • provide high-quality facilities locally and world class facilities for the elite • provide specialist training for specialist coaches aimed at increasing the number of coaches with disabilities • increase liaison between organisations involved with disability sport • ensure equality and ease of access, e.g. ramps, lifts etc. • continue to subsidise fees at sports clubs and centres • increase funding for potential elite performers through the World Class Performance Pathway
Women	
• opportunity (e.g. funding in families, communities and schools as well as prize money and sponsorship) • provision (quality and quantity of facilities, coaching, media coverage for example) • esteem (the need to keep changing social attitudes, smash myths and end stereotyping)	• increased opportunity, e.g. reduced entrance fees, more choice of activities at suitable times • increased provision, e.g. improved crèche facilities • increased esteem, e.g. respect and encouragement from others

continued ▶

Factors to consider	Possible measures to increase participation and excellence
Ethnic minority groups	
• Britain is a multicultural and multi-racial society • racial discrimination/racism stems from prejudice (intolerance and narrow mindedness) linked with the power of one racial group over another • discrimination still exists on the grounds of colour, language and cultural differences • performers from ethnic minorities are highly visible on the track, football pitch and cricket field so many (inaccurately) believe that there is not a problem	• raise awareness of racial inequality in sport; for example, back in 1993 the Professional Football Association (PFA) started a campaign (with the Commission for Racial Equality) to 'Kick Racism out of Football'; It is now called 'Kick it Out' (see www.kickitout.org) • promote positive role models • increase the number of black and ethnic minority decision makers and organisers in sport • challenge stereotypical thinking, perhaps through race-awareness training • provide for different cultural groups to pursue their own cultural activities, for example Kabaddi

Table 9 Possible measures to increase participation and excellence

EXAM TIP

If you really know and understand the impact of your three key terms – opportunity, provision and esteem – you will be able to have a good go at most exam questions relating to the elderly, people with a disability, women and ethnic minority groups.

KEY TERMS

Attitudes – Outlooks, feelings or thoughts about something.

Myths – Untruths, such as the view that males cannot do cartwheels or women cannot park cars.

Stereotyping – Typecasting, labelling or pigeon-holing people.

Social exclusion – The negative result of factors such as low income, discrimination, poor housing, etc. that put communities at a disadvantage.

Positive discrimination – Favoritism or special treatment for the focus group in order to give them a chance.

Socialisation – The process by which people learn acceptable cultural beliefs and behaviour including how to interact with people who are different from themselves.

Need to know more? For more information on opportunity, provision and esteem see Chapter 11, Part I, pages 280–293 in your Student Book.

Danny Crates – what challenges do elite paralympic performers face in terms of opportunity, provision and esteem?

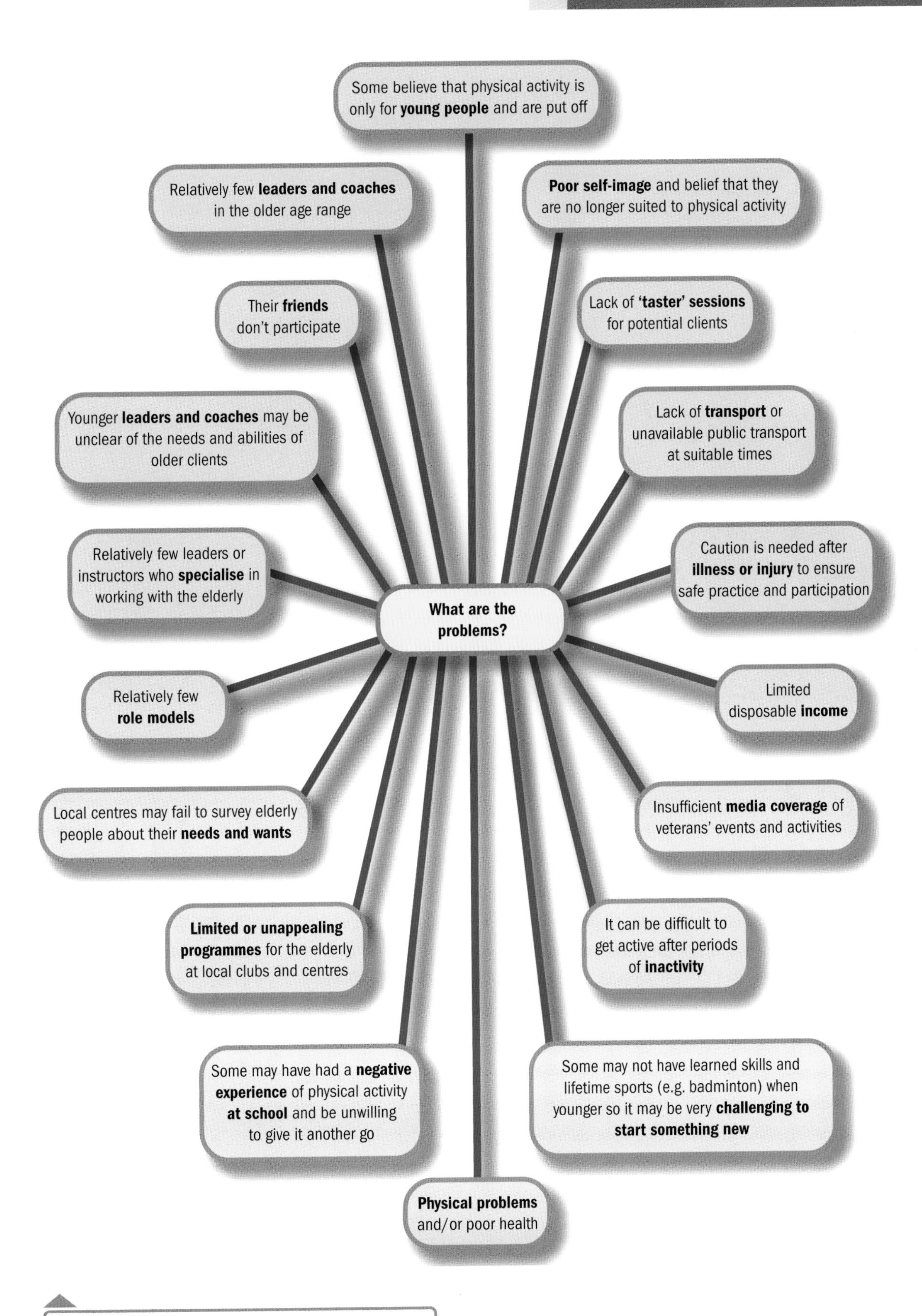

Fig 11.1.10 Socio-cultural factors impacting upon participation and the pursuit of excellence by elderly people

English netball has had a funding boost since its coverage on Sky TV

CHECK

If you are satisfied with your knowledge and understanding, tick off the sections that you have revised so far. If you are not satisfied, then revisit those sections and refer to the pages in the 'Need to know more?' features.

- ☐ Public, private and voluntary funding (including the National Lottery).
- ☐ UK Sport; the UKSI and home country organisations such as Sport England.
- ☐ Current Government and National Governing Body initiatives that influence and promote participation in physical activity.
- ☐ The sports development pyramid and the continuum from mass participation to sporting excellence.
- ☐ Opportunity, provision and esteem – in the context of mass participation and sporting excellence.

EXAM PRACTICE

Q.1 Outline the aims and activities of the following two bodies that are involved in sport in the UK:

a) UK Sport

b) Home Country Councils such as Sport England

5 marks

See page 184 for answers.

CHAPTER 11: PART II

Drugs, the media, sponsorship and violence in sport

LEARNING OBJECTIVES

By the end of this part you should be able to demonstrate knowledge and understanding of:

- The reasons for and the consequences of the use of drugs in sport
- Possible solutions to the use of drugs in sport
- The impact on performance in sport of modern technological products
- The roles and the impact of the media on sport
- The relationship between sport, sponsorship and the media
- Possible causes and solutions to violence in sport.

PERFORMANCE-ENHANCING PRODUCTS

Drugs in sport

The oath sworn on behalf of all Olympic athletes includes:

> *'In the name of all competitors, I promise that we shall take part in these Olympic Games ... without doping and without drugs in the true spirit of sportsmanship.'*

Yet the attraction and trappings of success are huge and the penalties for cheating comparatively small so the issue of drugs and sport continues to be an important contemporary sporting issue.

EXAM TIP

If a question asks for solutions to the problem of drugs in sport, make sure you don't list all the different types of drugs and explain what they are used for – this is not needed and will not gain you marks.

Remember, answer the question set!

Depending on the exact question, you may be able to make relevant mention of the following.

- 100% ME – the programme that promotes drug-free competitive sport throughout the UK by providing high-quality information on anti-doping and by promoting positive attitudes and values in sport.
- The World Anti-Doping Agency (WADA) – the organisation that promotes, co-ordinates and monitors the fight against doping in sports at international level.
- Examples of performers who have been found guilty of a doping offence.

The impact on performance of modern technological products

Modern sport bears little resemblance to the simple, natural activities of the past. Modern technological products have revolutionised sport and include up-to-date materials, machines and even medical techniques that influence and impact upon sports performance.

The key impacts are:

- increased safety
- increased comfort
- improved performance.

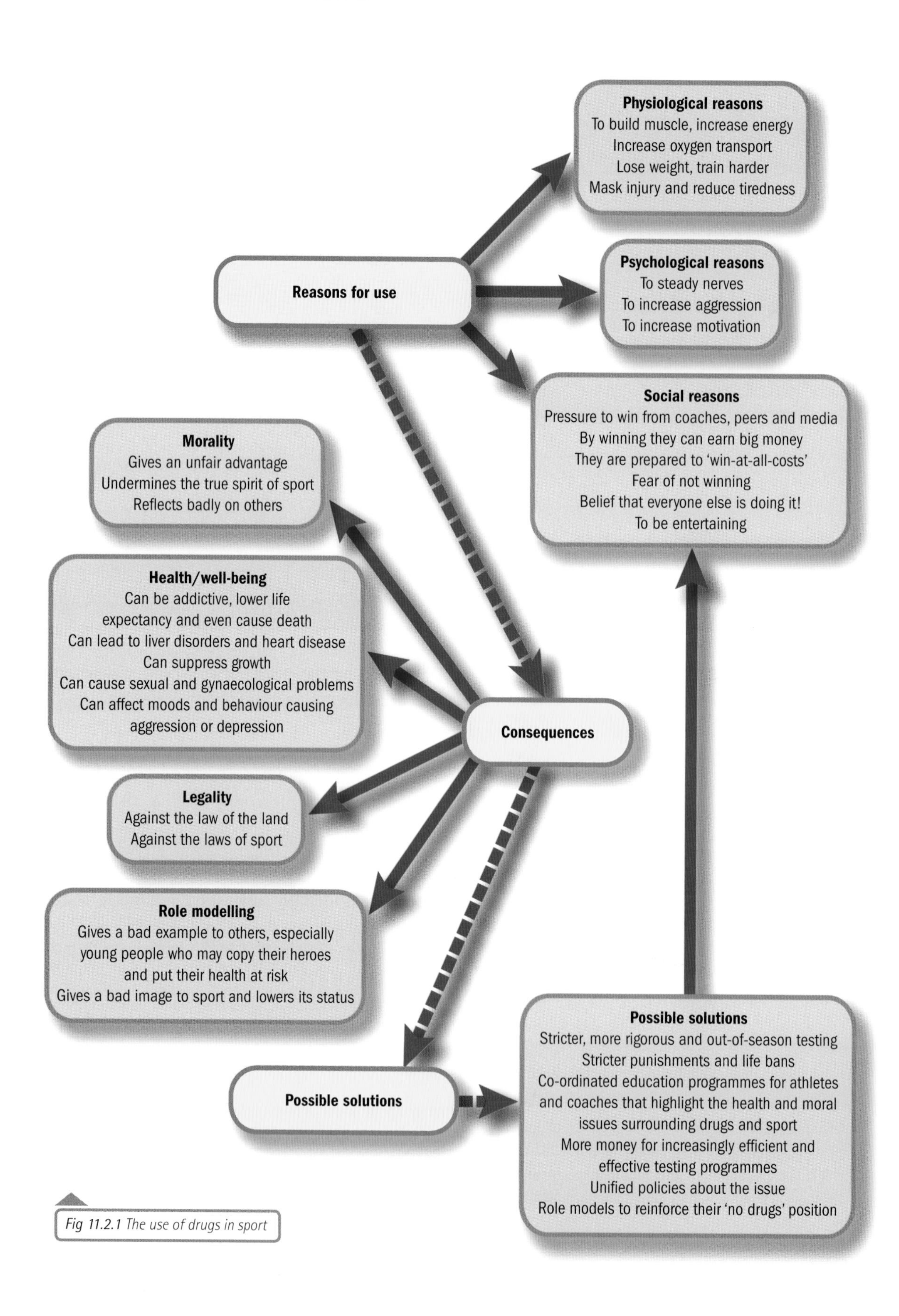

Fig 11.2.1 The use of drugs in sport

Examples of modern technological products		
Safety: • gum shields • rugby scrum caps • cricket head gear • padded equipment for hockey goal keepers and rugby players	Technology: • high-tech super bikes • bobsleigh and F1 car manufacture • gym equipment, e.g. treadmills and rowing machines • ball feeding machines for tennis and cricket • items that become part of popular culture, e.g. skateboards • arenas with retractable roofs	Materials: • carbon fibre and titanium for various items of equipment, e.g. poles for pole vault, golf clubs, racquets • large-headed clubs and racquets • astroturf, rubberised, bouncy tracks that give fast times and sprung floors in indoor venues • soft landing areas
Officiating: • electronic timing equipment that measures fractions of seconds • sports 'watches' for performers • 'Hawk-eye' – the officiating tool/ball tracking device system used in cricket and tennis	Shoes: • boots with bladed studs • track shoes that dampen muscle vibration and are said to boost performance	Clothing: • lycra body suits and hooded swift suits for track athletes • hydrodynamic swimming caps • full body suits for swimming • socks with an anti-microbial finish to help prevent the fungus that causes athlete's foot
Motion analysis: • motion analysis, e.g. of golf swing or discus throw which can be computer analysed	Comfort: • new fabrics that draw sweat away from the body, insulate, cool or breathe as needed	Science/medicine: • improved physiotherapy and sports medicine techniques including ultrasound, ice baths etc. • nasal strips, e.g. for athletes • improved/advanced surgery including artificial ligaments and joint replacements • lycra for compression bandages

Table 1 Modern technological products

EXAM TIP

Be aware that modern technological products are up-to-date technical, scientific or high-tech pieces of equipment that impact on sport. The impact is usually considered to be good – but in some cases might increase the chance of injury. What about football boot design?

SPORT, SPONSORSHIP AND THE MEDIA

The roles of the media

The media has four key roles.

1. **To inform** – e.g. informing about a match result, team analysis or player preparation or behaviour.
2. **To educate** – e.g. on global sporting issues, sport, skills, coaching techniques, sporting issues or local sporting provision.
3. **To entertain** – e.g. with live coverage of an event or information about stars' private lives, or a documentary on a particular team's pre-competition preparation.
4. **To advertise** – either directly or indirectly through sponsorship.

THE ROLES AND IMPACT OF THE MEDIA ON SPORT

Points to consider.

- Is sport now simply a branch of the advertising industry?
- Can sport retain its traditional nature and values and benefit from the money offered by the media?
- Has money corrupted sport or saved it from economic disaster?
- Has the need to win for money led to corruption and cheating?

EXAM TIP

If you are asked to 'critically evaluate' the impact of the media on sport – it simply means that you should weigh up (in good written form) the advantages and disadvantages of the media in sport.

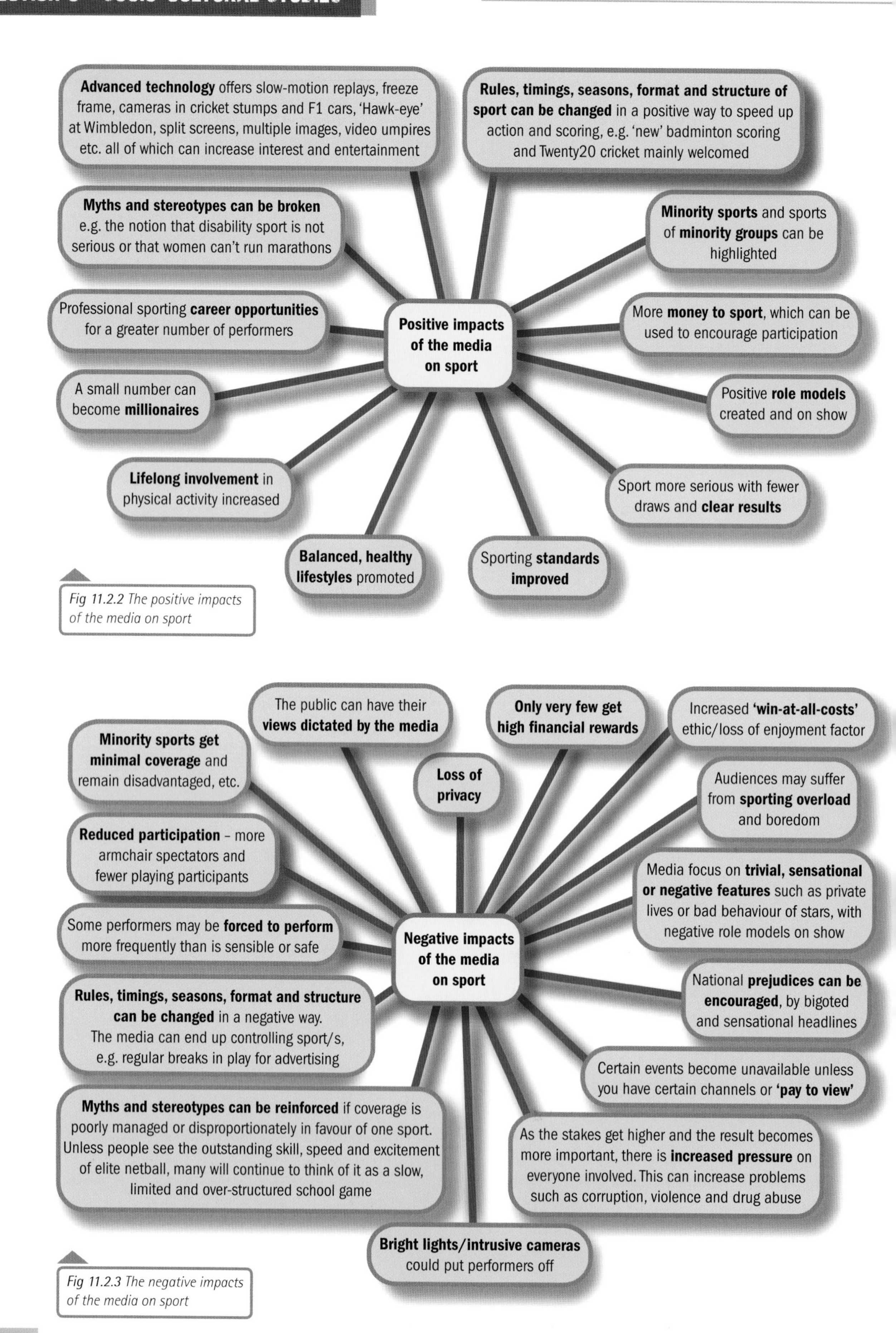

Fig 11.2.2 The positive impacts of the media on sport

Fig 11.2.3 The negative impacts of the media on sport

THE RELATIONSHIP BETWEEN SPORT, SPONSORSHIP AND THE MEDIA

The complex links between sport, sponsorship and the media are often referred to as the 'golden triangle'. Each needs the other for success. The relationship, which has strengthened in recent years, has both advantages and disadvantages.

Big sporting events in the UK are now full-blown entertainment driven by commercialism, reflecting what has been happening in the USA for many years. Winning becomes more and more significant – coming second can mean losing millions.

EXAM TIP

You need to be able to explain and discuss the relationship between sport, sponsorship and the media.

Need to know more? For more information on sport, sponsorship and the media see Chapter 11, Part II, pages 303–305 in your Student Book.

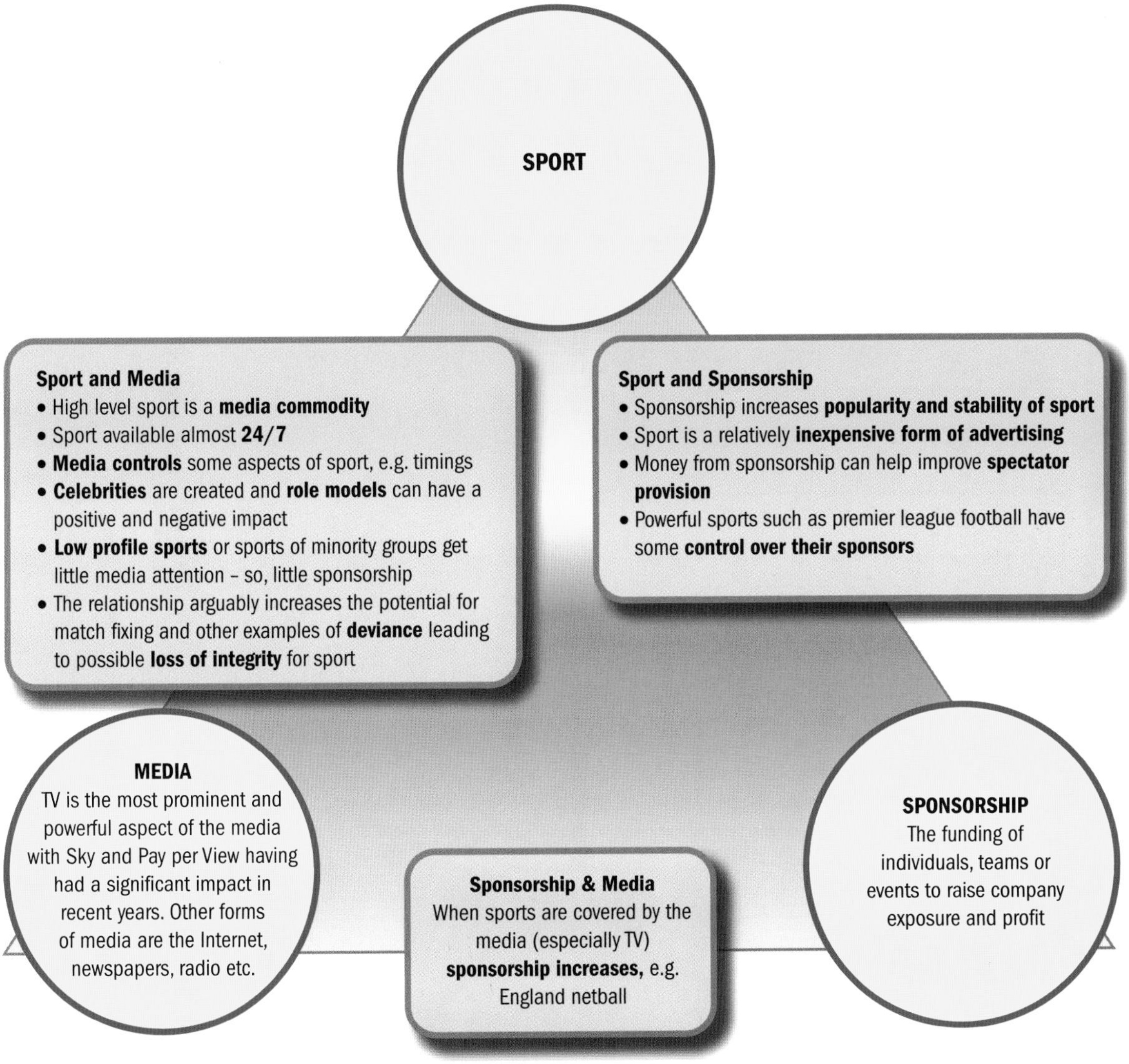

SPORT

Sport and Media
- High level sport is a **media commodity**
- Sport available almost **24/7**
- **Media controls** some aspects of sport, e.g. timings
- **Celebrities** are created and **role models** can have a positive and negative impact
- **Low profile sports** or sports of minority groups get little media attention – so, little sponsorship
- The relationship arguably increases the potential for match fixing and other examples of **deviance** leading to possible **loss of integrity** for sport

Sport and Sponsorship
- Sponsorship increases **popularity and stability of sport**
- Sport is a relatively **inexpensive form of advertising**
- Money from sponsorship can help improve **spectator provision**
- Powerful sports such as premier league football have some **control over their sponsors**

MEDIA
TV is the most prominent and powerful aspect of the media with Sky and Pay per View having had a significant impact in recent years. Other forms of media are the Internet, newspapers, radio etc.

Sponsorship & Media
When sports are covered by the media (especially TV) **sponsorship increases,** e.g. England netball

SPONSORSHIP
The funding of individuals, teams or events to raise company exposure and profit

Fig 11.2.4 *The inter-relationships between sport, sponsorship and the media*

VIOLENCE IN SPORT

Controlled aggression is a fundamental part of many sports and games. Sometimes, however, this spills over into uncontrolled violence both on and off the pitch.

You need to know and understand possible causes of violence by both players and spectators and be able to suggest possible solutions to the problems.

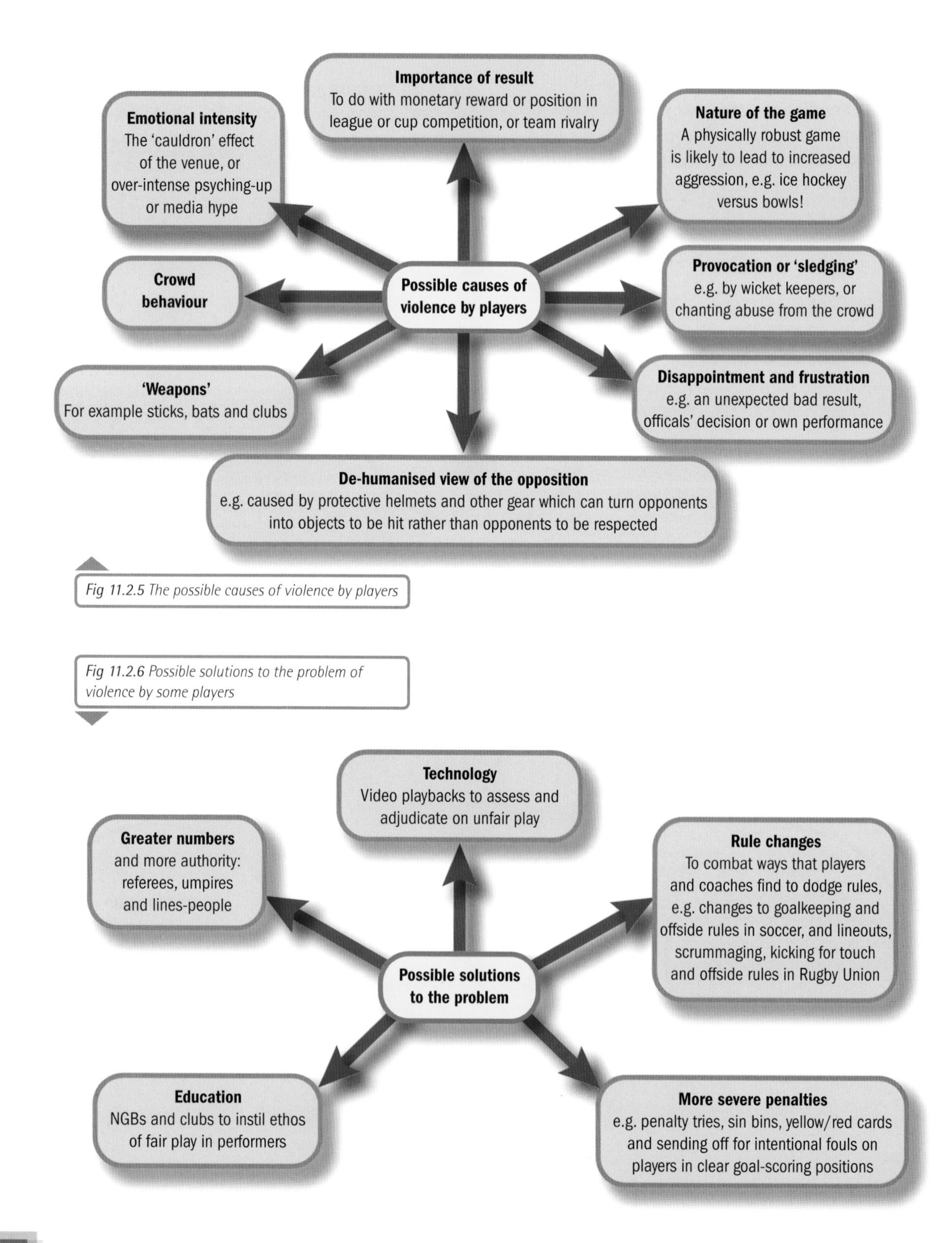

Fig 11.2.5 The possible causes of violence by players

Fig 11.2.6 Possible solutions to the problem of violence by some players

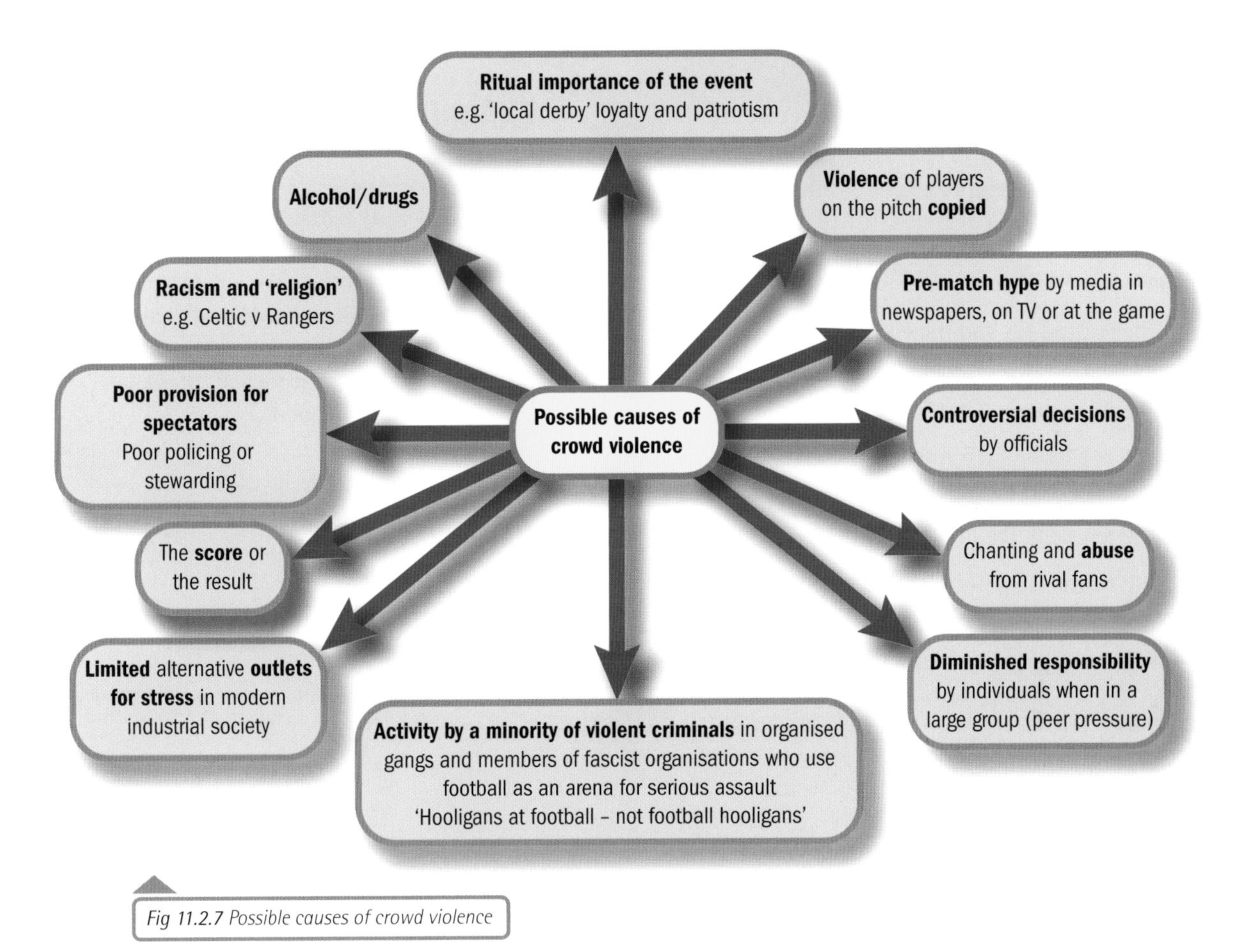

Fig 11.2.7 Possible causes of crowd violence

Solutions to the problem of crowd violence

- Promotion of sporting events as **family entertainment**
- Improvement of facilities
- **Responsible media** coverage
- **Control of alcohol**
- **Use of CCTV** and other security measures
- Liaison by police *within* areas of a country and *between* countries
- **Tougher deterrents** and more severe punishments
- **Separation of fans** from different clubs

Fig 11.2.8 Solutions to the problem of crowd violence

CHECK

If you are satisfied with your knowledge and understanding, tick off the sections that you have revised so far. If you are not satisfied, then revisit those sections and refer to the pages in the 'Need to know more?' features.

- ☐ The reasons for and the consequences of the use of drugs in sport.
- ☐ Possible solutions to the use of drugs in sport.
- ☐ The impact on performance in sport of modern technological products.
- ☐ The roles and the impact of the media on sport.
- ☐ The relationship between sport, sponsorship and the media.
- ☐ Possible causes and solutions to violence in sport.

EXAM PRACTICE

Q.1

a) Identify particular modern technological products that impact on performance in a named sport.

b) With reference to morality, health, legality and role modelling outline possible consequences of the use of drugs in sport.

6 marks

See page 185 for answers.

CHAPTER 11: PART III

The Olympic Games

LEARNING OBJECTIVE

By the end of this part you should be able to demonstrate knowledge and understanding of:

- The background to the Olympic Games including:
  - The vision of Baron Pierre de Coubertin in establishing the Modern Olympic Games (1896)
  - The principles, aims and philosophy of the Modern Olympic Movement
  - Summer and winter format of the Games
  - The British Olympic Association and the International Olympic Committee – two bodies involved with Olympic organisation and administration.
- Commercialisation of the Olympic Games after 1984
- London 2012 – opportunities and implications for UK sport and society
- The Olympic Games as a vehicle for nation building.

EXAM TIP

You need to be clear about the vision of De Coubertin and the principles, aims and philosophy of the modern Olympic movement.

THE MODERN OLYMPIC GAMES: BACKGROUND

The Ancient Olympics Games – these festivals of sport, religion and music took place throughout the Mediterranean region over 2000 years ago.

The Cotswold Olympic Games (England 1600s) – these were established by Robert Dover and were based upon the ancient Greek games.

The Much Wenlock Olympian Games (Shropshire, England 1890s) – founded by Dr William Penny Brookes, the aim of these games was to 'promote the moral, physical and intellectual improvement of the inhabitants of the town and neighbourhood of Wenlock'.

De Coubertin visited Much Wenlock in 1890 and was impressed and inspired by both the sport and the ceremony.

Baron Pierre de Coubertin – this wealthy French aristocrat wanted to educate young people and bring them together to increase international understanding.

The English Public Schools (19th Century) – De Coubertin was impressed by the spirit and ethos of these schools and the central place and values of games in them. He wanted similar 'character development' opportunities for the young people of France.

EXAM TIP

You will not be asked direct closed questions on the Ancient Olympic Games, Robert Dover's Cotswold Games or on the Much Wenlock Olympian Games. You could, however, be asked a question that tests your knowledge and understanding of the background to the modern Olympics and the vision of De Coubertin in which you could include some of this information.

Baron Pierre de Coubertin (1863–1937), seated 2nd left – Frenchman, educator and William Penny Brookes (1809–1905), seated to de Coubertin's left – Englishman, visionary

THE PRINCIPLES, AIMS AND PHILOSOPHY OF THE GAMES

KEY TERMS

Olympic Charter – The 'rule book' that governs how the Olympic Games and the IOC are run.

Principles

According to the International Olympic Committee (IOC) the principles of the Olympic Games are:

'To contribute to building a peaceful and better world by educating youth through sport practiced without discrimination of any kind and in the Olympic spirit, which requires mutual understanding with a spirit of friendship, solidarity and fair play.'

The British Olympic Association adds:

'The modern Olympic Movement was designed to link sport with culture and education. The founders wanted to promote the practice of sport and the joy found in effort. The Olympics would help to build a better world by bringing together people from around the globe to compete to the best of their abilities in the spirit of fair play and friendship. These core values are still at the heart of the Olympic Games today.'

We can learn more from the Olympic Creed, which states: *'The most important thing in the Olympic Games is not to win but to take part, just as the most important thing in life is not the triumph but the struggle. The essential thing is not to have conquered but to have fought well.'*

Aims

Baron Pierre de Coubertin himself explained:

'Why did I restore the Olympic Games? To ennoble and strengthen sports, to ensure their independence and duration, and thus to enable them better to fulfill the educational role incumbent upon them in the modern world. For the glorification of the individual athlete, whose muscular activity is necessary for the community, and whose prowess is necessary for the maintenance of the general spirit of competition.'

Philosophy

The philosophy of the Olympic Games is known as Olympism, which promotes:

- balance between body, mind and will
- effort – for the joy it can bring
- role modelling to educate and inspire others
- tolerance, generosity, unity, friendship, non-discrimination and respect for others.

The Olympic symbol of five interlocking rings is said to represent the coming together of the world's five continents with the white background of the Olympic flag symbolising peace throughout the festival.

The principles, aims and philosophy of the Olympic Games can be summed up as follows.

- Peace, unity, friendship, respect, fair play.
- Equality.
- Effort and appreciation of effort.
- Education through inspiration.
- Strengthening sport.
- Appreciation of physical excellence.
- Linking sport with culture and education.
- Development of a sound mind in a health body ('*mens sana in corpore sano*').
- Amateurism.

Summer and winter format

The Olympic Games has summer and winter events, each held every four years. The first winter games were in Chamonix, France in 1924. Up until 1992 the summer and winter games were held in the same year. Since then they have been held two years apart.

THE INTERNATIONAL OLYMPIC COMMITTEE (IOC)

The IOC was founded in Paris on June 23, 1894 and is now based in Lausanne, Switzerland. It is an international, non-governmental, non-profit organisation and receives no public money, being funded by profits from marketing and TV broadcasting rights.

Members of the IOC include athletes, administrators, lawyers and journalists who are ambassadors of the IOC in their own countries rather than being delegates representing their countries at the IOC.

Responsibility

The main responsibility of the IOC is to supervise the organisation of the summer and winter Games. It tries to ensure that commercialisation of the Games is well managed and controlled and that events are not exploited to the detriment of the Games as a whole.

It makes decisions about future Olympic Games and on any changes to the Olympic Charter. It works in areas such as sport science and sports medicine; women in sport; Olympic education; 'Sport for All' and environmental issues affecting sport.

The IOC supports and supervises the running of each Olympic Games by National Olympic Committees (NOCs) such as the British Olympic Association (BOA) and owns all rights to the Olympic symbols, flag, motto, anthem and Olympic Games.

Need to know more? For more information on the principles, aims and philosophy of the Olympic Games see Chapter 11, Part III, pages 313–316 in your Student Book.

THE BRITISH OLYMPIC ASSOCIATION (BOA)

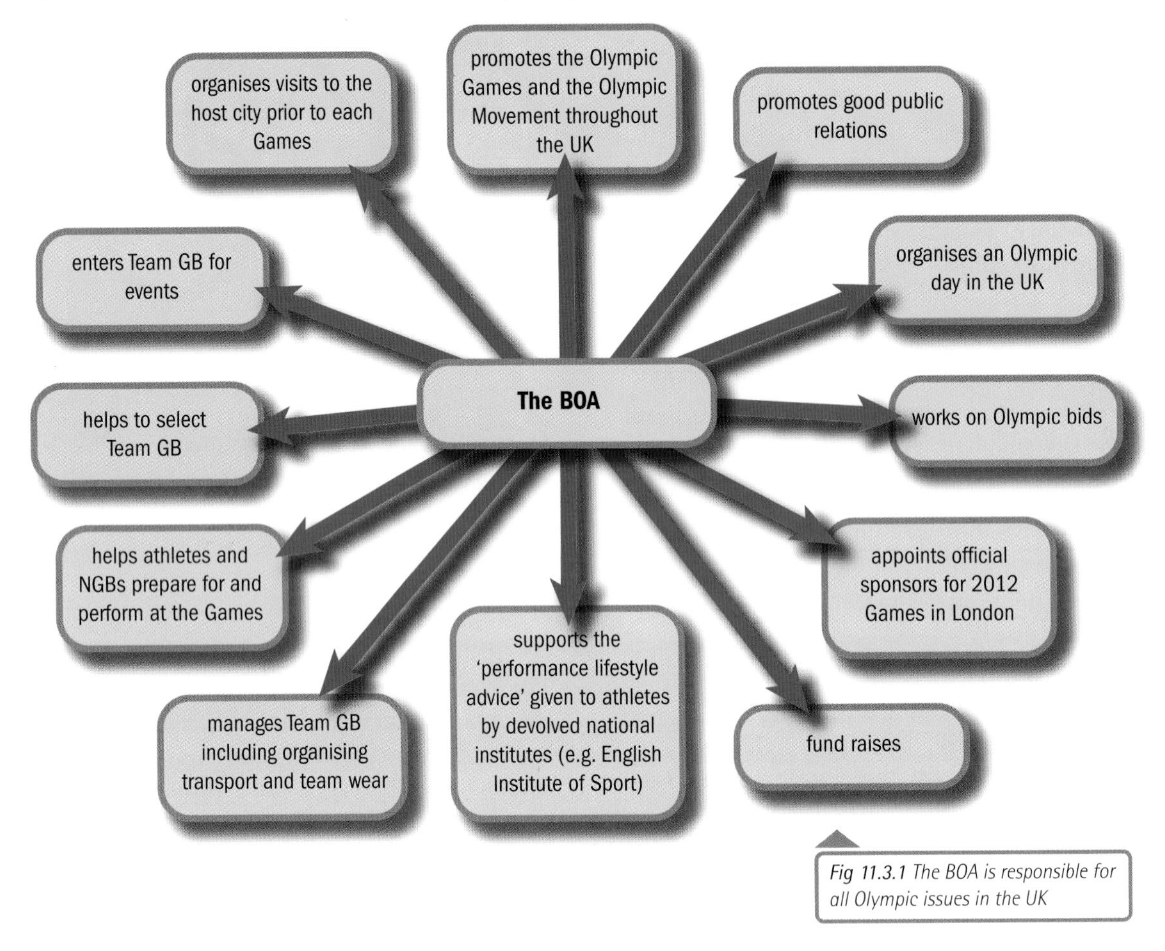

Fig 11.3.1 The BOA is responsible for all Olympic issues in the UK

COMMERCIALISATION OF THE OLYMPICS

The Olympic Games are now a giant commercial spectacle but that hasn't always been the case. From around the 1960s amateurism was causing problems for athletes from certain countries. Some athletes were well funded, e.g. those from the USA (funded by university scholarships) and from former Communist bloc countries such as the USSR and East Germany (funded by government).

British athletes, however, were still running for love (pure amateurism) and lagged behind. To compete realistically on the world stage amateur performers had to commit more time and effort to training. And therefore less time and effort to paid work.

Beginnings

The first Olympic Games to be seriously associated with commercialism were the Los Angeles Summer Games of 1984. Previous host cities, notably Montreal, Canada (1976) had lost millions through hosting the Games. The Los Angeles Games were a turning point in terms of marketing and sponsorship. Eventually, the IOC accepted commercialism.

Peter Uberroth was appointed to make the 1984 Games a commercial success. He charged huge sums of money for TV and radio rights, persuaded private companies to build the major facilities and invited sponsors to invest. This was when TV was building a huge global audience and so was able to make the Games attractive to sponsors. TV also gave nations, political groups and individuals a prominent stage or 'shop window' on which to make their point (see page 145).

Private funding

The 1996 Atlanta Olympic games showed the world that the Olympics could be handled by entirely privately funded profit-making commercial organisations. This is now the norm. Big companies get financially involved as official sponsors, official suppliers or official licensees of the Games.

Appointed companies become part of The Olympic Partner (TOP) Programme which is managed by the IOC. In return for their investment, TOP companies can use Olympic logos on their products and get exclusive worldwide marketing opportunities. TOP companies also get the first choice of advertising slots on TV and are allowed to showcase their products at the Games.

EXAM TIP

In the exam you will not be asked specific questions about the Paralympic Games.

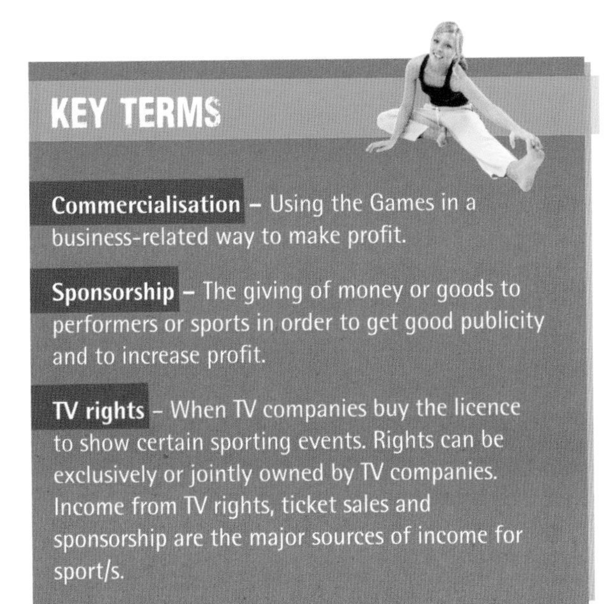

KEY TERMS

Commercialisation – Using the Games in a business-related way to make profit.

Sponsorship – The giving of money or goods to performers or sports in order to get good publicity and to increase profit.

TV rights – When TV companies buy the licence to show certain sporting events. Rights can be exclusively or jointly owned by TV companies. Income from TV rights, ticket sales and sponsorship are the major sources of income for sport/s.

THE OLYMPIC GAMES AS A VEHICLE FOR NATION BUILDING

The Olympic Games is an ideal stage on which to showcase a country and/or its political system. The one-party Communist state of China has done this. Some say that China used the Beijing Olympics as a coming-out party to highlight its economic rise and emergence as a world power.

Many hoped that the 2008 summer Games would force reforms and make the Communist Party open up Chinese society further. Others believed that the Games would simply validate/legitimise the Communist regime and its poor record on human rights.

'Shop window' effect

The 'shop window' effect is when a country is promoted; this is linked with 'nation building'. The outcome of the shop window effect can be national pride, greater morale and a feel-good factor, and appeasement or pacification of the people can be achieved. The country's status can also increase along with wealth, often in the form of tourism.

Government control and funding of sport

Prior to the 1990s all sport in China, as in some other Communist countries, was controlled and funded by the government. In 1994 Chinese soccer went professional and commercial followed by basketball, volleyball and table tennis. The 'golden triangle' (the strong relationship between sport, sponsorship and the media) thus began to operate in China. Even so, their government still funds sport heavily.

Sport as a political tool

Sport can be used to promote a political system or to make a political point, with sporting success able to increase the popularity of a government.

The following are examples of when the Olympic Games has been used as a political platform.

- Berlin, 1936 – Hitler and Jesse Owens.
- Mexico City, 1968 – the Black Power salute.
- Munich, 1972 – 11 Israeli athletes killed by terrorists.
- Moscow, 1980 – boycotts due to the Soviet invasion of Afghanistan.
- Los Angeles, 1984 – the Soviet Union boycott in return for 1980.

Need to know more? For more information on the Olympic Games and nation building see Chapter 11, Part III, pages 325–327 in your Student Book.

KEY TERMS

Centralised system – A system where political and administrative power is held centrally with no regional or local government control.

Shop window effect – When sporting success equates with political success and positive role models promote the country's status.

Communism – A centralised political system that opposes capitalism and democracy.

Elitism – To be exclusive or to select the best and to forget the rest.

Appeasement – To pacify or provide a feel-good factor.

LONDON 2012 – OPPORTUNITIES AND IMPLICATIONS FOR SPORT AND SOCIETY IN THE UK

EXAM TIP

This area of work about London 2012 is evolving. In an answer include points about the impact of being a host nation (both advantages and disadvantages) as you come across them in the time leading up to the Games. You will be given credit for relevant points that answer the question that has been set.

Impact on UK Society
- Potential increased participation in sport and physical activities particularly among young people.
- Improved health, fitness and well-being.
- Improved 'feel-good' factor.
- Improved infrastructure such as road and rail networks.
- Income from increased tourism.
- Business profit.
- Reduced discrimination due to high profile of Paralympics.

Impact on sport in the UK
- Increased funding and investment at all levels of sports development pyramid.
- A legacy of world class facilities for London.
- Improved facilities in regional training camps which will remain after Games.
- A higher profile for sport.
- Increased participation at the base of the sports development pyramid from which elite performers can later be selected.
- Improved organisation and administration of sport.
- Improved NHS provision particularly of high-quality sports medicine services – London/regional training camps.

london

Impact on Local Area
- Urban renewal.
- London promoted as a business area.
- Improved employment and skills opportunities for local people.
- Increased social integration and co-operation.
- Reduced crime.
- Increased sense of well-being and belonging.
- Housing from 'Olympic village' left for residential community.

Arguments against hosting the Games
- High council tax bills for locals.
- Soaring costs and potential legacy of debt.
- Few long-term job opportunities.
- A focus on elitism rather than participation.
- Regional areas such as Cornwall or the Lake District gain little, if any, direct benefits.
- An emphasis on nationalism which could lead to discrimination.
- Increased housing and rental prices discriminate against local people.
- Gypsy and travelling community evicted from area.

Fig 11.3.2 Possible impacts of being a host nation

KEY TERM

Legacy – What remains after an event. Among other things the Olympic legacy should include world class sporting facilities, improved road, rail and communication networks and increased participation in physical activity.

CHECK

If you are satisfied with your knowledge and understanding, tick off the sections that you have revised so far. If you are not satisfied, then revisit those sections and refer to the pages in the 'Need to know more?' features.

- ☐ Background to the Olympic Games.
- ☐ The vision of Baron Pierre de Coubertin in establishing the Modern Olympic Games (1896).
- ☐ The principles, aims and philosophy of the Modern Olympic Movement.
- ☐ Summer and Winter format of the Games.
- ☐ The British Olympic Association and the International Olympic Committee – two bodies involved with Olympic organisation and administration.
- ☐ Commercialisation of the Olympic Games after 1984.
- ☐ London 2012 – opportunities and implications for sport and society in the UK.
- ☐ The Olympic Games as a vehicle for nation building.

EXAM TIP

You will only get direct examination questions on the Olympic Games as a vehicle for nation building in China.

EXAM PRACTICE

Q.1

a) Who was Baron Pierre de Coubertin and what did he achieve?

b) Outline the commercialisation of the Olympic Games in the 1990s.

5 marks

See page 186 for answers.

CHAPTER 12

Performance

LEARNING OBJECTIVES

By the end of this chapter you should be able to demonstrate knowledge and understanding of:

- The roles you can be assessed in
- Which practical activities you can choose to be assessed
- How you will be assessed in each of these roles
- How you can improve your performances
- How you can improve your coaching/leading
- How you can improve your officiating.

POSSIBLE ROLES FOR ASSESSMENT

You will be assessed in:

1. **performing** two chosen activities from two different activity profiles and **evaluating and planning** for the improvement of performance

   or,

2. **performing** one chosen activity and **coaching/leading** one chosen activity from two different activity profiles together with evaluating and planning for the improvement of performance

   or,

3. **performing** one chosen activity and **officiating** one chosen activity in two different activities together with evaluating and planning for the improvement of performance.

In performing, coaching/leading and officiating you will be assessed out of 30 marks while your evaluating and planning for improvement response is assessed out of 20 marks, which enables you to score a maximum of 80 marks in this coursework unit.

CHOICE OF ACTIVITIES

The activities are grouped together by profile into 11 categories. You must choose two activities, each from a different category unless you are being assessed in officiating when you must choose two different activities.

These are the categories.

- Athletic activities.
- Combat activities.
- Dance activities.
- Invasion games.
- Net/wall games.
- Striking/fielding games.
- Target games.
- Gymnastic activities.
- Outdoor and adventurous activities.
- Swimming activities.
- Safe and effective exercise activities.

You can find out the activities in each of the 11 categories by visiting the OCR website.

Performing an activity

You have to be assessed in performing at least one practical activity, although you can choose to be assessed performing two practical activities.

Content of the practical activities

The specification indicates that the focus of your activities will be on 'acquired and developed skills'. This means that you will have to work specifically on the techniques and skills of your activities. These skills, however, will not be performed in isolation but in a situation where you are put under some pressure either from opponents or have to apply them to circumstances relevant to that particular activity. These are called conditioned competitive situations.

Conditioned competitive situations

These allow you to show that you are able to:

- select and perform the correct skill for a particular situation, e.g. choose the correct stroke when batting in cricket
- repeat skills consistently, e.g. get the skill right each time you perform it
- adapt skills where and when required, e.g. adjust your pass in netball to avoid the opponent marking you intercepting it
- show some tactical awareness
- perform all the above when under pressure
- apply the relevant rules, regulations and code of practice of the activity.

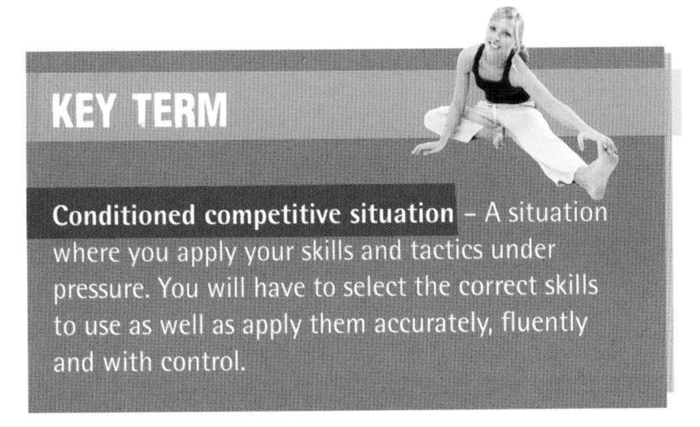

KEY TERM

Conditioned competitive situation – A situation where you apply your skills and tactics under pressure. You will have to select the correct skills to use as well as apply them accurately, fluently and with control.

The conditioned competitive situations also allow you to show how well-learned your skills are and how well they stand up to the pressure provided by these situations. It is important to realise that the pressure of competition is not the same for all activities and that the conditioned competitive situations will differ according to the category the activity belongs to.

For example, in gymnastics, in the conditioned competitive situation, students have to perform vaults and agility sequences. The 'competition' is to get your vaults and agilities as close as possible to the perfect model, and for them to flow and look aesthetically pleasing when linked together.

In invasion games the competition will be from opponents in a small sided game, while in outdoor adventurous activities it will be a situation where you have to combine your skills in an amended version of the 'normal' situation. For example, in mountain walking you will complete a two-day, 14-hour walk which covers 36 kilometres.

PERFORMING AN ACTIVITY: HOW YOU WILL BE ASSESSED

Your teacher will focus on the following criteria when assessing you.

- How good your range of skills is and the accuracy, control and fluency with which you perform them under pressure.
- Whether you have advanced skills and can use them when appropriate with accuracy, control and fluency.
- Your understanding of tactics and strategies, shown by your application of them.
- Your overall standard of performance.
- Your levels of physical and mental fitness.
- Your knowledge and understanding of the rules/regulations and conventions of your activity and your ability to apply them when you perform.

HOW CAN I IMPROVE MY PRACTICAL ACTIVITY PERFORMANCES?

You should be aware of how and when you will be assessed as well as the focus for your assessment. This understanding will help you plan how you should use your time to improve your performances in your practical activities and thereby increase the marks you are awarded.

Preparation

You should try to get someone to video one of your performances so that you can analyse it yourself, probably with the help of your teacher or coach. This analysis should identify the good aspects of your performance together with the weaknesses. It should cover skills, tactics and fitness. This will enable you to structure an action plan to improve your performance.

It is essential that you are able to perform, under pressure, both the basic skills of your activity and a range of advanced skills if you are to do well when assessed. You should ensure that you are aware of what the basic and advanced skills are and can perform them with accuracy, control and fluency. You should ensure that you are able to do this by practising these skills.

Because you are assessed in 'conditioned competitive situations' you will be required to use tactics, strategies/compositional and choreographical ideas and you can develop these through practice and receiving coaching.

Practice

Your skill practices can be done in a variety of ways but it is unlikely that there will be enough time in your lessons for you to perfect your skills. You must therefore look for additional opportunities to practise.

Within your centre there will be clubs and teams which will offer valuable opportunities to improve your skills. Other opportunities may be found by joining a local club where you will receive coaching and performing experience. It is important that you and your teacher talk to the coaches to make them aware of exactly what you have to do in your practical activity and how you will be assessed.

Joining a local club is particularly important if you do not have the opportunity in your centre to perform your activity 'competitively'. This could be a small sided game in hockey or an expedition in mountain walking. This experience, under the guidance of a teacher or coach, is important in developing your awareness and understanding of strategies and tactics/compositional and choreographical ideas.

Physical fitness

This is an important aspect in any practical activity and will be a key part of your preparation for both your performance activities. Different activities have different fitness requirements and through your training and by talking to your teacher/coach you should be able to identify which of the four main fitness components below are important in your activity.

- Strength
- Speed
- Stamina
- Suppleness

You will be able to use your knowledge from your anatomy and physiology studies to help you appreciate how you can work on your fitness. You will be able to use fitness tests to measure your fitness and any improvement.

If you can increase your levels of fitness in the relevant components then you will undoubtedly improve the standard of your performance and therefore your marks.

You will notice that you are also assessed in your mental fitness. Your mental fitness will develop by practising and gaining an understanding of tactics/compositional ideas and experiencing the pressures of competitive/challenging situations.

COACHING/LEADING AN ACTIVITY

The specification indicates that the focus of the assessment of your coaching/leading is on a range of applied and acquired skills, abilities and qualities. These skills will be assessed while you lead safe, purposeful and enjoyable activities. A suitable arena for these activities could be with primary school children in Top Sport or Dragon Sport activities or with other similar groups.

Practice

As with your performance you will need to practise your coaching/leading if you are to improve and will also need someone to observe you and give you feedback on your performances. There may be opportunities for practice created by your centre but you may have to seek opportunities with local clubs or with your local sports development officer.

Recording

In order to produce evidence for your assessment you will have to keep a log and record the following information in detail.

- A record of your coaching/leading activities over a three-month period.
- A scheme of work for ten hours of coaching in which the participants and activities show progression.
- Evaluations of your sessions.
- A video record of you coaching/leading for at least 40 minutes.
- Issues of Health and Safety relating to the activity and your sessions, together with risk assessments undertaken.

- Details of your First Aid qualification.
- Child protection procedures relevant to the activity.
- The health and fitness benefits of the activity for both participants and coaches/leaders.

If you have undertaken and successfully completed either the Community Sports Leader's Award or a Governing/Organising Body level two coaching qualification then you can include this in your log. (You don't have to have done either of these.)

EXAM TIP

You will need to complete this log as you do your coaching particularly in keeping the record of your coaching sessions and their evaluations. You should not leave it to the end, near the final date for the submission of assessments, before you put your log together.

Assessment

The focus of your assessments will be on your:

- ability to apply your coaching/leading skills in delivering sessions
- organisational and planning skills
- use of a range of coaching/leading strategies
- overall performance in coaching/leading
- awareness of Health and Safety
- implementation of risk assessments
- awareness of child protection
- awareness of the fitness and health benefits of the activity
- organisational skills in planning and delivering sessions
- knowledge of the rules/regulations of the activity
- evaluative skills.

HOW CAN I IMPROVE MY COACHING/ LEADING?

You should now be aware of how and when you will be assessed as well as the focus for your assessment. This understanding will help you plan how you should use your time to practise and improve your coaching/leading and thereby improve the marks you are awarded.

You may, within your centre, undertake the British Sports Trust Community Sports Leader's Award, and successfully completing this award may allow you to develop many of the skills on which your assessment will be based. Alternatively you could undertake a level two Governing/Organising Body coaching/leading award.

Observe, evaluate

You should observe and evaluate the sessions you are taught as part of your A level Physical Education course and any additional coaching/ leading courses you may undertake. This will allow you to see how other coaches operate and pick up ideas – preferably the ones that work and that you enjoy!

Any practices that other coaches use and you don't enjoy you can decide not to use or determine how you would change them to make them better so that you could use them.

Organising the skills you have to develop into groups might be helpful. Try these.

- Planning and organisation.
- Skill delivery.
- Evaluation.
- Technical knowledge.

Planning and organisation

These skills mainly concern things that you will do before your sessions. They usually ensure that your sessions have a good chance of being safe, enjoyable and successful. Knowing that you have planned and organised your sessions gives you confidence and allows you to concentrate on actually delivering the session and on the participants.

Planning properly enables the sessions to run smoothly, and although the participants might not be aware of all the planning time you have spent, they will appreciate being involved in a purposeful, safe and enjoyable session.

You should focus your planning on the following.

- Scheme of work.
- Session plans.
- Long- and short-term objectives.
- Facility details.
- Equipment details.
- Participant information.
- Health and Safety issues.
- Risk assessments.
- Warm-up and cool-down.
- Child protection details.

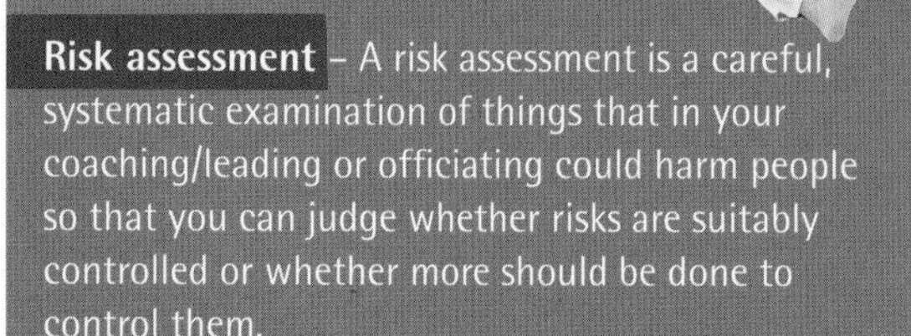

KEY TERMS

Risk assessment – A risk assessment is a careful, systematic examination of things that in your coaching/leading or officiating could harm people so that you can judge whether risks are suitably controlled or whether more should be done to control them.

Hazard – Anything or any situation that can cause harm, if uncontrolled.

Risk – The chance that somebody will be harmed by the hazard.

Delivery

When you deliver your sessions you will need to have prepared a detailed plan to follow. You will probably be given a session plan outline by your teachers or, if you undertake one of the courses already mentioned, by your tutor.

In your delivery of coaching/leading sessions you should focus on:

- appearance
- presence and personality
- communication
- voice tone
- quality of demonstrations
- control
- positioning
- motivation/praise
- enthusiasm
- a positive relationship with participants
- equal treatment of participants
- inclusion
- timekeeping.

Evaluation – overall

In your evaluation and reflection you should focus on identification of strengths and weaknesses of:

- the participants' performances
- your own performance
- the session itself.

Participants

During and after your session you will need to apply your evaluative skills – these enable you to decide what is good about a performance, and what is weak and needs to be improved. In your session you will have demonstrated and explained to the participants what it is you want them to do. You will then watch their practices, identifying good features – for which you will give praise – and observing anything that is wrong. Participants will need to be given extra practices so that these points can be put right.

Personal

Another major focus for your evaluative skills will be your evaluation of your own performance. Again you will identify what you did well, what was not so good and how you need to change things so that you do better next time.

It is important that you do this post-session evaluation as soon as possible after your session so that things are fresh in your mind. Your teacher, coach or fellow students may also evaluate your session and give you feedback.

Once you have received your feedback both from yourself and others who have observed the session, you will need to decide how you are going to apply this to future sessions.

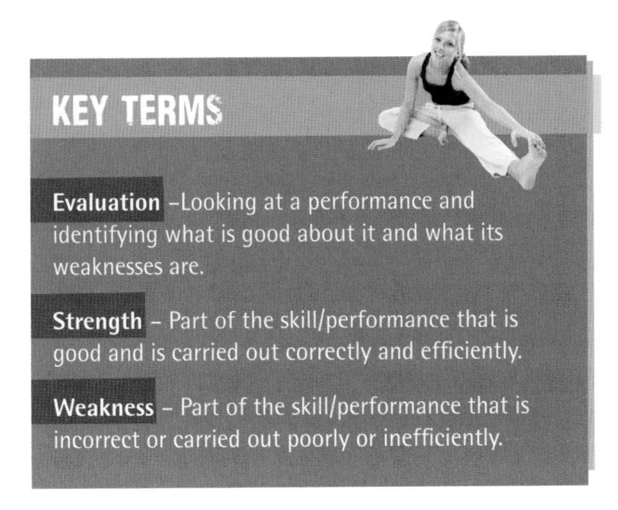

KEY TERMS

Evaluation –Looking at a performance and identifying what is good about it and what its weaknesses are.

Strength – Part of the skill/performance that is good and is carried out correctly and efficiently.

Weakness – Part of the skill/performance that is incorrect or carried out poorly or inefficiently.

Evaluation – technical

When you are looking at your technical knowledge of the activity you should focus on your knowledge of:

- correct technical models for the skills of the activity
- progressive practices to develop skills, together with the coaching points
- your ability to demonstrate/explain the technical models.

You will need to know the correct technical models for the skills of the activity, the phases they break down into, the coaching points together with the progressive practices to develop them. You can learn these from the sessions you take part in as part of your A level Physical Education course or you can find them in the coaching manuals that most governing bodies produce.

It also improves your credibility with the participants if you can demonstrate the skills that you are coaching so you will need to practise these skills to ensure that you can demonstrate them correctly.

You will have to have some knowledge of the tactics and strategies or compositional ideas that are applied in you activity. These will be covered in coaching manuals. You can develop an appreciation and understanding of these by observing the performance and coaching of your activity.

EXAM TIP

Watching other coaches/leaders is also a good way of improving your own coaching/leading. You can observe how they approach situations and see the practices they use for different skills. You can then use the good parts of these sessions in your own coaching and make sure that you do not make the mistakes that you see them make!

OFFICIATING AN ACTIVITY

The specification indicates that the focus of your assessment is on a range of applied and acquired skills, abilities and qualities. These skills will be assessed while you officiate safe, purposeful and enjoyable activities. Suitable opportunities for such activities would be primary school sports, local junior sports, inter-form sports or youth groups.

Practice

You will need to practise your officiating if you are to improve and you will need someone to observe you to give you feedback as to what you have done well and areas you need to improve on. While there may be opportunities for practice in your centre you may have to seek opportunities for practice in your local clubs or through your local sports development officer.

Recording

You will need to keep a log that contains evidence for your assessment. The log needs the following detailed information.

- A record of your officiating over a three-month period.

- Four evaluations by qualified assessors of sessions officiated.
- Risk assessments undertaken.
- A video record of 40 minutes of you officiating.
- Information relating to Health and Safety issues of your activity.
- Information relating to child protection procedures in the activity.
- The fitness and health benefits both from participating and officiating in the activity.

Complete your log as you officiate – don't leave it until your final assessment! It is far easier to put together information relating to your officiating sessions as you do them than to wait until your log is due to be assessed by your teacher.

EXAM TIP

Put your evidence log together as you do your officiating sessions rather than leaving it to the submission date. Make sure it has all the detail required.

Assessment

The focus of your assessment will be on your:

- ability to apply your officiating skills in sessions
- organisational and planning skills
- use of a range of officiating strategies
- overall performance in officiating
- awareness of Health and Safety
- implementation of risk assessments
- awareness of child protection
- knowledge of the rules and regulations/ conventions of the activity
- evaluative skills
- awareness of the fitness and health benefits of the activity.

HOW CAN I IMPROVE MY OFFICIATING SKILLS?

You should now be aware of how and when you will be assessed as well as the focus of your assessment. This understanding will help you plan how you should use your time to practise and improve your officiating and therefore increase the marks you get in your assessment.

Observe, evaluate

As well as practising your skills and strategies yourself by officiating it is useful to observe and evaluate others officiating. You can pick up ideas on how to deal with situations, different approaches to interacting with participants, etc. Sometimes when you are observing others you also find out approaches and ways you should not use!

You may within your centre undertake a Governing Body officiating award and successfully completing this course will allow you to develop many of the skills on which your assessment will be based.

Development

As with coaching and leading, try and identify and organise the skills you need to develop into groups.

1. Planning and organisation.
2. Officiating.
3. Evaluation.
4. Technical knowledge.

Let's have a look at these in more detail.

1. Planning and organisation

You need to do your planning and organising prior to your officiating sessions in order that you will be able to officiate successfully. In your planning and organising for your officiating you need to create habits. You should develop routines that you go through prior to officiating. The areas you are looking at are:

- knowledge of participants
- knowledge of rules of competition
- knowledge of venue/facility
- Health and Safety
- risk assessment
- child protection
- preparation of equipment.

2. Officiating

Once the session starts you will need to ensure that in your officiating you pay particular attention to your:

- appearance
- interaction with participants
- managing of participants
- decision-making
- positioning
- equity
- fitness
- teamwork with other officials (if appropriate).

3. Evaluation

You need to identify the strengths and weaknesses of your performance in terms of:

- planning and organisation
- officiating
- technical knowledge.

Once you have officiated your session you should evaluate your performance. You will identify what you did well, what was not so good and how you need to change things so that you do better next time. It is important that you do this post-session evaluation as soon as possible after your session so that things are fresh in your mind. Your teacher, assessor or fellow students may also evaluate your session and give you feedback.

It is also important to realise in your evaluation and other people's evaluations that very few officials or indeed performers and coaches/leaders get everything right all the time. What you are doing in your evaluation is identifying areas where you can improve and make yourself a better official as well as praising yourself for the things you did well.

In your evaluation you should cover your preparation and planning for the session, your officiating skills and strategies, your knowledge of the rules and regulations and your fitness.

Once you have received evaluative feedback both from yourself and others you should decide on how you are going to use this to improve your performance.

EXAM TIP

Make sure you have an up-to-date copy of your activity's rules and regulations from the governing body.

4. Technical knowledge

- Knowledge and application of the rules and regulations.
- Appropriate level of fitness.

The fourth category of skills you need to look at concerns your technical knowledge and your fitness. It is essential that an official in any activity has a good, up-to-date knowledge of the rules, regulations and conventions of that activity.

Also, you'll need to study the current rules, etc., and ensure that you know these and how to apply them. Most governing bodies publish their rules and regulations and you must have an up-to-date copy of these for your activity.

In activities that require you to be physically fit it is obviously essential that you ensure that you reach a required fitness level and maintain it. Some activities actually carry out fitness tests on their officials!

It does not do your credibility any good if you are unable to keep up with play or last the whole of the activity.

How can I improve my officiating?

Watching other officials, particularly experienced ones, is a good way to improve your own officiating. You can observe how they apply the rules, communicate with participants and position themselves, to see whether they do it differently to you.

Remember, however, that we all have different personalities, and that other people's approaches to officiating may not necessarily work for you.

CHAPTER 13

Evaluating and planning for the improvement of performance

LEARNING OBJECTIVES

By the end of this chapter you should be able to demonstrate knowledge and understanding of:

- The structure and contents of the evaluating and planning for the improvement of performance response
- Practicing your response
- How you will be assessed.

IMPROVEMENT OF PERFORMANCE: WHAT DO I HAVE TO DO IN MY EVALUATION AND PLANNING?

You will choose one of the two activities in which you are being assessed and on which you wish to focus for this aspect of your assessment. You will then:

- watch a fellow student performing the activity
- evaluate the performance, identifying the strengths and weaknesses
- select a major weakness and create an action plan to rectify/improve it
- discuss the opportunities locally and nationally for participation and improvement in the activity
- discuss the health and fitness benefits of the activity.

You will do this by talking to your teacher.

How do I do this?

Evaluation

When you evaluate you identify what is:

- good about the performance – the strengths
- poor about the performance – the weaknesses.

You will focus on the following areas.

- Skills.
- Tactics/compositional ideas.
- Fitness.

To help you do this you may want to refer to the phases that are used to analyse the activity and its skills (see Chapters 4 and 5 in your Student Book).

Action planning

Initially, you have to select one of the major weaknesses identified in your evaluation to be the focus of your action plan. Having selected the focus, your action plan should have:

- a clear realistic goal – to improve a major weakness you have identified
- a timescale
- a method for achieving the goal – detailed coaching points and progressive practices.

You now have a clear structure or plan of what it is that you have to do. This can be identified as follows.

- Accurately describe the major strengths of the performance.
- Accurately describe the major weaknesses of the performance.
- Construct a viable action plan to remedy a major weakness which has:
  - detailed coaching points
  - detailed progressive practices
  - a timescale for the plan.

In addition to your evaluation of the performance you will also have to discuss the opportunities that there are in your area and nationally to participate in this activity. You also need to talk about opportunities to improve your performance standard and the level at which you participate. This will obviously require you to undertake some research to establish what these opportunities are. Finally you will also need to discuss the health and fitness benefits to people who participate in this activity.

You now have a clear structure for your response.

1. Describe the strengths.
2. Describe the weaknesses.
3. Select a major weakness.
4. Create a viable action plan to include coaching points, progressive practices and a timescale.
5. Discuss **opportunities for participation and progression – locally and nationally.**
6. Discuss health and fitness benefits of activity.

How can I improve my evaluation and appreciation of performance?

Like your practical performance, this aspect of your assessment is a skill and to improve it you need to practise it and receive feedback. Like other skills, it can be broken down into parts for you to practise.

Analytical phases

You need to know the movement phases that are used to analyse the activity. This will help you analyse the skills. These can be found in the OCR's Teacher Support: Coursework Guidance.

Coaching points

You should know the coaching points for the major skills of your activity. You should make a note of these when your teacher covers them in your sessions or refer to coaching manuals to find them. You need to compare these coaching points to the performance you observe.

EXAM TIP

Make sure that you know the coaching points of all the major skills in your activity.

Identification of strengths and weaknesses

Focus	Strengths	Weaknesses
skills	it is important that you know the 'technical' models you are comparing the performance to – these can be found in the relevant governing or organising body coaching manuals knowledge of how the skill should be performed enables you to judge how good it is, and to justify your evaluation by identifying why it is good you will also use this knowledge when you are identifying weaknesses and constructing your action plan.	you will need to focus on the skills in which, when under pressure, the performer either performs poorly or chooses not to use at all you will be able to identify those performed poorly by comparing them to the correct technical models and the coaching points as well as the level of success when under pressure, some performers will be very inconsistent in some aspects of their skill production; this means they will be successful on one occasion and unsuccessful the next time when under pressure, do they choose not to perform advanced skills, indicating they are unsure or lack confidence in them?
tactics/ compositional ideas	as performers gain a greater grasp of the skills within the activity, they are able to devote more attention to the tactics and strategies involved; they show an increased perceptual awareness accompanied by an increased capacity for decision-making the majority of these increased capacities will be devoted to the performer attempting to influence the outcome of the activity through their use of tactics and strategies/ compositional ideas sometimes this may be shown through better teamwork or better compositional ideas; you will need to have a good understanding of the major tactics and strategies/compositional ideas used in the activity to be able to evaluate the performer you are observing this understanding will be gained from your own involvement in the activity but should be further improved by reading the appropriate coaching manuals and talking to coaches you will be comparing the performer you are looking at to what you know they should be doing; this will enable you to identify what they are doing correctly if they are part of a team, you will probably want to comment on the team's effective use of strategies as well as the individual's contribution	these will vary a great deal from activity to activity they will focus on attempting to outwit the opposition or the environment and in team activities they will also include teamwork again, you will be comparing what your performer does against what you know to be good tactics and strategies/compositional ideas; this will enable you to identify where he or she is going wrong this may be focused on the individual you are observing or the team in general

continued ▶

Focus	Strengths	Weaknesses
fitness	you should apply your knowledge of fitness to your evaluation; this should enable you to identify accurately the components of physical fitness appropriate to the performance you are evaluating as well as the skill-related fitness components you should evaluate the fitness of the performer you are observing under the following headings as appropriate: a) physical fitness • strength/power • suppleness/flexibility • stamina • speed b) skill-related fitness • agility • co-ordination • balance • timing you will be focusing on the aspects of fitness you know are important in the activity to assess whether or not the performer you are observing has good levels in these areas some of the areas suggested above will be more relevant in some activities than others and you need to adapt them to suit the activity you are observing there may be other fitness aspects that are appropriate to your activity and these should be included not only will you comment on the fitness aspects for which the performer has good levels, but also on their application of them to their performance	using the areas of fitness you have determined are important for the activity, you will identify those areas in which, in your opinion, the performer has weaknesses or in which you consider they could perform better by having increased levels of fitness

Table 1 Skills – strengths and weaknesses

It should have become apparent to you by now that in identifying strengths and weaknesses you are using the same information to determine both aspects. You should, however, ensure that you identify the strengths before the weaknesses, as it is easy to overlook them!

EXAM TIP

You need to know the tactics/compositional ideas of your activity.

CONSTRUCTING A VIABLE ACTION PLAN TO IMPROVE A MAJOR WEAKNESS

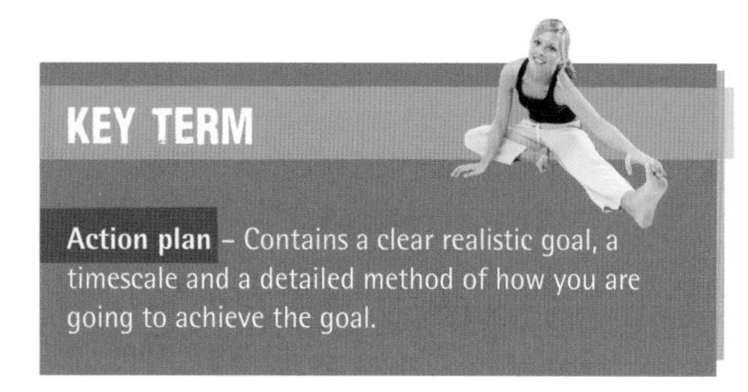

KEY TERM

Action plan – Contains a clear realistic goal, a timescale and a detailed method of how you are going to achieve the goal.

This is where you will select one of the major weaknesses you have identified and create a plan to remedy it, thereby improving the performance as a whole.

You will remember that your action plan had to include:

- clear, achievable, realistic goals
- timescale
- method for achieving the goals – detailed coaching points and practices.

These must appear in your action plan.

Clear, realistic goals

This will, in fact, be to remedy the major fault you have identified and thereby improve the performance. All you have to do is select one of the major faults you have identified. You may, in addition, identify more specific goals – for example, to achieve a specific level on the multi-stage fitness test rather than just to improve stamina.

When choosing the fault you should ensure you are able to suggest ways in which you will be able to remedy it – that is, to construct an action plan. Sometimes it is easier to focus on weaknesses within a skill or fitness area, as these are easier for creating action plans than tactics/compositional ideas.

EXAM TIP

Ensure that you identify a clear, realistic goal in your action plan.

Timescale

You need to identify how long your action plan will take, how often the practices or training will be, and so on. Different action plans will have different timescales. Those designed to develop aspects of fitness will usually be over a longer period than those to develop skills.

Make sure you know the correct technical models you are comparing the skill to.

You should give an indication of the overall length of the action plan – that is, the number of weeks or months – together with the frequency of the sessions (e.g. number of times a week).

Method for achieving the goals

Here you will describe the practices and drills you will suggest that the performer does to remedy the weakness. This should be done in detail, identifying the coaching points for the skills you wish to be improved as well as each of the practices you will use.

The practices you identify should show progression, going from simple to complex and from closed to open. You should, however, be realistic, starting the practices at a level that is appropriate to the performer you are observing. Remember that you will probably take the performer back to the cognitive stage of learning.

KEY TERM

Progressive practices – A practice that starts with a skill in its simplest, closed situation and goes through a series of stages to practise the same skill in its natural, open situation.

If you decide that the major weakness is an aspect of fitness, you should demonstrate your knowledge of training by identifying exactly the aspects of fitness you are going to focus on together with their relevance and application in the activity. You should include the detailed exercises, etc. that you would put in your plan to improve these fitness aspects and also detail how you would test them to see if they have improved.

OPPORTUNITIES TO PARTICIPATE AND PROGRESS IN THE ACTIVITY

In addition to this evaluation and action planning you must also discuss the opportunities for participation and improving performance both locally and nationally. This will mean that you will have to do some research both in your own local area and in your country.

You will probably already have some information about opportunities locally but could find out more by talking to your teachers and coaches as well as approaching your local sports development officer or department. They may also be able to give you information about the national picture that you can supplement by accessing the governing body's website.

Opportunities to participate

Health and fitness

The criteria also require you to discuss the health and fitness benefits participants get from taking part in the activity. In your AS Physical Education course you will have talked about a balanced, active and healthy lifestyle and you are being asked to say what contribution taking part in this activity makes to this. This will include not only the physical benefits but also the social and emotional benefits, both short- and long-term.

Your own experiences should help you in this area but, again, talking to your teachers/coaches and reading the coaching manuals will help you build up information.

Evaluation, and planning for improvement: practising

You should practise your evaluation and planning for the improvement of performance as many times as you can.

It may be that you can practise by looking at a video of the activity you are focusing on and you can record your response on tape so that you can listen to it and evaluate it yourself.

What will happen when I am assessed?

Your teacher will ask you to watch one of your fellow students performing the activity. They will then ask you to focus on particular aspects of the performance or a particular performer, and will select the aspects they wish you to focus on.

After you have watched the performance for some time, they will ask you to comment on it. You can make notes as you watch the performance to help you with your response – you cannot use any prepared notes. When you have started your response, you may well be able to look at the performance again to refresh your memory as well as referring to your notes.

After you have observed the performance, the teacher will say something like:

'You have just observed the effective performance of Sophie. Describe the strengths and weaknesses of the performance and create an action plan to improve a major weakness of the performance. You should also talk about the opportunities to take part and progress in this activity, as well as its health and fitness benefits.'

You will be expected to go through the six stages you have already identified.

1. Identify the strengths of the performance.
2. Identify the weaknesses of the performance.
3. Select the major weakness.
4. Create a viable action plan on which you:
   a) have clear, realistic, achievable goals
   b) identify a timescale
   c) identify the detailed coaching points you will use
   d) identify the detailed practices you will use
5. discuss the opportunities for participation and progression locally and nationally
6. discuss the health and fitness benefits of participating in the activity.

If you get stuck or miss out a stage, the teacher will probably ask questions to help direct you. These questions would probably be of the type that would guide you to think about a particular stage or area rather than requiring a specific answer.

Remember, this is your opportunity to tell your teacher how much you know and understand by applying it to the performance you observe. Ideally, once your teacher has asked you the starting question you should be able to keep talking about what you have seen and know, until they ask you to stop!

THE ASSESSMENT CRITERIA

Your teacher will be using the following criteria to assess you.

- Accuracy of the description of the major strengths of the skills, tactics/compositional ideas.
- Accuracy of the description of the major weaknesses of the skills, tactics/compositional ideas.
- Accuracy of prioritising an area of the performance that needs improvement.
- Creating a viable action plan which has detailed coaching points, detailed progressive practices and a timescale.
- Accuracy of the description of opportunities locally and nationally for participation and progression in the activity.
- Accuracy of the description of the health and fitness benefits of the activity.

They will use these criteria to firstly put you into one of four bands: 0–5, 6–10, 11–15, 16–20. They will then give you a mark from within this band.

ANSWERS TO EXAM PRACTICE QUESTIONS

CHAPTER 1

Offers all types of movements

The arm and front of the body at Shoulder

Q.1 (Shoulder joint extension analysis – tennis serve)
4 marks

- **a)** Joint type .... ball and socket
- **b)** Articulating bones .... humerus and scapula
- **c)** Muscle working as agonist .... posterior deltoid/latissimus dorsi
- **d)** Agonist contraction type .... concentric

Q.2 (Fast glycolytic (type 2b) muscle fibres: two structural/two functional characteristics)
4 marks total (1 mark for each point made)

Structural characteristics.

- Size – large.
- Glycogen store – large.
- Myosin ATPase activity – fast.
- Motor neurone size – large.
- Fibres per motor neurone – many.
- Phosphocreatine store/ATP stores – large/high.
- Mitochondria – few.
- Capillaries – few.
- Myoglobin stores – low.

Functional characteristics.

- Force production – high.
- Relaxation time – fast.
- Contractile speed – high.
- Fatigue resistant – low.
- Aerobic capacity – low.
- Anaerobic capacity – high.

Q.3 (Two structures of hip joint – role of each during performance of physical activity)
4 marks (1 mark for each point made)

Structure	Role
Description of spherical shape of bone/ball and socket/deep cup-like socket.	Allows wide range of movement, namely flexion, extension, circumduction, abduction, adduction and rotation. Structure also aids stability.
Strong ligaments.	Hold the joint in place/give stability by joining bone to bone.
Cartilage (hyaline/articular).	Helps to prevent wear and tear of the articulating bones.
Muscles/tendons.	Provide strength or support/allow greater range of movement.
Synovial fluid.	Lubricates the joint/nourishes cartilage/rids joint of waste debris.

continued ▶

Pads of fat.	Absorb shock/protect from wear and tear.
Bursae (sacs containing synovial fluid).	Help reduce friction.
Joint capsule/fibrous capsule.	Stabilises the joint.
Synovial membrane.	Secretes synovial fluid.

Table 1

Q.4

a) Type of contraction – bicep brachii in downward phase of bicep curl,
b) downward phase of sit-up – muscle that performs similar contraction)
2 marks

a) Eccentric contraction.
b) Rectus abdominus.

CHAPTER 2

Q.1 (Hitting a ball – how is force exerted so ball moves straight/spins?)
2 marks total

1 mark for each of:

- moves straight – a force is applied through the centre of mass/the player must hit the ball through the middle (centre of gravity) of the ball
- spins – a force is applied off centre/eccentric force/hitting a ball on the side will make the ball spin.

Q.2 (How position of centre of mass can affect balance of performer)
3 marks total

1 mark for each of the following:

- to hold a balance the centre of mass must be over the base of support
- the centre of mass/line of gravity must pass through the base of support
- the lower the centre of mass the more stable the balance
- the more points of contact are made the more stable the balance
- the larger the area of support the more stable the balance.

Q.3 (Apply Newton's Three Laws of Motion to weightlifting exercise)
3 marks

- (Newton's 1st Law) The performer will not move the weight unless a force is applied.
- (Newton's 2nd Law) The more force applied the greater weight lifted/weight lifted more quickly/more weight lifted requires more force to be applied.
- (Newton's 3rd Law) The performer exerts force against resistance/weight and force applied back against performer.

CHAPTER 3: PART I

Q.1

5 marks total

a) (Taking part in physical activity is considered essential…)

1 mark

- Many types of activity will have a positive impact but the health benefits gained are more significant if the activity is: aerobic/of a higher aerobic intensity.

b) (…positive impacts on the heart …)

4 marks for four of:

- main impact is hypertrophy
- decreases resting heart rate/bradycardia
- increasing SV
- to maintain the same Q at rest
- potential to increase the supply of O_2 during exercise.
- healthy heart (bradycardia) under less effort/strain at rest/over the period of one's lifetime
- slows down heart's deterioration in efficiency due to the natural ageing process
- improves length of an individual's quality of life (not necessarily longevity)
- sustaining a more active and healthy lifestyle.

CHAPTER 3: PART II

Q.1

5 marks total

a) (Difference between blood pressure and hypertension)

Max 3 marks from:

Blood pressure	Hypertension
• 'Pressure exerted by blood against the (arterial) blood vessel walls'/also expressed as: 'blood flow (Q) × resistance'.	• **Long-term, enduring** high Bp (do **not** accept just high Bp)
• **Systolic Bp – highest** arterial pressure/reflects ventricular systole (contraction phase).	
• **Diastolic Bp – lowest** arterial pressure/reflects ventricular diastole (relaxation phase).	
Resting average = $\frac{120 \text{ mmHg}}{80}$	Above $\frac{140 \text{ mmHg}}{90 \text{ mmHg}}$

Table 2

b) (Changes to blood pressure during physical activity)
Max 3 marks – no more than two from systolic or diastolic
Systolic:

- Sub-maximal
  – systolic Bp increases in line with exercise intensity and may plateau during sub-maximal exercise (around 140-160)
  – may decrease gradually if this sub-maximal intensity is prolonged.
- Maximal
  – systolic Bp continues to increase in line with intensity, from 120 mmHg to above 200 mmHg during exhaustive exercise intensity.

Diastolic:

- Sub-maximal
  – diastolic Bp changes little during sub-maximal exercise
  – localised muscular diastolic Bp may fall to around 60–70 mmHg.
- Maximal
  – diastolic Bp may increase a little (max 12%/>10 mmHg) as exercise intensity reaches maximum levels
  – resistance training involving isometric contractions increases both systolic/diastolic Bp/can exceed 480/350 mmHg.

CHAPTER 3: PART III

Q.1 (1968 Mexico Olympics; new world records, but none in distance events)

a) (Effects of altitude on the respiratory system)

3 marks for three of:

- percentage of oxygen within the air remains the same at sea level and altitude
- PP oxygen drops as altitude increases/hypoxic air
- diffusion gradient between air and lungs is reduced at altitude
- at altitude the diffusion gradient between the alveoli and blood is reduced/PP oxygen in lungs at altitude is lower than PP oxygen in lungs at sea level
- at altitude not as much oxygen moves from alveoli into the blood
- as a result haemoglobin is not fully saturated/reduced oxygen-carrying capacity of the blood
- at altitude not as much oxygen is delivered to the working muscles
- decreases muscle contraction force/decreased power outputs.

b) (How altitude may influence performance)

2 marks for two of:

- decreases aerobic performance for distance events
- anaerobic events do not rely on aerobic energy provision dependent upon O_2
- air is also thinner at altitude and offers less resistance to jump/throw/sprint events, improving performance.

CHAPTER 4

Q.1 (Describe discrete, serial etc. skills)

1 mark per point (5 marks max) – each must be accompanied by a suitable practical example

- **Discrete** – clear begining and end, if the skill is to be repeated it must start again, e.g. catching a ball in cricket/rounders, penalty in football or hockey.
- **Serial** – a movement skill with a number of discrete elements put together in a definite order, e.g. triple jump, trampolining sequence.
- **Continuous** – a movement skill that has no definite beginning or end. The end of one cycle of the movement is the start of the next, cyclic, e.g. running, cycling, swimming.
- **Simple** – movement skills that have low perceptual and decision-making aspects, small number of sub-routines to organise in which timing and speed are not critical, e.g. swimming, sprinting.
- **Complex** – movement skills that are intricate, highly perceptual with many decisions to be made. Many sub-routines to be organised in which timing and speed are critical. Feedback is important, e.g. tennis serve, somersault.

Q.2 (Progressive part method: practical example/advantages)

5 marks total (3 marks if no practical example)

- Used with serial skills/skills low in organisation/skills easily broken down/sometimes referred to as chaining, e.g. triple jump, gymnastic/trampolining sequence, lay-up shot in basketball.
- Learn part 1 – perform part 1, learn part 2 – perform parts 1 and 2, learn part 3 – perform parts 1, 2 and 3, learn part 4 – perform parts 1, 2, 3 and 4.
  - Example – Learn run-up in triple jump, practice it. Learn hop, then practice run-up and hop. Learn step, then practice run-up, hop and step. Learn jump, then practice run-up, hop, step and jump.
- Reduces the information load.
- Helps the flow of the skill.
- Helps the transfer of the skill into the whole.

Q.3 (Characteristics of abilities; examples – gross motor/psychomotor)

1 mark per point (max of 5)

- Innate/genetic/natural/born with them.
- Enduring/stable/underlying/a potential.
- Specific (to groups of movements)/underly/support/underpin.
- Gross motor ability – speed/power/flexibility/endurance.
- Psychomotor ability – decision-making/reaction time/hand–eye co-ordination/spatial awareness.

Q.4 (Compare/contrast methods of manipulating skills; critically evaluate their effectiveness)
This is a 'levels' question – see Table 4, which follows the Indicative content table below.

Practice type	Characteristics	Example	Advantages	Disadvantages	Additional info
Part practice	Working on and perfecting isolated sub-routines. Once the sub-routines are perfected they are put back together.	Practising body position, leg action, and breathing of swimming strokes and then putting them all together.	• Reduces the information to be processed and therefore reduces the possibility of overload. • Reduces the complexity and if the skill is dangerous reduces the risk and fear. • Success in the parts of the skill motivates the learner and gives confidence. • Good for learning serial skills and skills low in organisation.	• Takes longer than other methods. • Transferring the parts back into the whole can sometimes be difficult. • Learners can lose kinaesthetic sense and flow of the skill.	• Sub-routines must be divided into meaningful parts. • Learner must see the whole skill demonstrated prior to learning so they have an image of what they are learning.
Whole practice	The skill is learned in its complete form without being broken down into sub-routines or parts.	Basketball dribble, cartwheel, golf swing, sprinting.	• Good for skills high in organisation or continuous. • Good for skills low in complexity. • Allows the learner to get the flow and timing (kinaesthesis) of the skill. • Helps the learner understand the movement. • Also can be quicker than other methods. Good for ballistic skills.	Not suitable for complex or dangerous skills.	Ideally all skills should be taught by this method.

continued ▶

Practice type	Characteristics	Example	Advantages	Disadvantages	Additional info
Progressive practices	Parts of a complex skill are practised in isolation. They are then linked together to form larger and larger parts before finally becoming the whole skill: 1 Learn part 1 – perform part 1. 2 Learn part 2 – perform parts 1 & 2. 3 Learn part 3 – perform parts 1, 2 & 3. 4 Learn part 4 – perform parts 1, 2, 3 & 4.	Gymnastic floor routine, triple jump, lay-up shot in basketball.	• Good for complex skills as it reduces the information load. • Good for skills low in organisation. • Good for serial skills. • Helps the flow of the skill and can also help the transfer of sub-routines into the whole skill.	Not suitable for skills high in organisation.	Sometimes known as chaining.
Whole-part-whole	• Learner tries the whole skill first to get the feel of the performance. • Teacher identifies the weak parts of the skill and these are practised in isolation. Once the weak parts are perfected the whole skill is tried again.	Tennis serve – coach identifies that the ball is not being tossed up high enough and practices and perfects this before returning to the whole serve.	Learner gets the feel for the skill and the flow. This method can be quicker than the part method as only the parts which the learner has difficulty with are practised.	Not suitable for highly organised or dangerous skills.	

Table 3 Indicative content

L3 **8–10 marks**	• There is detailed knowledge and good understanding of the topic. • There is effective comparison and critical evaluation. • Knowledge is clearly and consistently linked to practical performance throughout the answer if appropriate. • Accurate technical and specialist vocabulary is used throughout. • There is a high standard of written communication. *Discriminators from L2 are likely to include:* • *understanding of the methods of practice* • *detailed knowledge of advantages and disadvantages* • *good comparison/contrast of one or more relevant factors.*	
L2 **5–7 marks**	• There is satisfactory knowledge and understanding of the topic. • Comparison and critical evaluation is attempted with some success. • Knowledge has been linked to practical performance with some success where appropriate. • Technical and specialist vocabulary is used with some accuracy. • Written communication is generally fluent with few errors. *Discriminators from L1 are likely to include:* • *explanation rather than mere description* • *knowledge shown for at least two methods* • *satisfactory comparison/contrast of one or more relevant factors.*	
L1 **0–4 marks**	• There is basic knowledge but little understanding of the topic. • Little or no attempt to compare and evaluate critically. • Little or no attempt to link knowledge to practical performance. • Technical and specialist vocabulary is used with limited success. • Written communication lacks fluency and there will be errors, some of which may be intrusive.	

Table 4 Level descriptors

CHAPTER 5

Q.1 (Distributive practice – use and advantages)

5 marks total

a) 'What' – 1 mark: Practice sessions with rest periods/breaks included.

b) 'When' – 1 mark: Used with beginners/less experienced/task is dangerous/complex/gross/continuous/physically demanding/learners are unfit.

c) Advantages – 3 marks for three from:

- not as tiring/can help maintain motivation/allows for recovery/not as boring
- mental rehearsal can occur between sessions
- allows for sessions to be varied
- corrections/feedback can be made at each session/mistakes are not compounded
- allows sessions to be progressive/increasingly demanding
- distributed practice more effective than massed.

Q.2 (Manual and mechanical guidance: meanings and advantages)

5 marks total

1 mark for each of:

- mechanical guidance – involves the use of equipment to help support the learner and shape the skill
- manual guidance – involves the teacher/coach holding or physically manipulating the body of the learner through the correct pattern of movement.

3 marks – at least one from each section:

Advantages

- reduces fear/develops confidence
- increases safety
- allows for kinaesthetic awareness/feel of movement.

Disadvantages

- swimmer begins to rely on arm bands/support
- poor technique could give incorrect kinaesthetic information
- swimmer does not have to try as hard/demotivating
- restricts feeling of wholeness.

Q.3 (Associative phase of learning)

4 marks (total) for four of:

- practice is important at this phase
- performer begins to identify own mistakes/reference made to the mental picture created in cognitive phase
- movement becomes less jerky and more flowing
- motor programme being formed and stored in long-term memory
- performer can use kinaesthetic/internal/proprioceptive feedback
- some attention can be focused away from the skill itself
- some performers never progress beyond this phase
- mental rehearsal/positive reinforcement important.

Q.4 (Massed and distributed practice: advantages and disadvantages)

10 marks

See Levels Table 5 below, then the Indicative content that follows.

L3 **8–10 marks**	• There is detailed knowledge and good understanding of the topic. • There is effective comparison and critical evaluation. • Knowledge is clearly and consistently linked to practical performance throughout the answer if appropriate. • Accurate technical and specialist vocabulary is used throughout. • There is a high standard of written communication. *Discriminators from L2 are likely to include:* • *understanding of the methods of practice* • *detailed knowledge of advantages and disadvantages* • *good comparison/contrast of one or more relevant factors.*	
L2 **5–7 marks**	• There is satisfactory knowledge and understanding of the topic. • Comparison and critical evaluation is attempted with some success. • Knowledge has been linked to practical performance with some success where appropriate. • Technical and specialist vocabulary is used with some accuracy. • Written communication is generally fluent with few errors. *Discriminators from L1 are likely to include:* • *explanation rather than mere description* • *knowledge shown for at least two methods* • *satisfactory evaluation of one or more relevant factors.*	
L1 **0–4 marks**	• There is basic knowledge but little understanding of the topic. • Little or no attempt to compare and evaluate critically. • Little or no attempt to link knowledge to practical performance. • Technical and specialist vocabulary is used with limited success. • Written communication lacks fluency and there will be errors, some of which may be intrusive.	

Table 5 Level descriptors

Indicative content:

a) (Advantages/disadvantages of massed and distributed practice)

Massed practice

Repeated/continuous attempts at a skill without breaks or rest intervals. The sessions are usually long.

Advantages

- Good for the grooving in of habitual/closed skills.
- Good for experienced performers.
- Good for highly motivated performers with good fitness levels.
- Suitable for discrete skills of short duration.
- Time saving as skills do not have to be reintroduced after breaks.
- Good for coach to simulate performance conditions where fatigue is a factor.

Disadvantages

- Can cause fatigue, boredom and demotivation which lead to poor performance and learning.

Distributive practice

Practice sessions with rest periods/breaks included.

Advantages

- Used with beginners/less experienced/short attention spans.
- Used if task is dangerous/complex.
- Used if task is physically demanding or performers unfit.
- Can help maintain motivation – good for those with low motivation.
- Allows for recovery – mental and physical.
- Not as boring as massed.
- Mental rehearsal/practice can occur during rest intervals.
- Allows sessions to be varied.
- Feedback can be given and corrections made between sessions.
- Mistakes are not grooved in.
- Allows for sessions to be progressively demanding.
- Research shows it to be more effective than massed.

Disadvantages

- Time-consuming.
- Skills may have to be reintroduced at the start of each session.
- Can lead to negative transfer.
- Not good for discrete skills.

b) (Mental practice: when to use; advantages compared with physical practice)

Mental practice

- The learner goes through the movement in their mind without any physical movement occurring.
- It can be used during rest intervals in distributed practice. In the early/cognitive stages it is used to build up a mental picture of the skill to be learned. Advanced performers use it to rehearse complex skills and to go over strategies and tactics. It can also be used for reinforcing successful movements and experienced performers use it for emotional control and to establish optimum levels of arousal.
- It is not an alternative to physical practice as when used on its own it is not as effective as physical practice. It should be used in conjunction with physical practice, i.e. rest intervals in distributed practice. It is more effective with skills with a cognitive element than simple skills.

CHAPTER 6

Q.1 (Components of the multi-store model)

6 marks total

a) Short-term sensory stores

2 marks for two from:

- all information entering the information processing system is held here for a very short time (0.25–1 second)
- these stores have a very large capacity
- there is a separate store for each sense
- the perceptual mechanism determines which of the information is important to us and we direct our attention to it; this filtering process is called selective attention
- this is the recognition aspect of perception
- irrelevant information is quickly lost from the sensory stores to be replaced by new information.

b) Short-term memory

2 marks for two from:

- this is known as the 'work place'
- it is here that the incoming information is compared with that previously learned and stored in the long-term memory
- this is the comparison aspect of perception
- the short-term memory has a limited capacity in terms of how much information it can store and for how long
- generally these limits are between five to nine pieces of information for up to 30 seconds
- you can increase the amount of information by linking or 'chunking' bits of information together and remembering them as one piece of information
- you can extend the period of time by rehearsing or repeating the information
- information considered important is rehearsed or practised and by this process passed into the long-term memory for future use; this process is called encoding.

c) Long-term memory

2 marks for two from:

- long-term memory holds the information that is well rehearsed and practised
- it has a limitless capacity and the information is held for a long time, perhaps permanently
- motor programmes are stored in the long-term memory as a result of practising them many times; think of how you never forget how to swim or ride a bike
- the long-term memory is the recognition part of the perceptual process when the information stored in the long-term memory is retrieved and compared with the new information to see if it can be recognised.

Q.2 (Intrinsic and extrinsic feedback)
4 marks total (1 mark for each point)

- Intrinsic – information about the task comes from within the performer; proprioceptive; kinaesthetic information is internal; performer uses sense of balance or touch to gain information about the perfomance.
- Extrinsic – information from external sources is used; visual and auditory senses give information about the task.
- Intrinsic – swimmer feels their legs kicking on the surface of the water; gymnast feels themselves overbalancing in a handstand.
- Extrinsic – basketball; netball player sees that their shot has been successful; coach/teacher tells trampolinist how good their routine was.

Q.3 (Quick reaction time/movement skills)
4 marks total

1 mark for (important to develop quick reactions):

- to produce skilled movement at speed; outwit your opponent; get away from opponents; get a good start; improve overall speed; be able to cope with the situation effectively.

1 mark per point (factors that could affect response time) – max 3:

- number of stimuli; number of possible alternative responses; number of decisions to be made; open, complex, externally paced skills; psychological refractory period; single channel hypothesis
- distractions; ability to selectively attend; focus; spectator distractions; social inhibition
- age; gender
- level of personal fitness; health; somatotype; length of neural pathways
- past experience; presence of motor programme; level of skill/ability
- relevant environmental factors not covered in any of the points above.

Q.4 (Identify two forms of anticipation)
4 marks total

1 mark for each of (max 2 marks):

- spatial anticipation – predicting what will happen
- temporal anticipation – predicting when it will happen.

(Effects of anticipation on response time)

2 marks for two of:

- can shorten response time if judgement correct
- can increase response time if judgement incorrect
- correct anticipation allows extra time to respond.

CHAPTER 7

Q.1 (Explain closed loop theory/control – handstand example)
1 mark for each of (max 5 marks):

- Level one is without feedback and is open loop control, e.g. this level would start the handstand.
- Level two involves sub-conscious control (via effector mechanism), e.g. this level would facilitate balance and correction if required.
- Level three involves conscious control requiring greater attention via cognitive processes, e.g. this level would complete and allow recovery from the handstand performance.
- Closed loop control involves feedback and this provides the performer with information about the 'feel' of the performance.
- The feel of the skill informs the performer about the position of the body during the handstand.
- This is called kinaesthetic or proprioceptive information and is a product of internal feedback.
- Information (perceptual trace) goes to the central control mechanism and a comparison is made with the memory trace (the grooved pattern of movement), e.g. the performance of the handstand must match the technical model stored as the memory trace.
- If, as a result of comparison, a change or adjustment is required the effector mechanism initiates the correction, e.g. any error in the handstand performance will be corrected.

Q.2 (Three functions of feedback… types used by advanced performer)
1 mark for each of (max 5 marks):

- Feedback helps to increase the confidence.
- Feedback motivates the sports performer.
- Feedback will help to prevent the onset of drive reduction and the associated reactive inhibition.
- The process of feedback is vital to learning as it detects and corrects errors.
- Actions can be reinforced through feedback so that learning bonds are strengthened and the athlete knows what to do in future situations.
- The advanced performer tends to operate by way of internal feedback (KP) as they have learned the association between the correct 'feeling tone' and successful performance.
- Kinaesthetic feedback or knowledge of performance (KP) ensures that the action is fluent.
- Extrinsic feedback can come from the coach for fault identification and knowledge of results helps to evaluate performance.
- Negative feedback can detect and correct errors to keep the skill finely tuned.
- Positive feedback will reinforce the correct motor programme and help to groove the skill.

CHAPTER 8: PART I

Q.1 (Drive/inverted U/catastrophe theories… arousal and performance of motor skills)

10 marks total

This is a 'levels' question. Level descriptors can be found in Table 6, after the answers for this question. Marks are awarded for three sections, a–c.

a) Drive theory submission – max 4 marks

- Drive theory indicates a linear relationship between arousal and performance.
- An increase in arousal is proportional to an increase in the quality of physical performance/ dominant response.
- The quality of performance/dominant response depends on how well the skill has been learned.
- Motor programmes that have already been learned are said to be 'learned behaviours' and are therefore termed dominant responses.
- A dominant response is a response that is most likely to emerge when a performer experiences an increase in arousal.
- The dominant response at the autonomous stage of learning would tend to produce a response that is fluent and technically correct.
- High arousal would be beneficial to the performer at the autonomous stage of learning.

b) Inverted U theory submission – max 4 marks

- The inverted U theory indicates or predicts that as arousal increases so does the quality of performance.
- Quality improves up to a point mid-way along the arousal axis/optimal point.
- The optimal point of arousal is a perfect state in which the potential to learn and perform well is maximised.
- At the optimal point the attention field of the individual adjusts to the ideal width and as a result the learner or performer is able to concentrate fully.
- With increased focus the performer detects only the most important information.
- This process of selective attentiveness is called cue-utilisation.
- When under-aroused, concentration is lost because the attention field of the performer widens excessively.
- This results in information overload.
- Over-arousal causes the field of attention to narrow excessively and as a result the relevant environmental cues are missed.
- This results in hypervigilence.

c) Catastrophe theory submission – max 4 marks

- Catastrophe theory, like the inverted U hypothesis, claims that as somatic arousal increases then the quality of performance improves.
- Catastrophe theory, however, also states that performance will reach maximum potential at the optimum level only if cognitive arousal is kept low.
- If high cognitive arousal coincides with high somatic arousal the athlete will go beyond the optimum level of arousal.

- Under these conditions performance drops vertically/catastrophically, not on a smooth curve as predicted in inverted U theory.
- After a catastrophe the performer can rejoin the upward curve of arousal and once again attain the optimal point of arousal.
- A reduction in cognitive anxiety is necessary before a return to the optimal is possible.
- When somatic arousal is low skill learning and performance can be enhanced if cognitive arousal is increased.
- Serious debilitation in learning performance will arise when low levels of physiological and psychological arousal converge.

L3 **8–10 marks**	• There is detailed discussion of a number of relevant factors. • There is detailed analysis of one or more relevant factors. • There is detailed knowledge and understanding of the topic. • There is a high standard of written communication evident. *Discriminators from L2 are likely to include:* • *qualitative comments* • *independent opinion and examples.*
L2 **5–7 marks**	• There is *satisfactory* discussion of some relevant factors. • There is *satisfactory* analysis of one or more relevant factors. • There is *satisfactory* knowledge and understanding of the topic. • There is relevant knowledge present that links to practical performance. • There is a *satisfactory* standard of written communication evident. *Discriminators from L1 are likely to include:* • *the number of points made by candidates/greater breadth* • *examples.*
L1 **0–4 marks**	• There may be *basic* discussion of one or more relevant factors. • There may be *basic* analysis of one or more relevant factors. • There is *basic* knowledge and understanding of the topic. • There may be relevant knowledge present that links to practical performance. • Written communication may lack fluency. Errors may be present.

Table 6 Level descriptors

Q.2 (Drive reduction/other motivational strategies… used to develop active etc. lifestyle)
This is a levels question. Level descriptors can be found in Table 6 above.
10 marks

a) Drive reduction submission – max 4 marks

- Drive reduction theory predicts that a performer develops a drive or the need to learn a new skill or to solve a sport-related problem.
- The learner will engage in practice until the skill has been learned.
- An S–R bond has now been formed and the skill can said to have been overlearned.
- Once this autonomous stage has been reached the drive to continue practising diminishes and too much practice leads to inhibition or boredom.
- A reduction in motivation results in the deterioration of performance.
- Motivation can be increased by introducing rest breaks (distributed practice).
- Motivation can be increased by setting new targets and bringing variety into learning (varied practice).

b) Motivational strategies submission – max 8 marks

- Extrinsic reward can motivate a novice performer to become involved e.g. certificates.
- Extrinsic reward can eventually be a drawback to the learning process as effort may only be applied if reward is given.
- Internal motivation involves giving learners positive feelings about their performance.
- People who are intrinsically motivated are more likely to continue participation than those who seek reward.

Other motivational strategies that will help to promote a balanced, active and healthy lifestyle include:

- fun activities: practices and activities should be enjoyable and provide fun
- positive reinforcement: praise from teachers, parents and peers encourages participation
- social experience: if young people perceive that sport is a social experience they are more likely to participate
- progression: learners are inspired if sports participation is leading somewhere
- attainable targets: if targets and goals are met during learning, motivation is enhanced
- transfer of skills: if new skills can be built on previously learned skills, they do not seem difficult
- skills and fitness: if young people feel that fitness and skill levels are improving, they are more likely to continue with sport
- role models: young people like to copy successful sports players.

CHAPTER 8: PART II

Q.1 (Example from PE/sport; how performer learns by operant conditioning; S–R bond)
6 marks (max 3 if no example)

- The teacher would first structure or manipulate the environment to bring about the desired response.
- For example, when learning to play a cross-court forehand in tennis a target may be drawn at the back of the opponent's court during practice.
- A period of trial and error learning will occur as the learner attempts to perform the desired action, e.g. to land the ball in the target.
- During this period the learner's response or behaviour is being shaped or modified.
- A good response is positively reinforced by the teacher in order to strengthen the S–R learning bond.
- Similarly, negative reinforcement can serve to strengthen a correct learning bond.
- Any response receiving no reinforcement will disappear.
- Complete reinforcement after every attempt increases the speed of learning.
- Partial reinforcement is a more effective way of remembering the skill.
- When the desired behaviour has been overlearned the target is taken away.
- A positive learning outcome facilitated by the process of reinforcement will promote behaviours associated with a balanced, active and healthy lifestyle.

Q.2 (Four key terms of cognitive learning theory; practical example of application of theory to teaching a skill in PE/sport)
5 marks total
4 marks max for key terms

- Intervening variables – refers to the mental processes or thoughts that occur between receiving a stimulus and making a response.
- Insight learning – using previous experience stored in the memory to solve an arising problem. Insight also depends upon having the perception and intelligence to understand the problem.
- Perception – the process of interpretation and understanding. It involves making sense of incoming data. Understanding the problem is necessary before it can be solved.
- Past experiences – previous experiences or schemas can be adapted and transferred to help with the solution of a current problem.
- Whole learning – learning is achieved more efficiently if the problem can be seen as a whole. Therefore, a skill is best learned as a whole.

1 mark max for example:

- Cognitive theories of learning can be applied by teaching the skill as a whole, e.g. teaching the whole swimming stroke as opposed to teaching leg and arm action separately.
- If the skill is too complex for a beginner to learn as a whole, problem solving can be facilitated by creating/adapting/conditioning games, e.g. Kwik cricket.

CHAPTER 8: PART III

Q.1 (Proactive/retroactive transfer; practical examples of each)
4 marks total (1 mark for each example)

- Transfer of training involves the influence that one skill has on the learning and performance of a separate skill. Proactive transfer occurs when a previously learned skill influences a skill that is currently being learned; a skill being learned at present will influence a skill learned in the future…

  Example – a throwing motor programme learned as a child transfers positively and proactively to the movement of the racquet arm in a tennis serve learned in later years.
- Retroactive transfer occurs when a newly learned skill influences a previously learned skill…

  Example – the acquisition of a successful tennis serve may influence the previously learned overarm throw.

Q.2 (Teaching a motor skill in sport: how teacher/coach can optimise effect of transfer)
6 marks total – 1 mark for each point

- For transfer to take place the teacher must ensure that there is similarity between two skills.
- For example, if a tennis serve is being taught, the racquet arm action is similar to an overarm throw.
- The learner must be made aware of the transferable elements of a previously learned skill.
- Clear and concise demonstrations must be used.
- Transfer of similar skills is predicted by the identical elements theory.
- The teacher must emphasise the elements that are transferable.
- If skills are to be transferred, the environmental conditions must be similar.
- The information processing requirements must be compatible, e.g. a netball skill drill must look like a game situation.
- Positive reinforcement will increase the likelihood of transfer.
- Previous skill needs to have been well learned if positive transfer to new skill is to be facilitated.
- Diverse experiences enhance the probability of transfer.
- Simplify the task during initial learning and transfer it later into the real situation.
- Learning situations need to allow for transfer.

CHAPTER 9

Q.1 (What is being described: i) physical activity requiring physical effort to improve health and fitness; ii) course-of-a-lifetime activities; iii) day to day life…)
6 marks total

a) 1 mark for each of:

- exercise/physical exercise
- lifetime sports
- healthy balanced lifestyles.

(Factors contributing to increasingly sedentary lifestyles)
b) 3 marks for three of:

- more desk bound jobs/less manual labour
- modern technology/reduced need to move around in everyday life
- cars/lifts/escalators/washing machines/sit-on mowers /TV remote controls/other labour-saving gadgets or machines
- computer use/shopping online
- children not walking to school.

Q.2 (Barriers to regular participation in physical activity…)
5 marks total (1 mark for each point)

Lack of:

- energy
- perceived ability/skills
- friends who participate
- suitable facilities nearby
- money, e.g. to join a gym
- suitable/correct kit.

Also:

- anxiety about being out after dark in winter
- want to stay inside during cold/wet times of the year
- dislike of exercise and/or sweating
- embarrassed to show body.

CHAPTER 10

Q.1 5 marks total

a) (What is meant by the following terms…)
1 mark for each of:

- amateurism – taking part for love/not being paid to take part/taking part more important than winning
- professionalism – the skill or character expected of a highly trained performer/being paid to take part/being highly organised or efficient in terms of (a 'professional approach').

b) (In UK sport… recent move from traditional amateur to professional approach)
3 marks for three of:

- due to government initiatives or government plans (local or national)
- due to the work of UK Sport
- due to the modernisation of NGBs
- due to London 2012 and the need to be well organised/professional
- the impact of The National Lottery.

Q.2 (Discuss American Football… origins/link with commercialism)
This is a 'levels' question. Level descriptors can be found in Table 7 below, which is followed by the Indicative content.

Level	Descriptors
L3 **8–10 marks**	• There is detailed discussion of a number of relevant factors. • There is detailed analysis of one or more relevant factors. • There is detailed knowledge and understanding of the topic. • There is a high standard of written communication evident. *Discriminators from L2 are likely to include:* • *qualitative comments* • *independent opinion and examples.*
L2 **5–7 marks**	• There is *satisfactory* discussion of some relevant factors. • There is *satisfactory* analysis of one or more relevant factors. • There is *satisfactory* knowledge and understanding of the topic. • There is relevant knowledge present that links to practical performance. • There is a *satisfactory* standard of written communication evident. *Discriminators from L1 are likely to include:* • *the number of points made by candidates/greater breadth* • *examples.*
L1 **0–4 marks**	• There may be *basic* discussion of one or more relevant factors. • There may be *basic* analysis of one or more relevant factors. • There is *basic* knowledge and understanding of the topic. • There may be relevant knowledge present that links to practical performance. • Written communication may lack fluency. Errors may be present.

Table 7 Level descriptors

Indicative content:

a) Origins

- The game developed in 'Ivy League' universities, e.g. Yale.
- In early 1800s there were no generally accepted rules.
- The first intercollegiate match was Rutgers v Princeton – 1869.
- Handling or carrying of the ball not allowed.
- Game became violent/sensational/dangerous.
- Winning dependent mainly on physical force.
- Game also called 'gridiron'.
- Original pitch markings formed grid of squares.

b) Links with commercialism

- A multi-billion dollar industry/big business.
- The National Football League (NFL) is a group (or cartel) of companies.
- Teams run as 'franchises'.
- TV networks compete for coverage.
- Teams relocate miles from fan base/'home' for profit.
- The Super Bowl is a big commercial event/linked with advertising.
- Companies compete to advertise during the Super Bowl.
- Super Bowl has half-time shows/entertainment.
- The game was redesigned (1960s) to suit television.
- Many commercial breaks.

CHAPTER 11: PART I

Q.1 (Aims and activities – two bodies involved in sport in the UK)
5 marks – submit max of three from section a) or b)

a) UK Sport

- Develop elite sport in UK.
- Promote ethical behaviour; eliminate drug use (runs anti-doping programme – 100% ME)
- Distribute National Lottery funding through the World Class Programme.
- Attract major sporting events.
- Encourage administrative efficiency in the UK system as a whole.
- Develop international sporting relationships.
- Help elite performers develop 'sporting lifestyle'.
- Support world class coaches.
- Support NGBs (Mission 2012).
- Develop the partnership between sport and higher/further education/TASS – Talented Athlete Scholarship Scheme.

b) Home country councils such as Sport England

- Promote community sport; mass participation; make their home countries 'active sporting nations'.
- Support government targets, e.g. support PESSCL strategy.
- Provide or distribute lottery funding/government funding.
- Promote volunteering/coaching/leadership/officiating.
- Focus on priority groups, e.g. people with disabilities/the elderly.
- Work with other organisations; share good practice.
- Work to ensure that the London 2012 Olympics and Paralympics leave a lasting sporting legacy.
- Responsible for funding elite performers in sports such as squash and netball that are non-Olympic (at time of writing).
- Provide information/have websites.

Accept any relevant project or campaign, e.g. (Get) Active, Sporting champions, Sport Action Zones.

CHAPTER 11: PART II

Q.1

6 marks total

a) (Modern technological products – impact on performance in named sport)
2 marks for any two of the following (any suitable modern technological product accepted, if given in context of named sport).

- Padded equipment for hockey goal keepers and rugby players.
- Ball feeding machines for tennis and cricket.
- Carbon fibre and titanium for various items of equipment, e.g. poles for pole vault, golf clubs, racquets.
- Hawk-eye ball tracking device in tennis and cricket.
- Full body suits for swimming.
- Motion analysis, e.g. of golf swing or discus throw, which can be computer analysed.
- Improved physiotherapy and sports medicine techniques including ultrasound, ice baths etc.

b) (With reference to morality, health etc. … possible consequences of the use of drugs in sport)
4 marks for four of the following – one from each category.

- Morality – cheating; gives an unfair advantage; undermines the true spirit of sport; reflects badly on other sports performers.
- Health – can be addictive; lowers life expectancy; is dangerous; can cause premature death; can lead to (various) disease(s); can suppress growth; can cause sexual or gynaecological problems; can affect moods or behaviour; can cause aggression or depression.
- Legality – against the law of the land; against the laws of sport.
- Role modelling – gives a bad example; young people might copy the behaviour or think it is acceptable; gives a bad image or lowers the status of sport.

CHAPTER 11: PART III

Q.1

Total 5 marks

a) (Who was Baron Pierre de Coubertin… achievements)
2 marks for two of (max 2 marks):

- De Coubertin was a wealthy French aristocrat; a keen sportsman
- he founded the Modern Olympic Games (1896)
- he was inspired by the English public schools (nineteenth century); he was inspired by the Much Wenlock Olympian Games (Shropshire)
- he used sport to educate young people/to bring young people together/to increase international understanding.

b) (…commercialisation of Olympic Games in 1990s)
3 marks for three of (max of 3):

- the first Olympics to be associated with commercialism (big business) were the Los Angeles (LA) Games (1984)
- Peter Uberroth was the man behind the change; Uberroth made the Games a commercial success
- Uberroth charged for TV and radio rights; he persuaded companies to build the facilities; he invited sponsors to invest
- since LA 1984, big business has been a major part of the Games; companies become official sponsors/or official suppliers/or official licensees of the Games
- appointed companies become part of The Olympic Partner (TOP) programme
- TOP companies can use the Olympic logo; the Olympic logo is a major marketing tool
- TOP companies get prime TV advertising slots; they are allowed to showcase or advertise their products at the Games
- it could be argued that the Games are now more about money than about sport.

(Give credit for any suitable personal analysis/judgement.)

Index